Lawyer HR
Vocabulary

영단어 공부
방법론

Lawyer Hong Rag Yun

충주고

한양대 법대, 동대학원

사법시험 제34회 (사법연수원 제24기)

New Zealand Permanent Resident

New Zealand Hamilton Waikato Law School 수학

USA Texas Houston Law School Master of Laws 수학

건국대학교 법학과 객원교수(영미법)

현 중원법무법인 대표 변호사

**Lawyer HR
Vocabulary**

영단어 공부 방법론

초판 1쇄 인쇄 2012년 01월 16일
초판 1쇄 발행 2012년 01월 23일

지은이 | 윤홍락
펴낸이 | 손형국
펴낸곳 | (주)에세이퍼블리싱
출판등록 | 2004. 12. 1(제2011-77호)
주소 | 153-786 서울시 금천구 가산동 371-28 우림라이온스밸리 C동 101호
홈페이지 | www.book.co.kr
전화번호 | (02)2026-5777
팩스 | (02)2026-5747

ISBN 978-89-6023-740-7 13740

Lawyer HR
Vocabulary

영단어 공부
방법론

윤홍락 지음

머리말

Vocabulary 학습은 영어 공부의 시작이자 마지막이며 전쟁에서의 총알이다. 영어공부를 한다고 하면서 Vocabulary 공부에 충실하지 아니하면 전쟁터에 빈총을 가지고 가는 것과 마찬가지이다. 수준에 맞는 영단어를 선정하여 효과적으로 활용하는 방안을 모색해보자. 고교 수준, 토익, 텝스, 토플 등 목표를 우선 선정한다. 가장 중요한 1,000단어를 선정하여 스스로의 Vocabulary 교재를 만들어 보자. 예를 들어, 다음 abdicate 에 대한 교재를 만들어 보자. 인터넷 사전에서 abdicate를 찾는다. 발음을 click 하면 (앱디케이트, 앱디케이트) 라고 두 번 발음 되는 것을 공 테이프에 녹음한다. 다음 대표 예문을 적고 원어민 발음을 녹음한다. He abdicated in favour of his son. 어느 정도 영어 실력을 갖춘 독자라면 스스로 원어민 테이프를 예문과 함께 만들어 보자. 책을 보지 아니하고 녹음만 듣고도 반복하여 따라할 수 있다면 금상첨화이다.

1. 암기 쪽지 만들기

A4 용지를 반으로 접어 한 면에 25단어씩을 표제어와 예문을 적어 한 장에 앞뒤로 100단어를 적어 10장을 만든다. (암기 쪽지) 접히는 부분을 유리테이프로 붙여 Paper 의 수명이 오래 가도록 한다. 처음에는 하루에 한 장씩 즉 100단어씩을 암기한다. 영단어를 따로 시간을 내어 암기하려고 하면 지겨워서 못한다. 등교, 출, 퇴근시간, 화장실에서, 점심시간, 잠자기 전, 일어난 직후 등 자투리 시간을 활용하여 필수단어를 암기한다. 다음에는 하루에 3장씩을 가지고 다니면서 암기한다. 마지막에는 하루에 10장을 다 암기할 수 있도록 하면 이제 지겨운 단어의 영역에서 해방하게 되는 것이다. 단어의 발음은 아무리 강조해도 지나치지 아니한다. 정확한 발음을 할 수 있을 때에만 진정한 자신의 단어가 되어 사용할 수 있다. 항상 인터넷 영어 사전에서 원어민의 정확한 발음을 확인하고 따라 한 연후에 길거리에서 큰 소리로 발음해 보면서 영단어를 암기하도록 하자.

* 단어 선정에 참조할 좋은 교재
 1. Vocabulary 22,000
 2. 문덕 MD Vocabulary

2. 공 테이프 녹음하기

1개는 영어 뉴스를, 1개는 토플 등 목표하는 시험용 Listening 부분을 원어민 발음으로 쉬는 부분 없이 녹음한다. 번갈아 가면서 무조건 듣는다. 의미를 모르더라도 조바심을 내지 말고 발음 지체를 듣기 위해 누력한다. 원어민 속도로 따라 할 수 있을 정도까지 반복(shadow 과정)한다. 받아쓰기를 한다. 의미를 확인하여 잘못된 부분을 교정한다. 실제 문장 속에서의 연음을 연습하기 위해서는 절대로 대본을 먼저 보지 말고 팝송을 따라하듯이 암기할 수 있을 정도로 들어 의미를 모르더라도 따라서 Shadow 할 수 있을 정도까지 반복하여 들어야 한다.

골프나 서예, 음악 등 한 가지 취미를 얻기 위해서도 수년간의 부단한 노력과 인내가 필요할 것이다. 하물며, 영어 공부함에 있어서 이 보다 더 한 노력이 필요할 것이다. 본 교재는 필자가 유학을 준비하면서 정리한 필수 Vocabulary 와 공부 방법 등을 소개한 것이다. 본 교재를 master 한 후 전공 단어를 정리한다면 외국 유학 생활에 아무 문제가 없을 것이라 확신한다. 우리 젊은이들이 세계로 뻗어나가는 기상을 펼치는 순간에 조금이라도 본 교재가 도움이 되었으면 하는 바람이다.

이 책을 공부하는 모든 이들에게
Good Lock !

2012. 새해에
중원법무법인 대표변호사실에서

Lawyer HR

contents

Part 1
기본단어

01 Bad weather _____s when good weather begins to return.

   a. abdicate   b.abeyance   c. ablution   d. abnegation

02 Tom's poverty kept his addiction to video games in _____.

   a. abdicate   b. abeyance   c. ablution   d. abnegation

03 Where our estates _____, we must build a fence.

   a. abound   b. abrogate   c. abscond   d. abut

04 _____ means the same thing as wealth and prosperity.

   a. accessory   b. accolade   c. acrimony   d. affluence

05 The major passenger airport in the US was closed about a month in the _____ of the September 11 attacks.

   a. aftermath   b. alacrity   c. allegory   d. altruism

06 The two nations reached an _____ agreement.

    a. amiable   b. amass   c. amicable   d. amorphous

07 The government intervention is _____ to the ideas of a market economy.

    a. anesthetic   b. antithetical   c. anonymous   d. anthology

08 He became an _____ when he left the church.

    a. aplomb   b. apathy   c. apotheosis   d. apostate

09 Climbing the mountain was _____.

    a. arduous   b. archaic   c. arbitrary   d. arid

10 The _____ was discovered in the ruins of Asia Minor.

    a. aspirant   b. askance   c. artifact   d. artifice

1. abase[1]

ad (to, toward), base (lower)

be abased, abase oneself 자신을 낮추다. humiliate, degrade

"The president is not willing to abase himself before the nation, and admit that he made a mistake." 대통령은 국민 앞에 자신을 낮추려 하지 않았으며 자기가 저지른 실수를 인정하려 하지 않았다.

2. abash

난처하게 하다 embarrass

She was abashed before him. 그녀는 그의 앞에서 수줍어했다

3. abate

bat (beat 치다) 누그러지다 lessen

abate the pain.

Bad weather abates when good weather begins to return.

나쁜 날씨는 좋은 날씨가 다시 돌아올 때 약화된다.

4. abbreviate

bre (short) 단축하다 curtail

abbreviate his speech 그의 연설을 단축하다.

5. abet

ab (to), bet (bait) 미끼를 달다, 선동하다, to help or encourage someone to do something wrong, especially to commit an offence.

방조와 교사 aid and abet.

abetting a criminal by giving her a place to hide.

그녀에게 숨을 장소를 제공함으로써 범죄를 교사하다.

---

1) abase, abash, abate, abbreviate, abet, abeyance

6. abeyance

bey (gape 놀라서 입을 벌림) 중지 a temporary stopping.

A's poverty kept his addiction to video games in abeyance

A의 가난이 비디오 게임에 대한 그의 중독을 잠시 중지시켰다.

7. abide²⁾

1)준수하다. abide by the newly enacted law,

새롭게 제정된 법을 지키다.

2)참다 tolerate, put up with,

We will not abide any violence in school.

우리는 학교에서 어떠한 폭력도 용인하지 아니할 것이다.

8. abjure

ab (away, from, off), jure (jury 배심원) swear, judge 도 같은 맥락.

공개적으로 안 하겠다고 선언하다. to promise solemnly, especially under oath,

to stop believing or doing something.

abjure alcohol. 금주하다.

9. ablution

ab(=intensive, away, off) + lu(=wash) 목욕, 목욕재계

the act of washing one's body or a part of it as a religious ceremony.

Islamic law which requires ablution before prayers.

기도 전에 목욕재계를 요구하는 이슬람 율법

10. abnegation

극기 self-sacrifice,

the act of giving up something one has or would like to have.

---

2) abide, abjure, ablution, abnegation, aboriginal

Ascetics practice self-abnegation.

금욕주의자는 스스로의 극기를 실행한다.

* ascetic 금욕주의자 someone who shuns or abstains from all physical comfort and pleasure, especiallysomeone who does so in solitude and for religious reasons.

11. aboriginal

ab (from), origin (oriri- rise, arise) 원시의, 토착의

primitive, native, **indigenous**

aboriginal Indians. 토착 인디언들

12. abound[3]

und (wave : inundate 침수시키다, redundant 여분의, undulate 물결치다.)

많이 있다.

Fish **abound** in the river. 물고기가 강에 많이 있다.

13. abrupt

1) 갑작스런 **happening suddenly**

an abrupt change, 갑작스런 변화

2) 퉁명스러운 brusque

an **abrupt** manner 퉁명스런 태도

14. abscond

abs(=from , away) + cond(=hide, recondite 뒤로 숨다 에서 심오한)

몰래 가지고 도망가다. **flee**

abscond with her jewels. 그녀의 보석을 가지고 도망가다.

15. abstruse

trus, trud (thrust : intrude 침입/강요하다, extrude 쫓아내다, obtrude 강요하다,

---

3) abound, abrupt, abscond, abstruse, abut, accessory, acclimate

protrude 불쑥 내밀다.) **difficult to understand**, profound 심오한

his **abstruse** works in philosophy 그의 철학에 있어서 심오한 작품들

16. **abut**

(어버트) 접경하다 인접하다 border upon; adjoin , **adjacent**

Where our estates **abut**, we must build a fence.

우리의 부동산이 인접하는 곳에 우리는 울타리를 쳐야만 한다.

17. **accessory**

부품 **additional object**, 종범 **accomplice**

He was made **accessory** to the crime 그는 그 범죄의 종범이다.

18. **acclimate**

(액클러메이트) ac, ad(=to) + clim(=slope, ladder) 적응시키다 **accustom** some-one or something to a new environment, climate,

acclimate themselves to their new and often strange environments.

그들의 새롭고 종종 이상한 환경에 적응하다.

19. **acquiesce**[4]

(액크위에스) ac, ad(=to, intensive) + quies(=quiet) 묵인하다

give consent silently, to accept it or agree to it without objection

They **acquiesced** in the decision. 그들은 그 결정을 묵인했다

20. **acquit**

1)무죄로 하다 **acquit** A of murder, A를 살인에서 무죄로 하다.

2)행동/처신하다. **acquit oneself well (badly)**

He **acquitted** himself like a pro. 그는 전문가와 같이 잘 처신했다.

---

4) acquiesce, acquit, acumen, adulation, adulterate, adventitious,

21. **acumen**

통찰력 <u>mental keenness</u>

his business <u>acumen</u> 그의 사업 통찰력

22. **adulation**

찬사 <u>flattery</u>, admiration

thrive on the <u>adulation</u> of his friends. 그의 친구들의 찬사에 의기양양하다.

23. **adulterate**

ad(=to, add) + ulter, alter(=other) 불순물을 섞다. <u>impure by mixing with</u>

<u>poorer quality.</u>

<u>adulterate</u> milk with water 물과 우유를 섞다.

*명사형 adultery는 간통 // commit adultery.

24. **adventitious**

우연의 happening by chance, <u>accidental</u>

<u>adventitious</u> meeting 우연한 만남.

25. **affluence**[5]

af, ab(=to, intensive) + flu(=flow) 풍요 <u>abundance</u>

<u>Affluence</u> means the same thing as wealth and prosperity.

풍요는 부와 번영과 동일이다.

26. **aftermath**

여파 <u>circumstances that follow and are a result of something, especially a</u>

<u>great and terrible event.</u>

---

5) affluence, aftermath, allay, amalgamate, ambidextrous, amicable

The major passenger airport in the US was closed about a month in the **aftermath** of the September 11 attacks.

미국에서 주요한 승객 공항이 11,11 공격의 여파로 한 달간 문을 닫았다.

27. allay

(얼레이) 가라앉히다 **calm, relieve**

allay the fears of the passengers 승객의 공포를 가라앉히다.

*alley (앨리) narrow passage

28. amalgamate

합병하다, **combine, unite**

amalgamate two groups into one. 두 그룹을 한 그룹으로 통합하다.

29. ambidextrous

ambi(=both, around) + dextr(=right hand) + ous(=having the quality of) 양손 잡이의 **able to use the left hand or the right equally well** ; unusually skillful

15

30. amicable

우호적인 **done in friendly way**

The two nations reached an **amicable** agreement.

두 나라는 우호적인 합의를 보았다.

31. anachronism [6]

chron(=time, age) 시대착오 **mistake in dating something**

Slavery is a sheer **anachronism** in the modern age.

노예제는 현대 시기에서 심한 시기착오이다.

---

6) anachronism, anesthetic, angst, anomaly, anonymous

32. **anesthetic**

(애너스 ;떼릭) 마취제 , 마치의 insensible

The Red Cross distributed a three-month supply of antibiotics, **anesthetics** and bandages to North Korean hospitals over the weekend. 적십자사는 지난 주 북한 병원에 3달간의 항생제, 마취제, 붕대를 공급했다.

33. **angst**

고뇌 **anxiety, apprehension.**

Adolescence is often marked by **angst.**
청년기는 고뇌로 종종 특징지어진다.

34. **annuity**

연금 **yearly allowance**

provide an **annuity** for its retired employees
은퇴한 직원에게 연금을 제공하다.

35. **anomaly**

변칙 **irregularity**

A rainy summer day is not an **anomaly.** 비오는 여름날은 변칙이 아니다.

36. **anonymous**

(어 ;나너머스) an(=not, without) + onym(=name, word ; antonym, synonym)

익명의 **without a name**

an **anonymous** benefactor donated 2 million dollars.
한 익명의 은인이 2백만 달러를 기증했다.

37. **antecedents**[7]

(앤터씨든트) (ced, cess 는 go; access, accede, concede, recede 퇴각하다, re-cess 휴식, proceed 앞으로 나아가다, precede 선행하다, cede 양도하다, prec-edent 전례) 전례 <u>preceding events or circumstances that influence what comes later; early life; ancestors</u>

a few questions about young man's birth and **antecedents**

(경력) 젊은이의 출생과 경력에 관한 몇 가지 질문

Your grandparents could be said to be your **antecedents**.

당신의 조부모는 당신의 조상이라고 말해진다.

38. **anthology**

(앤쌀러쥐) 모음집 <u>collection</u>

an **anthology** of his sayings 그의 어록의 모음집

39. **antipathy**

anti(=against, opposite) + path(=feel ; sympathy 공감, apathy 무감각, passion-ate 열정적인) + y(=that which) 반감/혐오 <u>strong dislike, aversion</u>

His extreme **antipathy** to dispute 논쟁에 대한 그의 극단적인 반감

40. **antithetical**

정반대의, 명사형은 antithesis (=opposite, contrary)

The government intervention is **antithetical** to the ideas of a market econo-my. 정부의 개입은 시장 경제의 정반대이다.

---

7) antecedents, anthology, antipathy, antithetical, aplomb, apocryphal

41. **aplomb**

(어플람) 태연함, 침착 <u>poise</u>

His nonchalance and <u>aplomb</u> in times of trouble always encouraged his followers.

어려운 시기에 그의 태연함과 침착함은 항상 그의 추종자를 격려했다.

42. **apocryphal**

(어파크러펄) cryph, crypt 가짜의 not genuine / sham

The legendary story is <u>apocryphal.</u> 그 전설적인 이야기는 허구이다.

43. **apostate**[8]

a (not) post(=stand) 배신자, <u>**one who abandons his faith**</u>

He became an <u>apostate</u> when he left the church.

그가 교회를 떠났을 때 그는 배신자가 되었다.

44. **apotheosis**

(어파티오시스) theo(=God) 신격화 <u>deification</u>

The <u>apotheosis</u> of a Roman emperor 로마황제에 대한 신격화

45. **arbitrary**

임의의 <u>dictatorial</u>(딕터토리얼)

oppose <u>arbitrary</u> executions without trial.

재판 없이 임의의 처형에 반대하다.

<u>* arbitrate 중재하다</u> arbitrate the dispute between - 사이에서의 분쟁을 중재하다.

46. **arcane**

이상한 <u>secret; mysterious</u>

---

8) apostate, apotheosis, arbitrary, arcane, archaic, arduous,

the rites of the secret cult were **arcane**. 그 비밀 사교의 의식은 이상했다.

47. archaic

고대의 **antiquated**

archaic words which are no longer part of our normal vocabulary.
더 이상 우리의 정상적인 어휘의 일부분이 아닌 고대 단어들

48. arduous

(아쥬어스) ardus 는 steep 경사 어원. 경사가 있는 곳으로 향하는 즉, 아주 힘드는 **toilsome,**

Climbing the mountain was **arduous.** 그 산을 오르는 것은 아주 힘들다.

49. arid[9]

마른 **dry; barren**

The cactus has adapted to survive in an arid environment.
선인장은 황폐한 환경에서 살아남도록 적응되어 왔다.

19

50. arraign

기소하다 **charge in court**

The accused man was **arraigned** in the County Criminal Court.
고소된 그 남자는 카운티 형사 법정에 기소되었다.

51. artifacts

공예품 **products of primitive culture**

the **artifacts** discovered in the ruins of Asia Minor
소아시아의 폐허지역에서 발견된 공예품들

---

9) arid, arraign, artifacts, artifice, ascetic, ascribe, aspersion

52. artifice

속임 __trickery__

resort to __artifice__ 계략에 의존하다.

53. ascetic

금욕의 __practicing self-denial;__

the __ascetic__ life led by the monks. 수도승에 의하여 영위되는 금욕 생활

54. ascribe

ad (to, d가 탈락), scribe (write) prescribe 사전에 쓰다. 처방하다, 규정/지시하다. circumscribe 한계를 정하다. conscript 징집하다. describe 묘사하다. depict 그림으로 그려서 묘사하다. __ascribe A to B 탓으로 하다.__

__ascribe__ one's success to good luck. 그의 성공을 행운의 탓으로 하다.

55. aspersion

a, ad(=to) + spers(=strew) 물 뿌리기, 비방/중상 __slander__

cast __aspersions__ on the corrupt president.

타락한 대통령에 대한 비방을 가하다.

__asperse__ a person with bitter words. 심한 말로 한 사람을 비방하다.

56. aspirant[10]

(에스퍼런트) (spire 는breathe ; conspire 공모하다, suspire 한숨 쉬다, expire 기간 다하다, respire 호흡하다.) 지위나 신분을 열망하는 사람 __seeker after position or status__

an __aspirant__ for public office 공직을 열망하는 자

__aspire__ to the leader of the party. 그 정당의 지도자를 열망하다.

---

10) aspirant

11 The refugees sought _____ from religious persecution.

    a. asylum   b. assessment   c. atrocity   d. atrophy

12 A clear sky morning is an _____ sign.

    a. austere   b. auspicious   c. autonomous   d. attenuate

13 An all-out war was _____ed by the last-minute compromise.

    a. bate   b. barrage   c. avert   d. aver

14 Her behavior _____ed her story.

    a. belie   b. beguile   c. barrage   d. bereft

15 Despite the salesperson's _____, the customer did not buy the outfit.

    a. cacophony   b. benediction   c. cache   d. blandishment

16 He was _____ to the suffering in the wards.

a. bombastic b. bumptious c. callous d. callow

17 The enemy was warned to _____ or face annihilation.

a. circumspect b. chide c. capitulate d. cajole

18 Her remarks were_____ and to the point.

a. colloquial b. cognizant c. clandestine d. cogent

19 _____ on this problem; the solution will come.

a. cogitate b. cohort c. condone d. conjecture

20 She was still angry despite his _____ words.

a. commodious b. complacent c. compliant d. conciliatory

57. **assail**[11]

공격하다 <u>assault</u>

He was <u>assailed</u> with questions after his lecture.

그는 그의 강연 후에 질문으로 휩싸였다.

58. **assessment**

(sess, sens 는 sit ; obsess, obsession 강박관념, session 학기, sedentary 앉아있는, supersede 대신하다, sediment 침전물) 평가

<u>assess</u> the damage caused by the storm

그 폭풍에 의해 야기된 손해를 평가하다.

59. **asslduous**

(어씨쥬어스) as, sid (sit ; insidious 음흉한, 잠행성의, preside 사회보다, subside 누그러뜨리다, reside 살다, resident 거주자), u (full), ous

한쪽으로만 향하여 전적으로 앉아 있는 즉, <u>diligent</u>, working steadily 부지런한, 끈기 있게 애를 쓰는 work assiduously.

the only <u>assiduous</u> student 단 하나의 부지런한 학생

60. **astringent**

심한 <u>harsh, severe</u>

The <u>astringent</u> quality of the unsweetened lemon juice

달지 않은 레몬주스의 신 맛

his <u>astringent</u> review 그의 신랄한 비평

61. **astronomical**

방대한, 천문학적인 <u>enormously large or extensive</u>

spend <u>astronomical</u> sums 방대한 금원을 소비하다.

---

11) assail, assessment, assiduous, astringent, astronomical, asylum

62. **asylum**

피난처 **place of refuge or shelter**

The refugees sought **asylum** from religious persecution

그 난민들은 종교적인 박해로부터 피난처를 구했다.

63. **atrocity**[12]

잔악행위 **brutality**

In time of war, many **atrocities** are committed by invading armies.

전시에는 많은 잔혹행위들이 침입 군대에 의해 자행된다.

64. **atrophy**

(애트러피) a, an(=not, without) + troph(=nourishment ; dystrophy 영양실조 malnutrition, hypertrophy 비대 obesity) 쇠약해지다. **waste away**

The athlete's muscle has dramatically **atrophied.**

그 운동선수의 근육은 심하게 쇠약해 졌다.

65. **attenuate**

at, ad(=to, intensive) + tenu(=thin ; tenuous 희미한, extenuate 정상참작하다)

가늘게 하다 make thin or slender ; **weaken**

attenuate the enemy lines 적의 전선을 약화시키다.

66. **auspicious**

au (avi, bird), spic (look), ious 새를 보고 길,흉 점을 침. **favorable**, fortunate 길조의, 순조로운

an **auspicious** moment. 길조의 순간

A clear sky morning is an **auspicious** sign

맑은 하늘 아침은 길조의 표식이다.

반대말은 inauspicious.

---

12) atrocity, atrophy, attenuate, auspicious, austere, autonomous

67. austere

엄격한 **strict**

His **austere** demeanor 단호한 태도

austere prison food 내핍의 죄수 음식

68. autonomous

nom(=law) 자치의 **self-governing**. 명사형은 autonomy

The east office of the firm was quite **autonomous**.

그 회사의 동쪽 사무소는 아주 자치적이다.

69. autopsy[13]

op(=eye) 검시 **postmortem examination of a body.**

The **autopsy** failed to discover the cause of the death.

그 검시는 그 죽음의 원인을 밝히는 데에 실패했다.

70. aversion

혐오 **firm dislike**

Their mutual **aversion** was so great. 그들 상호간의 반목은 아주 컸다.

71. avert

ab(=away, from) + vert(=turn, averse 싫어하는, adverse 역의, adversity 역경, convert 개종하다, converse 담화하다/ 거꾸로, conversant 정통한, divert 전환하다) 막다. **avoid, prevent**.

An all-out war was **averted** by the last-minute compromise.

전면전은 마지막 협상에 의해 방지되었다.

---

13) autopsy, aversion, avert, axiom, baleful, barrage, bastion

72. **axiom**

(액시엄) 공리 <u>**self-evident truth requiring no proof**</u>

"Everything that is living dies" is an <u>**axiom**</u>.

살아있는 모든 것은 죽는다. 는 것은 공리이다.

73. **baleful**

악의 있는 deadly; destructive, baneful, malign, <u>**pernicious,**</u>

a <u>**baleful**</u> omen 악의 있는 저주

74. **barrage**

탄막 ;a long burst of gunfire which keeps an enemy back while soldiers move forward.

a <u>**barrage**</u> of critical remarks 비평의 연발

75. **bastion**

<u>**fortress**</u>; defense 요새

a <u>**bastion**</u> of democracy 민주주의의 요새

76. **bate**[14]

억제하다. let down, <u>**restrain,**</u>

<u>**bate**</u> his curiosity. 그의 호기심을 억제하다.

77. **beguile**

속이다 즐겁게 하다 <u>**cheat**</u> ; amuse / <u>**delude**</u>;

A beguiled B into 속이다,

beguile oneself 즐기다.

beguile himself by playing a card game.

카드 게임을 즐김으로써 즐기다. guileless 순수한

---

14) bate, beguile, belie, bellicose, benediction, benign

78. belie

거짓임을 드러내다 **give a false impression**

Her behavior **belied** her story.

그녀의 행동은 그녀의 이야기가 거짓임을 드러내다.

79. bellicose

warlike, Bellona 그리스의 여신, war, beauty (belle 미인, embellish 장식하다.)

상징. 호전적인 **belligerent**.

80. benediction

dict(=say, addict, malediction, jurisdiction, abdicate 사임하다. verdict 평결,

predict, contradict, dictatorship 독재, indict 기소하다,) 축복, 축도

a prayer giving blessing, especially at the end of a religious service.

81. benign

gn, gen(=birth) generate 발생시키다. degenerate 퇴보하다, regenerate 갱생시

키다. congenial 같은 성질의, congenital 선천적인, cognate 같은 기원의, 상냥한

kind, gentle

his **benign** attitude 그의 선한 태도

a **benign** tumor 양성 종양, 반대는 **malignant** 악성의

82. bestow[15]

수여하다 **confer**

bestow great honors upon the hero. 그 영웅에게 큰 영광을 수여하다.

---

15) bestow, blandishment, blithe, boisterous, bombastic, broach, bucolic

83. blandishment

아첨 **flattery**; coaxing

Despite the salesperson's **blandishments**, the customer did not buy the outfit. 그 판매사원의 아첨에도 불구하고 그 고객은 그 물품을 사지 않았다.

84. blithe

유쾌한, 즐거운 **carefree** and gay lighthearted

a **blithe** spirit 유쾌한 정신

85. boisterous

거친, 시끄러운 violent; rough; **noisy**

The unruly crowd became even more **boisterous.**
그 통제 불가능한 군중은 심지어 더욱 거칠어 졌다.

86. bombastic

과장된, 허풍떠는 **pompous; using inflated language**

The orator's **bombastic** manner 그 연설자의 허풍떠는 태도

87. broach

끄집어내다 **open up**

broach the subject 그 주제를 꺼내어 내다.

88. bucolic

목가적인 **rustic; pastoral**, concerned with the countryside or people living there; pastoral; rustic.

89. **cache**[16]

은닉 장소 <u>hiding place</u>

He led them to the **cache** where he had stored his loot.

그는 그가 그의 약탈품을 저장해 놓은 은닉장소로 그들을 데리고 갔다.

90. **cadaver**

(커데버) 사체 <u>corpse</u>

It is illegal to dissect **cadavers.** 사체를 훼손하는 것은 불법이다.

cadaverous 창백한

his **cadaverous** appearance, 그의 창백한 모습

91. **callous**

(피부가) 굳어진, 못 박힌, 무삼각한, 냉담한 <u>hardened</u>; <u>unfeeling</u>

He was **callous** to the suffering in the wards.

그는 병동에서 고통 받는 자들에게 무감각하다.

29

92. **canvass**

유세하다 부탁하고 다니다, 세밀히 조사하다 inspect, scrutinize, <u>survey</u>

After **canvassing** the sentiments of his constituents, the congressman was confident that he represented the majority opinion of his district.

그의 선거구민의 감정을 세밀히 조사한 후에 그 의원은 그가 그 지역의 다수 의견을 대표한다고 확신하였다.

93. **capitulate**

cap(=head, captain, capital) 항복하다 <u>surrender</u> on stated condition

The enemy was warned to **capitulate** or face annihilation.

그 적은 항복하고 그렇지 아니하면 전멸당할 것이라고 경고 받았다.

---

16) cache, cadaver, callous, canvass, capitulate, chary

94. **chary**

조심스러운 <u>cautiously watchful</u>

She was <u>chary</u> of his favors because she had been hurt before.

그녀는 전에 감정을 상했기 때문에 그의 호의에 조심하였다.

95. **chasten**[17]

(체이슨)벌하다, 단련시키다 <u>discipline; punish in order to correct</u>

Whom God loves, God <u>chastens.</u> 신이 사랑하는 자를 신은 단련시킨다.

96. **chide**

꾸짖다 <u>scold</u>

<u>chide</u> Steven for his lying. 거짓말 했다고 꾸짖다.

97. **choleric**

화를 잘 내는 <u>hot-tempered</u>

a <u>choleric</u> nature. 화 잘 내는 성질

98. **coddle**

응석받이로 키우다 <u>pamper</u>

Don't <u>coddle</u> the children so much

그 어린아이들을 너무 응석받이로 키우지 마라.

99. **cogent**

설득력 있는 having a powerful appeal to the mind / <u>convincing</u>

Her remarks were <u>cogent</u> and to the point.

그녀의 말은 설득력이 있고 요점에 맞았다.

---

17) chasten, chide, choleric, coddle, cogent, cogitate, collusion

100. cogitate

숙고하다 **think over**

Cogitate on this problem; the solution will come.

이 문제에 숙고하라, 그러면 해결책이 나올 것이다.

101. collusion

공모 **complicity, connivance**

The police were acting in **collusion** with the drug traffickers.

경찰이 마약 거래상들과 결탁을 하고 있었다.

102. conciliatory[18]

달래는, 회유적인 **reconciling; soothing**

She was still angry despite his **conciliatory** words.

그녀는 그의 화해적인 말에도 불구하고 여전히 화를 낸다.

---

18) conciliatory

21 He was not a churchgoer; he was interested only in _____ matters.

    a. contumacious b. corporeal c. contrite d. contiguous

22 The _____ man resolved to reduce.

    a. craven b. covetous c. covenant d. corpulent

23 This _____ in the government can only result in anarchy.

    a. debonair b. debacle c. dearth d. debauchery

24 Luxury and self-indulgence _____ the Roman people and led to the fall of the empire.

    a. debilitate b. decimate c. decipher d. decry

25 Do not _____ at my request.

    a. default b. defunct c. demur d. demure

26 Thaksin was _____ed in a military coup on 19 September, and is currently living in exile in London.

a. depose   b. dilute   c. disparage   d. dissemble

27 an _____ liar

a. discreet   b. discrete   c. disperse   d. egregious

28 She is keen to _____ her sister's sporting achievements.

a. elucidate   b. emanate   c. embellish   d. emulate

29 He gave an _____ answer, typical of a politician.

a. enamored   b. enigmatic   c. equivocal   d. ephemeral

30 He was _____ of the crime when the real criminal confessed.

a. enthrall   b. exculpate   c. espouse   d. erudite

103. congenial[19)]

con(=with) + gen(=birth) 같은 성질의, 취미가 같은, 마음 맞는
<u>congenial</u> companions. 같은 성질의 동료들

104. congenital

타고난 <u>선천적인 existing at birth, but not hereditary</u>
His <u>congenital</u> deformity 그의 선천적인 질병

105. conjecture

con(=with) + ject(=throw) 짐작, 억측, 짐작하다, 추측하다 <u>guess</u>
It was based on a mere <u>conjecture.</u> 그것은 단순히 추측에 근거한 것이다.

106. contend

con(=together) + tend(=stretch) 다투다 <u>struggle</u>
contentious 호전적인 quarrelsome
Several teams are <u>contending</u> for the prize.
그 상을 놓고 몇 팀이 겨루게 된다.

107. contrite

회개하는, 잘못을 깊이 뉘우치는 <u>penitent</u>
Her <u>contrite</u> tears 그녀의 회한의 눈물

108. convoke

소집하다 <u>call together</u>
Congress was <u>convoked</u> at the outbreak of the emergency.
의회는 위급상황의 발발에 소집된다.

---

19) congenial, congenital, conjecture, contend, contrite, convoke, corporeal

109. corporeal

육체의 물질의 __bodily material__

He was not a churchgoer; he was interested only in <u>corporeal</u> matters. 그는 교회에 가지 않는다. 그는 단지 물질의 문제에만 관심이 있다.

110. corpulent[20]

corp(=body) 뚱뚱한 __fat and heavy__

The __corpulent__ man resolved to reduce.

그 뚱뚱한 사람은 줄이려고 결심했다.

111. culmination

최고점에 달함, 절정 __attainment of highest point__

marked the __culmination__ of his political career.

그의 정치 경력의 정점에 달하다.

112. daunt

겁나게 하다 __intimidate__

Your threats cannot __daunt__ me. 너의 위협은 나를 겁나게 할 수 없다.

__dauntless__ 불굴의 용감한 bold

the __dauntless__ soldier 불굴의 병사

113. dawdle

빈둥거리다 <u>loiter</u>

__dawdle__ over their homework 그들의 숙제에 빈둥거리다.

---

20) corpulent, culmination, daunt, dawdle, dearth, debacle, debauch

114. **dearth**

결핍 <u>scarcity</u>

The **dearth** of skilled labor 숙련된 노동의 결핍

115. **debacle**

깨짐 와해 <u>breaking up; downfall</u>

This **debacle** in the government can only result in anarchy.
정부의 와해는 단지 무정부를 결과할 수 있다.

116. **debauch**

타락시키다 더럽히다

A vicious newspaper can **debauch** public ideals.
그 사악한 신문은 대중의 이상을 더럽힐 수 있다.

117. **debilitate**[21)]

쇠약하게하다 <u>weaken; enfeeble</u>

Luxury and self-indulgence **debilitated** the Roman people and led to the
fall of the empire. 사치스러움과 방종은 로마 사람들을 쇠약하게 하고 그 제국
의 몰락을 가져왔다.

118. **decimate**

열 명에 한 명꼴로 죽이다, <u>kill many people</u> / usually one out of ten
Smallpox began to **decimate** the population.
천연두는 인구를 감소시키기 시작했다.

119. **decipher**

해독하다 <u>decode</u>

---

21) debilitate, decimate, decipher, decorous, decrepit, decry

I could not **decipher** the doctor's handwriting.
나는 그 의사의 필적을 해독할 수 없었다.

120. decorous

예의바른 점잖은 **proper**

lack of **decorum**. 예의의 결핍

121. decrepit

병약한 ; 노쇠한 **weakened by old age ; old and having no power**

Our Constitution is almost 200 years old, but far from being **decrepit**, it is still a valid, dynamic, and highly practical plan of government. 우리 헌법은 거의 200년이 되었지만 노쇠하기는커녕 아직도 유효하고, 역동적이고, 아주 실용적이 정부 계획이다.

122. decry

비난하다 헐뜯다 **disparage**

Do not attempt to increase your stature by **decrying** the efforts of your opponents. 너의 적의 노력을 비난함에 의하여 너의 위상을 올리려고 시도하지 마라.

123. default[22]

불이행, 재판정에서의 결석 **failure to do**

She was granted a divorce by **default**.
그녀는 불출석에 의해 이혼을 승인받았다.

---

22) default, deleterious, demur, demure, depose, depredation

124. **deleterious**

해로운 <u>harmful</u>

the <u>deleterious</u> effects of radioactive substances.
방사선 물질의 해로운 효과

125. **demur**

반대하다 <u>object</u>

Do not <u>demur</u> at my request. 나의 요구에 반대하지 마라

126. **demure**

수줍은 said of a person: <u>quiet</u>, modest and well-behaved.
She was <u>demure</u> and reserved. 그녀는 수줍고 소극적이다.

127. **depose**

면직하다 ; 퇴위시키다 ; 선서증언하다 de(=from, away) + pos(=put)
<u>put someone out of a high office</u> ; remove someone from a throne ; <u>declare</u>
<u>under oath</u>

Thaksin was <u>deposed</u> in a military coup on 19 September, and is currently
living in exile in London. 탁신은 11.19 군사 쿠데타에 의해 실각했고 현재 런던
에서 망명 생활을 하고 있다.

128. **depredation**

de(=intensive) + pred(=plunder) 파괴, 약탈 destruction or pillaging of property / <u>plundering</u>

the <u>depredations</u> of the invaders 침입자의 약탈

129. dichotomy[23]

이분법 di(=two) + cho(=into) + tom(=cut) + y(=that which) **division into two parts**

a simple **dichotomy** of right and wrong. 단순한 선과 악의 이분법

130. didactic

교훈적인 teaching; **instructional**

The **didactic** qualities of his poetry 그의 시의 교훈적인 자질

131. dilute

희석하다, 묽게 하다 **make less concentrated**; **reduce in strength**

preferred her coffee **diluted** with milk. 우유를 탄 그녀의 커피를 좋아하다.

132. disavowal

부인 거부 **denial**; disclaiming

His **disavowal** of his part in the conspiracy was not believed by the jury. 공모의 그의 부분에 대한 부인은 배심원에 의해 믿어지지 아니하였다.

133. disparage

dis(=not) + par(=equal) 멸시하다 say that someone or something is of small value or importance ; speak ill of / **belittle**

Do not **disparage** anyone's contribution; these little gifts add up to large sums. 어느 사람의 공헌을 멸시하지 마라, 이러한 작은 선물들이 모여서 큰 것이 된다.

---

23) dichotomy, didactic, dilute, disavowal, disparage, disperse

134. disperse

흩뜨리다 <u>scatter</u> in all directions

The police fired tear gas into the crowd to <u>**disperse**</u> the protesters.

그 경찰은 데모 자들을 해산하기 위해 군중에 최루탄을 발사했다.

135. divulge[24]

(디벌쥐) 나타내다 <u>reveal</u>

A person accused of a crime is not obliged to <u>**divulge**</u> anything that might tend to incriminate him. 범죄로 고소된 사람은 그를 죄 지우는 어떠한 것도 나타내도록 강요되어서는 안 된다.

136. dross

폐기물 불순물 <u>**waste matter; worthless impurities**</u>

separate the valuable metal from the <u>**dross**</u>. 귀금속과 폐기물을 구분하다.

137. drudgery

고된 일 <u>**hard, unpleasant, uninteresting work**</u> / menial work

It was <u>**drudgery**</u> washing dishes in the hot kitchen.

뜨거운 부엌에서 설거지를 하는 것은 고된 일이다.

138. egregious

지독한 e, ex(=out) + greg(=flock, mob) <u>**remarkably bad**</u>

an <u>**egregious**</u> liar 사악한 거짓말

139. empirical

경험적인 <u>**relying on observation and experiment, not on theory**</u>

<u>**empirical**</u> evidence 경험적인 증거

---

24) divulge, dross, drudgery, egregious, empirical, emulate, enamored

140. emulate

필적하다 rival; **imitate**; to try to equal or excel

She is keen to **emulate** her sister's sporting achievements.

그녀는 언니의 스포츠 업적에 필적하려고 열심이다.

141. enamored

매혹된 **in love**

Narcissus became **enamored** of his own beauty.

나르시스는 그의 자신의 아름다움에 매혹되었다.

142. enormity[25]

거대함 **hugeness** (in a bad sense)

the **enormity** of his crime 그의 범행의 서내힘

143. enthrall

매혹하다 노예를 만들다 **capture**; enslave

He was **enthralled** by her beauty. 그는 그녀의 아름다움에 매혹되었다.

144. ephemeral

덧없는 living for a very short time ; **transitory** / short-lived; fleeting

145. equivocal

모호한 doubtful; **ambiguous**; the equivocal statements

He gave an **equivocal** answer, typical of a politician.

그는 정치가들에게 전형적인 모호한 답변을 했다.

---

25) enormity, enthrall, ephemeral, equivocal, erudite, espouse, euphemism

146. **erudite**

e, ex(=out) + rud(=crude) 박식한

a witty and immensely **erudite** man 기지가 있고 엄청나게 박식한 사람

147. **espouse**

지지하다 adopt; **support**

espouse a worthy cause. 가치 있는 대의명분을 지지하다.

148. **euphemism**

완곡어법 **a mild or inoffensive term** used in place of one considered offensive or unpleasantly direct.

The expression "he passed away" is a **euphemism** for "he died."
"그가 지나갔다." 라는 표현은 "그가 죽었다." 의 완곡 표현이다.

149. **evanescent**[26]

e, ex(=out, intensive) + van(=empty) + esc(=becoming) 덧없는
fleeting; vanishing

as **evanescent** as snowflakes 눈송이처럼 순식간에 사라지는

150. **exculpate**

(엑스커페잇) 무죄로 하다 **clear from blame**

He was **exculpated** of the crime when the real criminal confessed.

---

26) evanescent, exculpate

31 Your statement is _____ and will upset the harmony that now exists.

a. explicit   b. extraneous   c. facetious   d. factious

32 The neglected wound became _____.

a. fetid   b. extrovert   c. fetter   d. fickle

33 They drove around in Rolls-Royces, openly _____ing their wealth.

a. foray   b. flaunt   c. flagrant   d. flout

34 The _____ report confused many readers.

a. garbled   b. futile   c. furtive   d. foible

35 Entrance is _____.

a. germane   b. gainsay   c. gratis   d. garrulous

36 In the _____ of a plumber, the detective investigated the murder case.

a. harbinger   b. halcyon   c. guffaw   d. guise

37 Filled with _____, Lear refused to heed his friend's warnings.

a. hieroglyphic   b. hedonism   c. hubris   d. hoary

38 The married couple argued incessantly and finally decided to separate

because they were _____.

a. impetuous   b. inarticulate   c. incessant d.   incompatible

39 The plot of the play is _____.

a. iniquitous   b. intrepid   c. jejune   d. itinerant

40 Let us be serious; this is not a _____ issue.

a. ludicrous   b. lugubrious   c. loquacious   d. licentious

151. exhume[27)]

발굴하다 <u>dig out of the ground;</u>

His body was **exhumed** in order that an autopsy might be performed.

그의 시체는 검시가 시행될 수 있도록 하기 위해 발굴되었다.

152. exonerate

ex(=out) + oner(=burden) + ate(=make) 면제 하다 ; 무죄로 하다

<u>absolve, acquit, vindicate</u>

A commission of inquiry **exonerated** him.

조사위원회가 그의 혐의를 벗겨 주었다.

153. expedite

촉진하다 <u>hasten</u>

expedite delivery 배달을 촉진하다.

45

154. expiate

(엑스피에잇) ex(=out, intensive) + pi(=holy, tender) 속죄하다

<u>make amends for</u>

expiate one's guilt 자기 죄를 속죄하다

155. expurgate

ex(=out) + purg(=clean, clear) 삭제하다 <u>take out</u> from a book what is considered to be improper

an **expurgated** edition 삭제 판

---

27) exhume, exonerate, expedite, expiate, expurgate, extraneous

156. **extraneous**

이질적인 <u>not related</u>

His point was **extraneous** to the argument.

그의 요점은 그 논쟁에서 벗어났다.

157. **extrapolation**[28]

추론 projection; <u>conjecture</u>

Based on their **extrapolation** from the results of the primaries on Super Tuesday, the net works predicted that George Bush would be the Republican candidate for the presidency. 슈퍼 화요일의 프라이머리 경선 결과로부터 추론에 근거를 두고 네트워크는 죠지 부시가 대통령직을 위한 공화당 후보가 될 것이라고 예상했다.

158. **extricate**

ex(=out) + tric(=petty obstacle) <u>release</u> or disentangle from a net, difficulty **extricate** himself from the trap. 그 자신을 덫으로부터 구출하다.

159. **extrovert**

vert(=turn) 외향적인 자 <u>person interested mostly in external objects and actions</u>

160. **fabricate**

조작하다. <u>build; lie</u>

fabricated evidence against them. 그에 대한 증거를 조작하다.

161. **factious**

당파적인 <u>causing dissension</u>

---

28) extrapolation, extricate, extrovert, fabricate, factious, factitious

Your statement is **factious** and will upset the harmony that now exists. 너의 말은 당파적이고 지금 존재하는 조화를 뒤집는다.

162. factitious

fact 는 make, do, **artificial**; sham 인위적인 가짜의

factitious tears 가짜 눈물

163. fallacious[29]

(fall ; fallen 은 타락한 a fallen woman, 정조를 잃은) 오류가 있는 **misleading**

Your reasoning must be **fallacious**.

너의 추론은 오류가 있음에 틀림이 없다.

164. fetid

냄새가 심한 **malodorous**

The neglected wound became **fetid**.

그 방치된 상처는 냄새가 심하게 났다.

165. fetter

속박하다 **shackle**

The prisoner was **fettered** to the wall. 그 죄수는 그 벽에 묶였다.

166. fickle

변덕스러운 **changeable**, vacillating, volatile

The taste of the public is so **fickle**, 대중의 기호는 너무 변덕스러워서, *pickle 오이지

---

29) fallacious, fetid, fetter, fickle, fidelity, filial, flagging, flagrant

167. **fidelity**

fid(=trust ; confidence 신용) loyalty, **faithfulness** ; exactness 정확성

Hi-Fi = high fidelity

168. **filial**

자식의

forget their **filial** obligations 그들의 자식의 의무를 잊다.

169. **flagging**

약한 **weak**; drooping / **unflagging** 굴하지 않는

170. **flagrant**

극악무도한 **conspicuously wicked** * fragrant 향내는

171. **flaunt**[30]

display ostentatiously 과시하다

They drove around in Rolls-Royces, openly **flaunting** their wealth.

그들은 롤스로이스를 주위로 몰았다. 그들의 부를 공개적으로 과시하면서,

172. **flout**

업신여기다 to defy (an order, convention, etc) openly; to **disrespect** (authority, etc).

flouted all authority 모든 권위를 무시하다.

173. **foray**

습격, (전문분야로의)진출 **raid**

staged a midnight **foray** against the enemy outpost.

적의 전초기지로 한밤중의 습격을 전개하다.

---

30) flaunt, flout, foray, forestall, forsake, furtive, futile

48

174. forestall

미리 막다 <u>upset</u> somebody or his plans by doing something unexpectedly early

<u>forestall</u> any demonstrations 어떤 데모를 미리 막다.

175. forsake

버리다 <u>abandon</u>; renounce

She <u>forsook</u> her notebook for new technology.

그녀는 새로운 기술을 위해 그녀의 노트북을 버렸다.

176. furtive

은밀한 <u>secretive</u>; stealthy; sly.

a <u>furtive</u> look at his classmate's test paper.

그의 급우의 시험지를 은밀히 보다.

49

177. futile

쓸모없는 <u>useless</u>

futile pursuits 무익한 추구

178. gainsay

반박하다 <u>to deny or contradict</u>

<u>gainsay</u> the truth of the report. 그 보고서의 진실성을 반박하다.

178. gainsay[31]

반박하다 <u>to deny or contradict</u>

<u>gainsay</u> the truth of the report. 그 보고서의 진실성을 반박하다.

---

31) gainsay, garbled, gratis, gregarious, guise, halcyon, hallowed

179. garbled

왜곡된 **mixed up; based on false or unfair selection**
The **garbled** report confused many readers.
그 왜곡된 보고서는 많은 독자들을 혼란시켰다.

180. gratis

(그래리스) 무료의 **free**
give one package **gratis** to every purchaser
모든 구입자에게 한 가지 패키지를 무료로 주다.
Entrance is **gratis**. 입장 무료.

181. gregarious

greg(=flock, mob) 군집성의 **living in groups or societies**
Human beings are naturally **gregarious**.
인간은 자연적으로 군집생활을 한다.

182. guise

모습 **appearance**; costume
In the **guise** of a plumber, the detective investigated the murder case. 배관공의 외양으로 그 탐정은 그 살인 사건을 조사했다.

183. halcyon

고요한 **calm; peaceful**
In those **halcyon** days 그런 고요한 날에

184. hallowed

신성한 **consecrated**
rest in **hallowed** ground. 신성 지역에서 휴식하다.

185. **harbinger**[32]

선구자 <u>forerunner</u>

an early **harbinger** of spring. 봄의 전령

186. **hibernal**

겨울의 <u>wintry</u>

Bears prepare for their long **hibernal** sleep by overeating.

곰은 과식에 의해 그들의 긴 겨울잠을 준비한다.

<u>* hibernate</u> 겨울잠을 자다. sleep throughout the winter

187. **hieroglyphic**

상형문자 <u>picture writing</u>

the ancient Egyptian **hieroglyphics** 고대 이집트의 상형문자

188. **hoary**

흰백이 된 <u>white with age</u>

The man was **hoary** and wrinkled when he was 70.

그 남자는 늙고 70이 되었을 때 주름이 졌다.

189. **hubris**

오만 <u>arrogance</u>; excessive self-conceit

Filled with **hubris**, Lear refused to heed his friend's warnings.

오만으로 가득 찬 레어는 그의 친구의 경고에 주의하는 것을 거절했다.

190. **hypothetical**

(하이퍼쎄리컬) hypo(=under) + thet(=put) + ical(=nature of) 가설의

By reference to **hypothetical** cases, 가설의 경우를 참조하여

---

32) harbinger, hibernal, hieroglyphic, hoary, hubris, hypothetical, hedonism

191. **hedonism**

hedon(=pleasure) 쾌락주의 <u>**belief that pleasure is the chief good**</u>

<u>Hedonism</u> and asceticism are opposing philosophies of human behavior.
쾌락주의와 극기주의는 인간 행동의 반대되는 철학이다.

192. **immutable**[33]

im, in(=not) + mut(=change) 불변의 <u>**unchangeable**</u>

discover the <u>**immutable**</u> laws of nature. 자연의 불변의 법칙을 발견하다.

193. **impetuous**

성급한 충동적인 violent; <u>**hasty**</u>; rash

We tried to curb his <u>**impetuous**</u> behavior.
우리는 그의 성급한 행동을 제한하기 위해 노력했다.

194. **impunity**

im, in(=not) + pun(=punish) 형을 받지 않음 <u>**exemption from punishment**</u>

<u>**with impunity**</u> 형벌을 받음이 없이

195. **inarticulate**

모호한 똑똑히 말을 못하는 <u>**unable to express oneself clearly or to speak distinctly.**</u>

He became <u>**inarticulate**</u> with rage. 그는 격노로 말을 똑똑히 못했다.

196. **incarcerate**

투옥하다 <u>**imprison**</u>

<u>**incarcerate**</u> the felon after conviction.
유죄판결 후에 그 중범죄 인을 투옥하다.

---

33) immutable, impetuous, impunity, inarticulate, incarcerate, incompatible

197. incompatible

양립할 수 없는 <u>inharmonious</u>

The married couple argued incessantly and finally decided to separate because they were **incompatible**. 결혼한 부부는 끝임 없이 논쟁했고 마침내 양립할 수 없어 헤어지기로 결심했다.

198. incongruity[34]

부조화 <u>lack of harmony; absurdity</u>

The **incongruity** of his wearing sneakers with formal attire,
그가 정식 복장에 운동화를 신은 부조화

199. inveterate

in(=in) + vet(=old) 고질적인 deep-rooted ; long-established / <u>habitual</u> an **inveterate** smoker 고질적인 흡연가

53

200. itinerant

소요하는 <u>wandering</u>; traveling

The farms relied heavily on **itinerants** during the harvest period.
그 농장들은 수확기에 일용직 노동자들에게 크게 의존했다.

201. jejune

지루한 <u>lacking interest</u>; barren; meager

The plot of the play is **jejune**. 그 연극의 구성은 지루하다.

202. kleptomaniac

병적도박자 <u>person who has a compulsive desire to steal</u>

---

34) incongruity, inveterate, itinerant, jejune, kleptomaniac, largess, latitude

203. largess

아낌없이 줌 **generous gift**

distributed **largess** to the poor 가난한 자에게 아낌없이 베풀다.

204. latitude

가. 위도 at a **latitude** of ten degrees north 북위 10도에.

* parallel (반의어는 longitude)

나. 자유재량 a wide **latitude** in his choice of college
그의 대학 선택에 있어서 광범위한 재량

205. laudable[35)]

칭찬할 만한 **praiseworthy**; commendable

His **laudable** deeds 그의 칭찬할 만한 행동

206. lithe

유연한 **flexible**; supple

lithe bodies 나긋나긋한 몸

207. loquacious

수다스런 **talkative**, garrulous, verbose;

208. ludicrous

우스운 **laughable**; trifling

Let us be serious; this is not a **ludicrous** issue.
심각하자. 이것은 우스운 주제가 아니다.

209. lugubrious

슬퍼하는, 우울한

have a **lugubrious** expression 슬픈 표정을 짓다

---

35) laudable, lithe, loquacious, ludicrous, lugubrious

41 She had undergone an amazing _____ from awkward schoolgirl to beautiful woman.

a. malediction   b. malinger   c. metamorphosis   d. mercurial

42 He was _____ in checking his accounts and never made mistakes. a. mordant   b. modish   c. meticulous   d. miscreant

43 He was concerned only with _____ matters.

a. mundane   b. munificent   c. mutilate   d. myriad

44 The people in the house had died from inhaling _____ smoke.

a. nebulous   b. nefarious   c. noxious   d. neophyte

45 He attacks the newspapers for their uncritical _____ to the rich and the powerful.

a. obfuscation   b. obtrusion   c. obloquy   d. obeisance

46 He's an _____ little man and widely disliked in the company.

a. palliate   b. palpable   c. officious   d. palatable

47 The _____ attached to this job

a. perquisite   b. peccadillo   c. paucity   d. penchant

48 His sudden and unexpected appearance seemed to _____ her.

a. placate   b. perpetrate   c. petrify   d. peruse

49 There is no _____ for it.

a. precaution   b. precedent   c. plethora   d. prerogative

50 She wanted to _____ these unhappy memories from her mind.

a. purge   b. propitiate   c. proliferate   d. prognosticate

210. **metamorphosis**[36]

(매러모퍼시스) morph(=form) 변신 **change** of form or character
She had undergone an amazing **metamorphosis** from awkward schoolgirl
to beautiful woman. 그녀는 꼴사나운 여학생에서 아름다운 여인으로 놀랍게
변신해 있었다.

211. **meticulous**

지나치게 세심한, 꼼꼼한 **excessively careful**; to be careful about detail
He was **meticulous** in checking his accounts and never made mistakes.
그는 그의 계좌를 체크하는 데에 꼼꼼하여 결코 실수를 하지 않는다.

212. **mitigate**

완화하다 **allay**, alleviate, assuage, mollify, palliate, relieve
mitigate her wrath 그녀의 화를 누그러뜨리다.

213. **modish**

유행하는 **fashionable**
discarded all garments which were no longer **modish**.
더 이상 유행이 아닌 모든 옷들을 버리다.

214. **multiplicity**

다양성
The **multiplicity** of the insect world is awesome.
곤충세계의 다양성은 놀랄만하다.

---

36) metamorphosis, meticulous, mitigate, modish, multiplicity, mundane

215. **mundane**

현세의, **ordinary**; dull; everyday.

He was concerned only with **mundane** matters.

그는 오직 현세 문제에만 관심이 있다.

216. **mutilate**[37]

불구로 만들다 **maim**

The torturer threatened to **mutilate** his victim.

그 고문하는 자는 그의 희생자를 불구로 만들겠다고 위협했다.

217. **noxious**

해로운 **harmful** , baneful, deadly, pernicious, pestilential, deleterious

The people in the house had died from inhaling **noxious** smoke.

그 집에 있던 사람들은 유독성 연기를 마시고 죽었다

218. **nullify**

폐지하다 **abolish**, abrogate, annihilate, annul, invalidate, vitiate

Once the contract was **nullified**, 일단 그 계약이 폐지된다면,

219. **obeisance**

(오베이썬스) 복종 deep bow of respect or **homage**

He attacks the newspapers for their uncritical **obeisance** to the rich and the powerful. 그는 신문이 부유하고 권력 있는 사람들에게 무비판적인 경의를 표한다는 것에 대해 공격을 가했다.

220. **officious**

참견하는 **very fond of giving unwelcome services or advice**

---

37) mutilate, noxious, nullify, obeisance, officious, ossify

He's an **officious** little man and widely disliked in the company.

그는 참견하기 좋아하는 유치한 남자로 회사에서 널리 미움을 받았다.

221. ossify

경화하다 <u>harden into bone</u>

Their ideas **ossified** into a rigid orthodoxy.

그들의 생각은 확고한 정설로 굳어졌다.

222. ostracize[38]

추방하다 <u>banish</u>, exile, expatriate, expel, relegate, oust

He was **ostracized** by his colleagues for refusing to support the strike. 그는 파업지지를 거부하여 동료들의 배척을 받았다.

223. palatable

맛좋은 <u>agreeable; pleasing to the taste</u>

Paying taxes can never be made **palatable.**

세금을 지불하는 것은 결코 기분 좋은 일일 수 없다.

224. palpable

palp(=touch) + able(=capable of) 명백한 <u>that can be felt or touched</u>

His statement is **palpable** nonsense. 그의 진술은 명백한 난센스다.

225. parley

회담 <u>conference</u>

The peace **parley** 평화회담

---

38) ostracize, palatable, palpable, parley, paucity, peccadillo, peripatetic, perpetra

226. **paucity**

부족 <u>scarcity</u>

a <u>paucity</u> of evidence 증거 부족

227. **peccadillo**

(패커딜로우) 경범죄 <u>slight offense</u>

minor sexual <u>peccadilloes</u> 사소한 성적 과오

228. **peripatetic**

여기저기 돌아다니는 <u>going about from place to place ; wandering</u>

The <u>peripatetic</u> peddler 돌아다니는 행상인

229. **perpetrate**

자행하다 <u>commit an offense</u>

<u>perpetrate</u> such a horrible crime. 그런 끔찍한 범죄를 자행하다.

230. **perquisite**[39]

팁 <u>any gain above stipulated salary</u>

The <u>perquisites</u> attached to this job 이 직업에 부수되는 팁

231. **petrify**

돌같이 굳게 하다 망연자실하게 하다 <u>turn to stone</u>

His sudden and unexpected appearance seemed to <u>petrify</u> her.
그의 갑작스럽고 예기치 않은 출현은 그녀를 망연자실하게 하였다.

232. **precedent**

(프리씨든트) 전례 pre(=before) + ced(=go)

---

39) perquisite, petrify, precedent, prerogative, pugnacious, pungent, purge

There is no **precedent** for it. 그것에 대한 전례가 없다.

233. **prerogative**

특권 **an exclusive right or privilege** arising from one's rank or position.

It is a woman's **prerogative** to bear children.

아이를 낳는 것은 여성의 특권이다.

234. **prognosticate**

pro(=before) + gno(=know) 예언하다 to foretell

235. **pugnacious**

호전적인 **combative**; disposed to fight, bellicose, belligerent, contentious,
militant, warlike

236. **pungent**

자극성의, 신랄한 **stinging; caustic**

The **pungency** of the cigarette smoke 담배연기의 자극성

237. **purge**

정화하다 **clean by removing impurities; purify**

She wanted to **purge** these unhappy memories from her mind.

그녀는 마음속에서 이 불행한 기억들을 깨끗이 지우고 싶었다.

51 The patient did not _____.

  a. repudiate b. recuperate c. reiterate d. recondite

52 Many scientific discoveries are a matter of _____.

  a. salient b. resurgent c. serendipity d. sanguine

53 More than 100 people have been killed this year in _____ outbursts of ethnic violence.

  a. sporadic b. sophomoric c. servile d. squander

54 The company was given a substantial _____ by the government.

  a. subsistence b. statute c. subsidiary d. subsidy

55 The _____ between a plant and the insect that fertilizes it

  a. surfeit b. surmise c. symbiosis d. surreptitious

56 He was _____ by bad luck.

a. trenchant   b. tenuous   c. taciturn   d. thwarted

57 Filling in a false tax return is not in itself a crime of gross moral _____ike lying in court would be.

a. turpitude   b. turgid   c. turbid   d. vacillation

58 The car suddenly _____ off the road.

a. venal   b. veer   c. vacuous   d. ubiquitous

59 Much of the region's _____ countryside has been destroyed in the hurricane.

a. verdant   b. verbose   c. verbatim   d. veracious

60 As was his _____, he jogged two miles every morning.

a. wean   b. zenith   c. wanton   d. wont

238. rampant[40]

만연한 rearing up on hind legs; unrestrained

rampant inflation 걷잡을 수 없는 인플레이션

239. recapitulate

요약하다 summarize, epitomize, review

240. rectify

교정하다. put right, take out mistakes from

rectify the errors 잘못을 고치다.

241. recuperate

회복하다 recover

the patient did not recuperate 그 환자는 회복하지 못했다.

242. relegate

re(=back) + leg(=send) send someone to a lower 지위를 떨어뜨리다,

relegate a person to an inferior post …을 좌천시키다

243. renegade

re(=intensive) + neg(=deny) deserter; apostate 배반자 (레너게이드)

a renegade priest 변절한 사제

244. requisite

(레큐어짓) re(=intensive, again) + quisit(=ask) 필요조건

the requisites for a good teacher. 좋은 스승의 필요조건

---

40) rampant, recapitulate, rectify, recuperate, relegate, renegade, requisite, ruminate

245. ruminate

되씹다 <u>chew the cud; ponder</u>

sit <u>ruminating</u> on recent events 앉아서 최근 사건들을 곰곰이 생각하다

246. serendipity[41]

(쎄런디퍼티) 뜻밖의 횡재 <u>gift for finding valuable things not searched for</u>

Many scientific discoveries are a matter of <u>serendipity.</u>
많은 과학적인 발견들이 우연한 횡재의 문제이다.

247. sophomoric

(싸퍼모릭) 미숙한 <u>immature;</u> shallow, callow, especially US a second-year
student at a school or university

248. sporadic

산발적인 <u>occurring irregularly; happening from time to time</u>

More than 100 people have been killed this year in <u>sporadic</u> outbursts of
ethnic violence. 100명이 넘는 사람들이 올해 산발적으로 터진 종족 간 폭력사
태에서 목숨을 잃었다.

249. squander

낭비하다 <u>waste</u>

<u>squander</u> a chance 기회를 허비하다

250. statute

법령 <u>law</u>, decree, ordinance, precept, regulation

---

41) serendipity, sophomoric, sporadic, squander, statute, subjugate, subsidy

251. **subjugate**

정복하다 <u>conquer</u>; bring under control

<u>subjugate</u> our foe 적을 정복하다

252. **subsidy**

(섭서디) 보조금 <u>direct financial aid by government</u>

The company was given a substantial **subsidy** by the government.

그 회사는 정부로부터 실질적인 보조금을 받았다.

253. **subsistence**[42]

호구지책 the means of existence; <u>livelihood</u>.

my salary provides a mere **subsistence**

많은 월급은 단지 생존수단 만큼만 지불한다.

254. **subversive**

반항적인 <u>insurgent</u>, mutinous, rebellious

255. **symbiosis**

공생 (심비오시스)

the **symbiosis** between a plant and the insect that fertilizes it

식물과 그것을 수분시켜 주는 곤충과의 공생

256. **theocracy**

(씨아크러시) 신권정치 <u>government of a community by religious leaders</u>

257. **thwart**

(쓰워트) 좌절시키다 <u>baffle; frustrate</u>

---

42) subsistence, subversive, symbiosis, theocracy, thwart, turbid, turgid

thwart his plans 그의 계획을 좌절시키다.

He was **thwarted** by bad luck. 그는 운이 나빠 좌절당했다.

258. **turbid**

혼탁한 **muddy**; having the sediment disturbed

259. **turgid**

부푼 **swollen; distended**

the **turgid** waters of the river (호우 등으로) 불어난 강물

260. **turpitude**[43]

(터피튜드) 사악함 **wickedness, depravity**

moral turpitude. 도덕적 타락

Filling in a false tax return is not in itself a crime of gross moral **turpitude** like lying in court would be. 거짓 납세 신고서를 작성하는 것은 그 자체로는 법정에서 거짓말을 하는 것처럼 도덕적으로 엄청나게 비열한 범죄행위는 아니다

261. **vacillation**

(배쌀레이션) 망설임 **fluctuation; wavering**

her **vacillation(s)** over whether or not to resign

사직을 할 것인가 말 것인가를 두고 그녀가 하는 망설임

262. **vacuous**

공허한 **empty; inane**

a charming but **vacuous** person 매력적이긴 하지만 멍청해 보이는 사람

---

43) turpitude, vacillation, vacuous, veer, venal, vendetta

263. **veer**

바꾸다 <u>change in direction</u>
The car suddenly <u>veered</u> off the road.
그 차가 갑자기 방향을 바꾸면서 도로를 벗어났다.

264. **venal**

뇌물을 받는 (비늘) <u>capable of being bribed</u>
The <u>venal</u> policeman 타락한 경찰

265. **vendetta**

(밴데타) 피의 복수 <u>feud; private warfare</u>
<u>a bitter feud in which the family of a murdered person takes revenge by</u>
<u>killing the murderer or one of their relatives.</u>
engaged in a bitter <u>vendetta</u> 심한 복수를 하다.

266. **veracious**[44]

정직한 <u>truthful</u>

267. **verbatim**

(버베이름) 말 그대로의
repeated the message <u>verbatim</u>. 그 전언을 그대로 반복하다

268. **verbose**

말 많은 wordy, **garrulous**, loquacious, prolix, talkative
He was renowned for being a <u>verbose</u> and rather tedious after-dinner
speaker. 그는 말이 많고 다소 지루한 식후 연설가로 잘 알려져 있었다.

---

44) veracious, verbatim, verbose, verdant, vicissitude, vindictive, virtuoso, viru

269. **verdant**

(버른트) 푸르른 **green**; fresh * vernal (봄의)

Much of the region's **verdant** countryside has been destroyed in the hurricane. 그 지역의 녹지대 대부분이 허리케인 때문에 파괴됐다.

270. **vicissitude**

(비씨써튜드) 흥망성쇠 **change**, especially in somebody's fortunes

You could say that losing your job is just one of the **vicissitudes** of life. 실직하는 것은 인생의 변화 중의 하나일 뿐이라고 말할 수도 있겠다.

271. **vindictive**

앙심을 품은 **revengeful**

She can be extremely **vindictive**.

그녀는 극도로 앙심을 품을 수 있는 사람이다.

272. **virtuoso**

거장 **highly skilled artist**

273. **virulent**

맹독의 **extremely poisonous**

a **virulent** infection 악성 전염병

274. **vitriolic**[45]

(비츄리알릭) 신랄한 **corrosive; sarcastic**

He launched a **vitriolic** attack on the prime minister, accusing him of shielding corrupt friends. 그는 총리가 부패한 친구들을 감싸고 있다고 비난하면서 총리에 대한 통렬한 공격을 시작했다.

---

45) vitriolic, vivacious, volatile, wallow, wan, wangle, wean

69

275. **vivacious**

> 명랑한 <u>lively</u>, high-spirited, gay, animated;
> She gave a <u>vivacious</u> laugh. 그녀가 명랑한 웃음을 터뜨렸다.

276. **volatile**

> 휘발성의 <u>evaporating rapidly; lighthearted; mercurial</u>
> a <u>volatile</u> political situation 변화가 심한 정치 상황

277. **wallow**

> 허우적거리다 <u>roll in; indulge in; become helpless</u>
> <u>wallow</u> in the mud. 진흙에서 허우적거리다.

278. **wan**

> (완) 창백한 <u>having a pale or sickly color; pallid</u>
> You look <u>wan</u>. 얼굴이 창백해 보이네요.

279. **wangle**

> (왱걸) 교묘히 손에 넣다 <u>to obtain something by persuasiveness</u>.
> She managed to <u>wangle</u> an invitation to the reception.
> 그녀는 교묘히 그 리셉션 초대장을 손에 넣었다.

280. **wean**

> (윈) 젖을 끊다. <u>accustom a baby not to nurse; give up a cherished activity</u>
> <u>wean</u> himself away from eating junk food 정크 음식을 먹는 것을 끊다.

281. **wont**[46]

> (원트) 습관 <u>custom; habitual procedure</u>

---

46) wont

As was his **wont**, he jogged two miles every morning

그의 습관대로 그는 매일 아침 2 마일을 조깅한다.

Part 2
용례

01 _____ a person with questions.

  a. berate   b. bereaved   c. beseech   d. besiege

02 The _____ old lady had a warm smile.

  a. benign   b. bounteous   c. circumlocution   d. circumspect

03 English, Dutch and German are _____ languages.

  a. cogent   b. cogitate   c. cognate   d. cognition

04 The two events _____ with each other.

  a. cohere   b. coincide   c. collate   d. collateral

05 a _____ aim of the government's industrial strategy.

  a. collateral   b. collide   c. colloquial   d. collude

06 They are _____ in size.

    a. commence   b. commend   c. commensurate   d. commodious

07 the winner's _____ smile.

    a. complacent   b. complaisant   c. complement   d. compliment

08 _____ a long story into a few sentences.

    a. concoct   b. condense   c. condescend   d. condole

09 _____ a friend's fault.

    a. condone   b. confer   c. confine   d. confiscate

10 _____ to the rules.

    a. conform   b. confound   c. confront   d. congenial

11 a work _____ to one's taste.

a. confound   b. confront   c. congenial   d. congenital

12 living in a state of _____ bliss

a. conjure   b. connubial   c. conscript   d. consecrate

13 It's been raining for five_____ days.

a. consecutive   b. consensus   c. conserve   d. consign

14 _____ with criminals.

a. console   b. consolidate   c. consort   d. constrict

15 Colds are _____.

a. construe   b. consummate   c. contagious   d. contaminate

16 The company's future is _____ on the outcome of the trial.

a. condemn   b. contiguous   c. contingent   d. contort

17 hold the _____ opinion.

a. convene   b. converse   c. convert   d. convict

18 _____ a chemical compound

decipher   b. decompose   c. decoy   d. decrepit

19 _____ to one's elders

a. defer   b. defunct   c. degenerate   d. deject

20 _____ somebody into believing

a. deliberate   b. delinquent   c. delude   d. demeanor

21 the dotted line on the graph _____ profits.

      a. demur   b. demure   c. denote   d. denounce

22 _____ the use of violence.

      a. deposit   b. deprecate   c. deputy   d. derange

23 _____ a ship in the dense fog

      a. descry   b. designate   c. desolate   d. despise

24 a series of _____ events

      a. discreet   b. discrepancy   c. discrete   d. discriminate

25 make _____ed decision

      a. dishearten   b. disillusion   c. disinterest   d. disoriented

26 I _____ myself with bowling

    a. dissipate   b. dissuade   c. distort   d. distract

27 coins _____ed with letters and figures

    a. emboss   b. embroider   c. embryo   d. empower

28 a disease _____ to the tropics

    a. endear   b. endemic   c. endorse   d. engender

29 _____ obedience on the soldiers.

    a. enhance   b. enjoin   c. enlist   d. enliven

30 Writing a history book _____ a lot of work.

    a. enslave   b. ensue   c. ensure   d. entail

31 She _____ him away from his wife.

    a. enthrall   b. enthrone   c. entice   d. entreat

32 _____ one's political philosophy.

    a. entrench   b. entrust   c. envoy   d. ephemeral

33 It takes many years to _____ the terrible memories of a war.

    a. epoch   b. eclipse   c. efface   d. effigy

34 Anyone over the age of 18 is _____ to vote.

    a. elicit   b. eligible   c. elucidate   d. elude

35 be _____ed from military service.

    a. exalt   b. exasperate   c. excerpt   d. exempt

36 I gave him an _____ instructions

    a. expend   b. expire   c. explicit   d. exploit

37 _____ toothpaste from the tube

    a. exterminate   b. extinct   c. extol   d. extrude

38 an _____ defeat

    a. exult   b. ignoble   c. ignominious   d. illegible

39 a boorish _____

    a. illicit   b. illiterate   c. immaculate   d. immature

40 _____ differences between the original painting and the copy

    a. imperceptible   b. impertinent   c. impotent   d. impracticable

41 shoes _____ with a party dress

    a. incognito   b. incompatible   c. incongruous   d. infamous

42 Germs are _____ animals.

    a. infallible   b. infamous   c. infinitesimal   d. infirm

43 an _____ part of the argument

    a. insolent   b. insolvent   c. intangible   d. integral

44 _____ the instructions before you fill out your application.

    a. pertain   b. peruse   c. pervade   d. perverse

45 a _____ for not going to school.

    a. prestige   b. pretext   c. prevail   d. proclivity

46 by _____ to violence

    a. recipe   b. reciprocal   c. recline   d. recourse

47 _____ me the money at once.

    a. remiss   b. remit   c. remnant   d. remorse

48 _____ school expenses

    a. restrict   b. reticent   c. retrench   d. retrieve

49 _____ oneself from society

    a. seclude   b. sedition   c. seduce   d. suffrage

50 _____ to the temptation

    a. subtract   b. succumb   c. suffocate   d. suffrage

51

_____ the judge to pardon him.

a. supplement   b. supplicate   c. susceptible   d. superlative

1. be **beguiled** by his flattery into trusting him.[47]

   속이다 (deceive) 아첨에 속아 믿다 / 즐겁게 하다 (amuse)

2. **belated** birthday greetings. 늦은 delayed

3. The newspaper **belied** the facts of the event.

   거짓 전하다 give a false idea of

4. **belittle** the explorer's great discoveries.

   과소평가하다 make unimportant, depreciate

5. **bemoan** one's bitter fate. 슬퍼하다 deplore, lament

6. His father **bequeathed** him a fortune.

   유증하다 give after death, hand down

7. **berated** the boys for teasing one's cat 꾸짖다 scold sharply, upbraid

8. a husband **bereaved of** his wife. 잃다 deprive, divest

9. I **beseech** you to forgive him.

   간청하다 implore, beg, appeal, supplicate, entreat

10. **besiege** a person with questions.

    포위하다, 질문을 퍼붓다 beset, harass

85

---

47) beguile, belated, belie, belittle, bemoan, bequeath, berate, bereave, beseech, besiege, betroth, bewail

11. **betroth** one's daughter to a rich man. 약혼시키다 engage

12. a girl **bewailing** the loss of her doll

    몹시 슬퍼하다 mourn for, lament, weep

13. **bewitch** a person with one's beauty.[48]

    마법을 걸다, 매혹시키다 enchant, charm

14. the **benediction** at the end of marriage ceremony 축복 blessing

15. become **benefactor** of an orphanage. 후원자 patron

16. The **benign** old lady had a warm smile.

    친절한 having a kind disposition, gracious

17. give **bounteous** gifts to the poor. 후한 generous

18. without **circumlocution.** 완곡어법 a roundabout or indirect expression

19. a **circumspect** action. 신중한 cautious

20. **circumvent** the tax law 회피하다 avoid

21. form a **coalition** government 연합 alliance

---

48) bewitch, benediction, benefactor, benign, bounteous, circumlocution, circumspect, circumvent, coalition, cogent, cogitate, cognate, cognition, cohere, coincide

22. **cogent** argument in favor of the proposal 설득력 있는 persuasive

23. **cogitate** on a problem. 숙고하다 ponder

24. English, Dutch and German are **cognate** languages. 동족의 kindred

25. in full **cognition** of the facts. 인식 perception, awareness

26. make two surfaces **cohere.** 붙다 stick together, adhere

27. The two events **coincided** with each other.
    동시에 발생하다 synchronize

28. **collate** two ancient manuscripts.[49] 대조하다 compare

29. a **collateral** aim of the government's industrial strategy.
    간접적인 secondary

30. The two cars **collided** with each other. 충돌하다 crash

31. a **colloquial** expression. 구어체의 conversational

32. **collude** with the terrorists. 공모하다 conspire, connive

---

49) collate, collateral, collide, colloquial, collude, commandeer, commence, commend, commensurate, commodious, commotion, compact, compassion, compatible

33. **commandeer** a taxicab to chase the criminal.

   징발하다 seize, confiscate

34. **commence** a lawsuit. 시작하다 begin

35. be **commended** for one's good conduct. 칭찬하다 acclaim

36. They are **commensurate** in size. 같은 크기의 equivalent

37. a **commodious** house. 넓은 spacious

38. make much **commotion.** 소요 tumult

39. **compact** between countries. 협정 agreement, contract

40. feel great **compassion** for the orphans. 연민 sympathy

41. Is this software **compatible** with Apple Macintosh?

   호환의 able to be used with another thing

42. **compensate** a person for loss. [50]

   보상하다 recompence, atone, reimburse, make amends for

43. **compile** an encyclopedia. 편찬하다 collect, assemble

---

50) compensate, compile, complacent, complaisant, complement, compliment, comprehend, compress, comprise, compunction, concave, concede, conciliate, concoct

44. the winner's **complacent** smile. 만족해하는 self - satisfied

45. the wife **complaisant** to her husband's will.
    고분고분한 compliant, obedient, meek, amenable

46. This wine **complements** the food perfectly. 보완하다 supplement

47. make a **compliment.** 칭찬하다 commend, praise, eulogize

48. do not **comprehend** the book's full meaning. 이해하다 grasp

49. **compress** one's report into three pages. 요약하다 abridge

50. The United States **comprises** 50 states. 구성하다 make up, compose

51. have a **compunction** about telling a lie.
    양심의 가책 remorse, regret, repentance, penitence, contrition

52. **a concave** mirror 오목한 hollow

53. **concede** one's defeat. 인정하다 admit, acknowledge

54. **conciliate** the crying baby with a candy. 달래다 soothe

55. **concoct** a splendid meal from the leftovers.
    만들다 devise, invent, contrive, make up

56. **condense** a long story into a few sentences.[51] 압축하다 compress

57. The king **condescended** to eat with the beggars.
자신을 낮추다 stoop, lower oneself

58. **condole** with him on his wife's death. 애도하다 lament

59. **condone** a friend's fault. 용서하다 excuse, forgive

60. **confer** a medal on the winner. 수여하다 grant

61. **confine** a criminal in jail. 감금하다 imprison

62. **confiscate** the property of the deposed leaders.
몰수하다 seize, appropriate

63. **conform** to the rules. 따르다 comply

64. **confound** liberty with license. 혼동하다 confuse

65. **confront** the criminal with the evidence. 증거를 제시하다 encounter

66. a work **congenial to** one's taste. 적합한 agreeable

67. a **congenital** defect 선천적인 inborn

---

51) condense, condescend, condole, condone, confer, confine, confiscate, conform, confound, confront, congenial, congenital, congregate, conjecture, conjure

68. **congregate** around the campfire. 모이다 assemble

69. **conjecture** what will happen next. 추측하다 suppose

70. **conjure** a rabbit out of one's hat.
    요술로 나오게 하다 cause to appear

71. living in a state of **connubial** bliss[52] 결혼의 conjugal

72. be **conscripted** for military service. 징집하다 draft

73. **consecrate** one's life to helping the poor.
    신성하게 하다, 바치다 hallow, devote

74. It's been raining for five **consecutive** days. 연속적인 successive

75. reach an **consensus** on an issue 의견 일치 concord, agreement

76. **conserve** forests for future generations. 보존하다 preserve

77. The thief was **consigned** to prison.
    넘겨지다 commit, hand over formally

78. **console** her daughter by promising to buy her a doll. 달래다 soothe

---

52) connubial, conscript, consecrate, consecutive, consensus, conserve, consign, console, consolidate, consort, conspire, constellation, constrict, construe, consummate

79. **consolidate** several local branches into one. 통합하다 merge

80. **consort** with criminals. 사귀다 keep company, associate

81. **conspire** to rob a bank. 음모를 꾸미다, 공모하다 plot

82. a **constellation** in the northern hemisphere. 별자리 asterism

83. The tight collar **constricted** his neck. 조이다 compress

84. **construe** somebody's silence as agreement. 해석하다 interpret

85. **consummate** one's ambition. 성취하다 accomplish

86. Colds are **contagious.**[53] 전염성의 infectious

87. Drinking water is **contaminated** when sewage seeps into the water supply. 오염시키다 pollute

88. He **condemned** the actions of the dictator. 경멸하다 despise

89. America and Canada are **contiguous.** 맞닿아 있는 touching

90. The company's future is **contingent** on the outcome of the trial. 조건으로 하는 conditional

---

53) contagious, contaminate, condemn, contiguous, contingent, contort, contour, contrite, convene, converse, convert, convict, convivial, convoke, convoy

91. **contort** one's face with pain. 비틀다 twist, distort

92. the irregular **contours** of the Britain coastline. 윤곽 profile

93. make a **contrite** apology to — 깊이 뉘우치는 penitent

94. **convene** the conference 소집하다 assemble

95. hold the **converse** opinion. 반대의 contrary, opposite

96. **convert** water power into electricity. 전환시키다 transform

97. **convict** the accused man of theft and arson.
    유죄를 선고하다 sentence, doom

98. a very **convivial** atmosphere. 즐거운 delightful

99. **convoke** all the members of the committee. 소집하다. assemble

100. be moved under **convoy** of armed guards. 호송(하다) escort

101. a **copious** harvest of rice.[54] 풍부한 plentiful

102. Witnesses **corroborated** the driver's statement.
    확증하다 confirm, verify

---

54) copious, corroborate, contradict, contravene, controversial, counterfeit, countermand, counterpart, debilitate, deceased, decipher, decompose, decoy, decrepit, defer, defunct

103. **contradict** a person's statement. 반박하다 deny

104. **contravene** the parking regulations. 위반하다 violate

105. a **controversial** decision. 논쟁적인 debatable

106. a **counterfeit** note. 위조의 fake

107. **countermand** a command. 취소하다 revoke

108. Night is the **counterpart** of day. 상대물 parallel

109. be **debilitated** by the extreme heat 쇠약하게 하다 weaken

110. the **deceased** 죽은 dead

111. **decipher** a person's signature 해독하다 decode

112. **decompose** a chemical compound 분해하다 analyze, decay

113. **decoy** ducks into the net 유인하다 lure

114. a **decrepit** old man 노쇠한 feeble

115. **defer to** one's elders 복종하다 yield

116. a **defunct** law 죽은 deceased

117. liberty is apt to **degenerate** lawlessness.[55] 퇴보하다 deteriorate

118. a **dejected** look 낙심한 depressed

119. **delegate** him to the convention 대리로 파견하다 depute

120. **deliberate** on what to do 심사숙고하다 ponder

121. **delinquent** taxes 체납된 overdue

122. **delude** somebody into believing 속이다 deceive

123. an arrogant **demeanor** 태도 behavior

95

124. **demolish** the slum district 파괴하다 destroy

125. **demur** at working overtime 반대하다 object

126. a **demure** young lady
    얌전한 체하는 quiet and not trying to draw attention to oneself, modest

127. the dotted line on the graph **denotes** profits. 표시하다 indicate

128. be **denounced** as a traitor 비난하다 condemn

---

55) degenerate, dejected, delegate, deliberate, delinquent, delude, demeanor, demolish, demur, demure, denote, denounce, deplore, deport, depose

129. **deplore** moral decline 개탄하다 lament

130. **deport** oneself like gentleman 처신하다 conduct, 추방하다 banish

131. The dictator was **deposed** by the people
     퇴위시키다 dethrone, 선서 증언하다 testify

132. **deposit** one's paycheck in a bank[56] 예금하다 bank

133. **deprecate** the use of violence. 반대하다, 비난하다 deplore

134. a **deputy** premier 대리 delegate, surrogate

135. **deranged** lines of communication 미친 insane, 혼란된 disarranged

136. a **derelict** old house 버려진 abandoned

137. **deride** one's opponent 조롱하다 ridicule

138. **derive** great pleasure from books 끌어내다 draw

139. **descry** a ship in the dense fog 알아보다 notice at a distance

140. be **designated** as the chairman 임명하다 appoint, 나타내다 indicate

---

56) deposit, deprecate, deputy, deranged, derelict, deride, derive, descry, designate, desolate, despise, destitute, desultory, detach, deteriorate, detrimental

141. The Vikings **desolated** the lands they attacked

황폐하게하다 devastate

142. **despise** a hypocrite 경멸하다 disdain

143. a **destitute** family 가난한 indigent

144. **desultory** conversation 산만한 discursive

145. **detach** oneself from the party 떠나다, 분리시키다 disconnect

146. His health is **deteriorating.** 악화시키다 depreciate, make worse

147. a **detrimental** effect on the environment 해로운 injurious

148. **devastate** the border towns[57] 유린하다 ravage

149. **deviate** from the usual flight path. 벗어나다 diverge

150. **devour** one's luncheon. 게걸스럽게 먹다 gorge

151. be **dismayed** to hear the news 당황하다 bewilder

152. **defer** the decision for a few weeks. 연기하다 delay

---

57) devastate, deviate, devour, dismay, defer, deluge, devoid, diffident, digress, dilapidated, dilate, dilatory, dilute, disable, disband, discard

153. a **deluge** of questions 쇄도 flood

154. He is **devoid** of human feeling 없는 empty

155. be **diffident** about expressing one's opinions 수줍어하는 shy

156. **digress** from the subject for a moment. 벗어나다 deviate

157. a **dilapidated** chair 황폐한 desolate

158. Her eyes **dilated** in surprise. 팽창시키다 expand

159. **dilatory** in replying 느린 tardy

160. **dilute** whisky with water 약하게 하다 attenuate

161. be **disabled** in the war 불구로 만들다 cripple

162. **disband** a club 해산하다 disperse

163. **discard** an old coat 버리다 abandon

164. become a **disciple** of Gandhi [58]제자 follower, apostle

165. be **disconcerted** by his opposition. 당황케하다 embarrass

---

58) disciple, disconcert, discord, discreet, discrepancy, discrete, discriminate, disdain, disentangle, disfigure, dishearten, disillusion, disinterested, disorient, disparage

166. the apple of **discord** 불화 dissension

167. a **discreet** answer 신중한 prudent

168. **discrepancies** between one's words and action 불일치 difference

169. a series of **discrete** events 분리된 distinct

170. **discriminate** between fact and theory 구별하다 distinguish

171. **disdain** the offer of a bribe 경멸하다 despise

172. **disentangle** oneself from an unhappy relationship 풀다 extricate

173. A scar **disfigured** his face. 흉하게 하다 deform

174. The long drought **disheartened** the farmer. 낙담시키다 discourage

175. be **disillusioned** about a romance 환상에서 깨어나게 하다 disenchant

176. make **disinterested** decision 공정한 objective

177. His mother's sudden death **disoriented** him.
    혼란스럽게 하다 embarrass

178. **disparage** the hero's brave attempt 얕보다 depreciate

179. a **disparity** in the rates of pay for men and women[59]

차이 difference

180. **dispel** one's fear 떨쳐버리다 disperse

181. **dispense** food and clothing to the flood victims

나누어 주다 distribute, 약을 조제하다 dispensary 약국

182. **disperse** the crowd 흩뜨리다 scatter

183. try to **disrupt** the assembly 해산시키다 shatter

184. **dissect** a frog 해부하다 anatomize

185. **dissemble** one's anger with a smile 가장하다, disguise

186. News is **disseminated** by means of television and radio

퍼뜨리다 diffuse

187. **dissent** from public opinion 의견을 달리하다 differ

188. the **dissidents** from public opinion 반체제인사 opponent

189. **dissipate** one's father's fortune

낭비하다 squander, 흩어지게 하다 scatter

---

59) disparity, dispel, dispense, disperse, disrupt, dissect, dissemble, disseminate, dissent, dissident, dissipate, dissuade, distort

190. **dissuade** the boy from running away from home

　　단념시키다 discourage

191. a face **distorted** by pain 비틀다 contort

192. I **distract** myself with bowling[60]

　　기분전환하다 entertain, 주의를 딴 데로 돌리다 divert

193. send out a **distress** signal 조난 calamity, 고통 anxiety

194. **diverge** from the rule 이탈하다 deviate

195. a person of **diverse** interests 다양한 various

196. **divulge** somebody's plan to the press 누설하다 reveal

197. put an **embargo** on the supply of oil 제재 prohibition

198. **embark** on a new career 시작하다 start, 승선하다 board

199. a white hat **embellished** with pink roses 장식하다 decorate

200. **embezzle** 50,000 from one's company 횡령하다 appropriate

201. The dove is an **emblem** of peace 상징 symbol

---

60) distract, distress, diverge, diverse, divulge, embargo, embark, embellish, embezzle, emblem, embody, emboss, embroider, embryo

202. **embody** the ideals of democracy 구체화하다 materialize

203. coins **embossed** with letters and figures
튀어 나오게 하다 decorate with a design that stands out from the surface

204. a dress **embroidered** in silk thread 자수하다 decorate

205. a plan still in **embryo** 초기 단계 an undeveloped stage, 태아 fetus

206. **empower** one's secretary to sign certain contracts[61]
권한을 주다 authorize

207. **enact** a bill to restrict the sale of guns. 제정하다 legislate

208. The music **enchanted** us all. 매혹시키다 charm

209. Rebel forces had **encircled** the airport. 둘러싸다 surround

210. The atmosphere **encompasses** the earth. 둘러싸다 encircle

211. **encounter** a friend on the plane. 우연히 만나다 meet unexpectedly

212. Be careful not to **encroach** on her authority. 침해하다 intrude

213. Heavy shoes **encumber** a runner in a race. 방해하다 hinder

---

61) empower, enact, enchant, encircle, encompass, encounter, encroach, encumber, endear, endemic, endorse, engender, engrave, engross, enhance

214. Her kindness **endeared** her to all of us. 애정을 느끼게 하다 love

215. a disease **endemic** to the tropics 한 지방에만 나타나는 indigenous

216. **endorse** the check

　　배서하다 write one's name on the back of, 승인하다 sanction

217. Racial inequality **engenders** conflict 야기 시키다 cause

218. a memorial **engraved** on the stone. 조각하다 carve

219. be **engrossed** in the story 몰두시키다 absorb

220. **enhance** the prospects of world peace.

　　향상시키다 increase, heighten

221. **enjoin** obedience on the soldiers.[62]

　　명령하다 command, 금지하다 prohibit

222. He **enlisted** in the navy. 입대하다 enroll

223. Spring **enlivens** all nature. 생기 있게 하다 animate

224. A good deed **ennobles** the person who does it.

　　품위 있게 하다 dignify

（103）

---

62) enjoin, enlist, enliven, ennoble, enrage, enroll, ensign, enslave, ensue, ensure, entail, entangle, enthrall, enthrone

225. Her rude behavior **enraged** him. 격노하다 infuriate

226. **enroll** one's son in a music school 등록시키다 register

227. the **ensign** of the Korea 국기 flag, symbol

228. **enslave** the captives 노예로 만들다 make a slave of, enthrall

229. Thousands of people were killed in the **ensuing** battle.
    결과로서 일어나다 follow

230. This medicine will **ensure** you a good night's sleep.
    보장하다 secure

231. Writing a history book **entails** a lot of work.
    수반하다 make necessary, involve

232. Threads are easily **entangled.** 엉키게 하다 tangle, involve

233. **enthrall** the audiences 매혹시키다 captivate

234. The insurgents **enthroned** their chief. 즉위시키다 seat on a throne

235. She **enticed** him away from his wife.[63] 유혹하다 tempt

---

63) entice, entreat, entrench, entrust, envoy, ephemeral, epidemic, epitome, epoch, eclipse, efface, effigy, elaborate, elapse

236. **entreat** him to help her 간청하다 implore

237. **entrench** one's political philosophy. 확립하다 confirm

238. **entrust** the children to baby-sitter. 맡기다 commit

239. a special **envoy** of the president. 특사 agent

240. His success as a singer was **ephemeral**. 일시적인 transitory

241. schools closed because of an **epidemic** of flu 유행병 plague

242. the **epitome** of all one's previous books 요약 summary

243. The years of the Civil War were an <u>epoch</u> in history of the United States. 시대 era

244. a total **eclipse** of the sun 일식

In sports he **eclipsed** his elder brother, 능가하다 surpass

245. It takes many years to **efface** the terrible memories of a war. 지우다 erase

246. burn an **effigy** of the enemy. 형상 image

247. make **elaborate** preparations for the party. 정성들인 worked out with great care

248. Many hours **elapsed** while he slept. 경과하다 pass

249. His success in the contest **elated** him.[64] 의기 양양 하게 하다 exalt

250. **elicit** laughter from the audience. 이끌어 내다 evoke

251. Anyone over the age of 18 is **eligible** to vote.
자격이 있는 competent

252. **elucidate** one's theory by a few simple demonstrations.
명료하게 하다 clarify

253. the sly fox **eluded** the hunter. 교묘히 피하다 evade

254. this new machine will **emancipate** us from all the hard work.
해방시키다 release

255. many people have **emerged** from slums.
벗어나다 escape, 나오다 appear

256. the sun **emits** light and heat. 방출하다 discharge

257. he was **enervated** by his long illness. 약화시키다 unnerve

258. **enumerate** the reasons for one's decision 열거하다 recount

---

64) elate, elicit, eligible, elucidate, elude, emancipate, emerge, emit, enervate, enumerate, eradicate, erode, erudite, erupt

259. **eradicate** weeds from the garden 근절하다 extirpate

260. the sea **erodes** the rocks. 침식하다 gnaw

261. an **erudite** teacher 박식한 learned

262. her face **erupted** in pimples(여드름) 분출하다 explode

263. **evacuate** all civilians from the war zone[65] 대피시키다 withdraw

264. **evade** pursuer by hiding in a cave 피하다 avoid

265. boiling water **evaporates** rapidly 증발하다 vaporize

266. **evoke** a dead man's spirit. 불러일으키다 elicit

267. she was **exalted** by success 의기 양양케하다 elate

268. the little child's constant noise **exasperated** his father.
몹시 화나게 하다 enrage

269. **excerpts** from her new book 발췌 extract

270. be **exempted** from military service. 면제하다 release

---

65) evacuate, evade, evaporate, evoke, exalt, exasperate, excerpt, exempt, exhale, exhort, exile, exorbitant, exotic, expedient

271. **exhale** clouds of smoke 내뿜다 emit

272. the general **exhorted** his men to fight bravely.

   타이르다 urge strongly, advise

273. a political **exile** 추방된 자 expatriate

274. the hotel charges **exorbitant** prices. 터무니없는 excessive

275. many **exotic** plants at the flower show. 이국적인 alien

276. get into the house by simple **expedient** of climbing through a window 편리한 수단, 편리한 useful

277. **expedite** the release for the political prisoners.[66]

   (엑스 퍼 다잇) 촉진하다 quicken

278. **expel** a traitor from a country. 추방하다 banish

279. **expend** energy on a useless job 쓰다 spend

280. **expire** of a heart attack from overwork

   죽다 die, 만료되다 terminate

281. I gave him an **explicit** instructions 명백한 definite

---

66) expedite, expel, expend, expire, explicit, exploit, expound, expunge, extemporize, exterminate, extinct, extol, extrude, exuberant, exult

282. **exploit** the country's mineral resources.

개발하다 develop, 착취하다 make unfair use of

283. **expound** objections to the bill 자세히 설명하다 explain

284. **expunge** certain remarks from the record 삭제하다 erase

285. **extemporize** instead of following the score 즉석에서 하다 improvise

286. this poison will **exterminate** roaches 근절하다 eradicate

287. an **extinct** volcano 죽은 extinguished

288. **extol** the merits of a new car 칭찬하다 commend

289. **extrude** toothpaste from the tube 밀어내다 push

290. receive an **exuberant** welcome 넘치는 lavish

291. the winners **exulted** in their victory 의기 양양해하다 rejoice

292. to betray a friend is **ignoble**[67] 비열한 without honor, 비천한 humble

293. an **ignominious** defeat 수치스러운 disreputable, disgraceful

---

67) ignoble, ignominious, illegible, illegitimate, illicit, illiterate, immaculate, immature, immemorial, immortal, immune, impartial, impassive, impecunious imperceptible

294. his handwriting is almost **illegible** 읽기 어려운 indecipherable

295. strictly prohibit an **illegitimate** behavior 불법의 unlawful

296. become rich with an **illicit** income 불법의 forbidden

297. a boorish **illiterate** 문맹의 ignorant

298. wear **immaculate** gym shoes 순결한 pure

299. **immature** apples are usually green 미숙한 undeveloped

300. from **immemorial** times to now 태고의 antique

301. write an **immortal** literary work 불멸의 everlasting

302. makes a person **immune** to an epidemic 면제된 exempt

303. a judge should be **impartial** 공평한 fair

304. endure pain with **impassive** face 무감각한 apathetic

305. an **impecunious** man from gambling 가난한 needy

306. **imperceptible** differences between the original painting and the copy 알아차릴 수 없는 impalpable

307. the suspect's **impertinent** manner[68]

뻔뻔한 impolite, 부적절한 inappropriate

308. man **impotent** against the hurricane 무력한 helpless

309. an **impracticable** plan for the problem 실행 불가능한 impossible

310. win the case with an **impregnable** argument

확고부동한 unconquerable

311. **imprudent** behavior to rush into something without thinking

경솔한 unwise

312. commit a crime with **impunity** 무사 immunity[69]

313. an **inadvertent** mistake ruined the experiment 부주의한 careless

314. a baby makes **inarticulate** sounds 불분명한 obscure

315. the **incessant** noise from the factory 끊임없는 continual

316. **inclement** weather is common in winter 혹독한 rigorous

317. the king traveled **incognito** to avoid crowds. 익명의 anonymous

(111)

---

68) impertinent, impotent, impracticable, impregnable, imprudent, impunity, inadvertent, inarticulate, incessant, inclement, incognito, incompatible, incongruous, inconsistent

69) indemnify, indignant, indiscreet, indiscriminate, indolent, indomitable, inert, inexorable, inextricable, infallible, infamous, infinitesimal, infirm, inhospitable, iniquitous

318. bad eating habits are **incompatible** with good health
양립할 수 없는 inconsistent

319. shoes **incongruous** with a party dress 어울리지 않는 inconsistent

320. the two statements are **inconsistent** 모순된 incongruous

321. **indemnify** him for his injuries 변상하다 recompense

322. an **indignant** expression on his face 성난 wrathful

323. the **indiscreet** girl revealed secrets to strangers 경솔한 imprudent

324. the terrorists' **indiscriminate** violence 무차별의 sweeping

325. an naturally **indolent** man 게으른 idle

326. show **indomitable** courage against overwhelming enemies
불굴의 unconquerable

327. a fat and **inert** woman 느릿느릿한 slow, 비활성의 inactive

328. the forces of nature are **inexorable** 냉혹한 relentless

329. **inextricable** financial troubles 벗어날 수 없는 insoluble

330. an **infallible** rule 확실한 certain

331. an **infamous** criminal 악명 높은 notorious

332. Germs are **infinitesimal** animals. 극소의 microscopic

333. an old and **infirm** man 허약한 feeble

334. **inhospitable** desert areas 불모의 barren, 불친절한 unkind

335. an **iniquitous** suggestion 사악한 wicked

336. an **innumerable** swarm of bees[70] 무수한 countless

337. **inordinate** demands for higher wages 부설제한 excessive

338. become **insensible** from cold 무감각한 senseless

339. heat is **inseparable** from fire 분리할 수 없는 indivisible

340. an **insolent** remark 무례한 arrogant

341. the bank was declared **insolvent** 파산한 bankrupt

342. sound and light are **intangible** 무형의 impalpable

343. an **integral** part of the argument 필수의 essential, 완전한 entire

---

70) innumerable, inordinate, insensible, inseparable, insolent, insolvent, intangible, integral, integrity, intrepid, invaluable, invariable, invincible, involuntary, irrational

344. a man of complete **integrity** 정직 honesty

345. the **intrepid** mountaineers 용감한 dauntless

346. good health is an **invaluable** blessing 매우 귀중한 priceless

347. an **invariable** habit 변하지 않은 unchangeable

348. the champion wrestler seemed **invincible**
이길 수 없는 unconquerable

349. give an **involuntary** yawn 무심코 automatic

350. a completely **irrational** decision. 비이성적인 unreasonable

351. a question **irrelevant** in a music lesson[71] 부적절한 inappropriate

352. an **irreparable** loss to the firm 돌이킬 수 없는 irrecoverable

353. **irresolute** persons make poor leaders 우유부단한 hesitant

354. his **irrevocable** decision 돌이킬 수 없는 irreversible

355. the room was **illuminated** by four large lamps.
조명하다 lighten, 계몽하다 edify

---

71) irrelevant, irreparable, irresolute, irrevocable, illuminate, imbibe, immerse, imminent, impair, impart, impassioned, impeach, impede

356. these graphs **illustrate** the results of the experiment
설명하다 clarify

357. **imbibe** moisture from the earth 마시다 quaff, 받아들이다 absorb

358. **immerse** feet in a bucket 담그다 dip, 몰두시키다 absorb

359. be in **imminent** danger of death 절박한 impending

360. his illness has **impaired** his efficiency.
손상시키다 damage, make worse

361. **impart** the secret to me. 주다 bestow, 전해주다 communicate

362. make an **impassioned** speech 감동적인 stirring

363. **impeach** a corrupt official 탄핵하다 charge

364. the rescue attempt was **impeded** by bad weather
방해하다 hinder

365. an **impending** war between two nations.[72] 절박한 imminent

366. an **imperative** manner 강제적인 commanding

---

72) impend, imperative, impetuous, implement, implicit, implore, impose, impoverish, impromptu, impute, inaugurate, inborn, incense, incipient, incite, incumbent

367. an **impetuous** torrent of water 격렬한 violent, 충동적인 impulsive

368. **implement** an order 이행하다 fulfill

369. their request seems to contain **implicit** threat 함축적인 suggestive

370. the prisoner **implored** pardon 애원하다 entreat

371. **impose** a fine on the guilty man 부과하다 put a burden or tax on

372. a long drought **impoverished** the farmers.
    가난하게하다 make very poor

373. give an **impromptu** speech 즉석의 improvised

374. **impute** his failure to laziness 탓으로 하다 attribute

375. a president is **inaugurated** every five years. 취임시키다 begin

376. an **inborn** sense of music 타고난 innate

377. he felt deeply **incensed** at her remark. 격분시키다 enrage

378. the children's **incipient** cough 시초의 initial

379. agitators **incited** the men to strike 선동하다 provoke

380. the **incumbent** president 현재의 present, 의무인 obligatory

381. an **indented** coast[73] 움푹 들어가게 하다 make notches in

382. lions are **indigenous** to Africa 토착의 native

383. become a legendary hero to the **indigent** 가난한 needy

384. **indulge** all one's desires 만족시키다 satisfy

385. **infer** his displeasure from his refusal 추측하다 reason, imply

386. **inflate** a tire 부풀리다 expand

387. **inflict** the severest possible penalty 고통을 가하다 strike

388. **infringe** the food and drug law 위반하다 break

389. their insults **infuriated** him 격노하다 enrage

390. **infuse** a liquid into a vessel 붓다 inspire

391. the **ingenious** boy made a radio set for himself. 재능이 있는 clever

392. an **ingenuous** smile 천진난만한 innocent

---

73) indent, indigenous, indigent, indulge, infer, inflate, inflict, infringe, infuriate, infuse, ingenious, ingenuous, ingrained, inhale, inherit, inject

393. **ingrained** habits 깊이 베어든 rooted

394. these days we can't help **inhaling** car exhaust gas. 흡입하다 breathe

395. she **inherited** the land from her grandfather 상속하다 succeed to

396. **inject** the invalid with the new drug
   주사하다 put into with a special needle

397. one of the **inmates** has escaped[74] 수감자 prisoner

398. an **innate** sense of humor 타고난 natural

399. spread his scandal by **innuendoes** 암시 insinuation

400. **inoculate** a virus into a person 접종하다 vaccinate

401. my father's words are **inscribed** on my memory 새기다 embed

402. **insidious** intent 음흉한 sly, 잠행성의 working secretly

403. **instigate** a quarrel 선동하다 urge

404. an **insurrection** aimed at the overthrow of the government
   반란 revolt

---

74) inmate, innate, innuendo, inoculate, inscribe, insidious, instigate, insurrection, intoxicate, intricate, intrigue, intrude, intuition, inundate, invert

405. driving while **intoxicated** 취하게 하다 make drunk

406. an **intricate** plot of the novel 복잡한 entangled

407. the royal palace was filled with **intrigue** 음모 conspiracy

408. do not **intrude** your opinions upon others 강요하다 force

409. by experience the doctor has developed great power of **intuition.**
     직관 insight

410. the river overflowed and **inundated** the village 범람시키다 overflow

411. catch the insect by **inverting** the cup 뒤집다 reverse

412. build canals to **irrigate** the desert[75] 물을 대다 water

413. **interdict** one's daughter from going out at night 금지하다 forbid

414. take **interim** measures to help unemployed. 임시의 temporary

415. If I may **interject** a few comments for this point 첨가하다 insert

416. **interrogate** the suspect for several hours. 심문하다 inquire

---

75) irrigate, interdict, interim, interject, interrogate, interrupt, intersect, malady, malediction, malefactor, malevolent, malice, malign, malinger, miscarry

417. The building **interrupts** the view from our window. 가로막다 stop

418. A path **intersects** the field. 가로지르다 cross

419. Cancer and Malaria are serious **maladies**. 질병 illness

420. cast a **malediction** of a person's arrogance. 저주 curse

421. The scoundrel is an incurable **malefactor**. 악인 villain

422. **malevolent** inclinations to destroy the happiness of others.
    사악한 wicked

423. bear a person a **malice** 악의 ill will

424. She was **maligned** by the press 중상하다 slander

425. He says he's got flu, but I think he's **malingering.**
    꾀병을 부리다 feign illness

426. Their strike miscarried. 실패하다 miss

427. The theft of a small amount to money is a **misdemeanor.**[76]
    경범죄 wrongdoing

---

76) misdemeanor, obdurate, obese, oblige, oblique, obliterate, oblivion, obloquy, obnoxious, obscene, obsequious, obsess, obsolete, obstinate, obstruct, obtrude

428. an **obdurate** refusal 고집 센 intractable

429. an **obese** child 비만의 very fat

430. I was **obliged** to go at once. 강요하다 compel

431. an **oblique** line 비스듬한 inclined

432. **obliterate** landmarks. 말소하다 delete

433. many ancient cities fell into **oblivion.** 망각 forgetfulness

434. glory and **obloquy** 불명예 dishonor

435. **obnoxious** smell 불쾌한 hateful

436. an **obscene** book 외설의 lewd

437. **obsequious** behavior 비굴한 flattering

438. be **obsessed** by a fixed idea 망상이 들다 haunt

439. an **obsolete** word 구식의 out of date

440. as **obstinate** as a mule 고집 센 stubborn

441. **obstruct** a person's plan 방해하다 hinder

442. **obtrude** one's opinions upon others 강요하다 intrude

443. an **obtuse** person[77] 무딘 blunt, dull

444. **obviate** danger 제거하다 eliminate

445. **occult** powers 신비로운 magical

446. defeat one's **opponent** in the election 대립자 antagonist

447. an **opportune** advice 시기적절한 timely

448. **ostensible** purpose 표면적인 seeming

449. His religion was sincere, not **ostentatious.** 허세부리는 pretentious

450. **overhaul** a government department 철저히 조사하다 investigate

451. **overhear** some cruel remarks 어쩌다 듣다 hear by accident

452. anger **overpowered** every other feelings. 눌러버리다 overwhelm

453. the **overrun** in the capital expenditure 초과 excess, 만연하다 infest

454. a great wave **overwhelmed** the boat

---

77) obtuse, obviate, occult, opponent, opportune, ostensible, ostentatious, overhaul, overhear, overpower, overrun, overwhelm, outburst, outgoing, outlay, outrageous

덮치다 cover completely, 압도하다 overcome completely

455. an **outburst** of laughter 폭발 explosion

456. a very **outgoing** person 외향적인 sociable

457. a large **outlay** for education 지출 expense

458. **outrageous** treatment of prisoners 잔인무도한 egregious

459. an **outright** expression of opinion.[78] 솔직한 obvious

460. the book fascinated the reader from the **outset.** 시작 start

461. The advantages of the plan **outweigh** its disadvantages.
     뛰어나다 overweigh

462. read the **parable** of the lost sheep 우화 allegory, fable

463. "The child is father to the man" is a **paradox**. 역설 contradiction

464. The accident left him with **paralysis** of the legs. 마비 cripple

465. This task is **paramount** to all others. 최고의 supreme

---

78) outright, outset, outweigh, parable, paradox, paralysis, paramount, peremptory, perennial, perjury, permeate, pernicious, perpendicular, perpetrate, perquisite

466. a **peremptory** order. 단호한 imperative

467. the **perennial** beauty 영원한 perpetual

468. commit **perjury** 위증 false witness

469. the rain has **permeated** the sand. 스며들다 penetrate

470. smoking is a **pernicious** habit. 해로운 noxious

471. a **perpendicular** line 수직의 vertical

472. **perpetrate** a crime 범하다 commit

473. the **perquisites** of the college president including a home and car. 수당 bonus

474. **persecute** pagans.[79] 박해하다 torment

475. a **perspicacious** comment 통찰력 있는 clear-sighted

476. documents **pertaining** to the case. 관련하다 belong or be connected as a part or possession

477. **peruse** the instructions before you fill out your application.

79) persecute, perspicacious, pertain, peruse, pervade, perverse, pervert, precept, precinct, preclude, precursor, predicament, predilection, predispose, predominate

정독하다 read

478. the odor of pines **pervades** the air. 퍼지다 permeate

479. angered by his **perverse** attitude 외고집의 obstinate

480. **pervert** the order of nature. 왜곡하다 distort

481. follow few basic **precepts** 격언 maxim

482. a police **precinct** 관할 구역 province

483. **preclude** possible retaliatory attack later 미리 막다 prevent

484. a **precursor** to recession 선구자 forerunner

485. be in a dangerous **predicament** 곤경 plight

486. a **predilection** for dangerous sports 편애 preference

487. her kindness **predisposed** me to like her. 마음이 생기게 하다 incline

488. sunny days **predominate** over rainy days in desert regions.
우세하다 excel

489. the country **preeminent** in the field of medical research[80]

탁월한 excellent

490. she was **pregnant** with her second child.

임신한 having an unborn young in the body

491. play the **prelude** to the music 전주 overture

492. the baby was two months **premature**. 시기상조의 untimely

493. the **premise** that an accused person is innocent until he's proved

guilty, 전제 assumption

494. a vague **premonition** of disaster. 예감 foreboding

495. it would be **preposterous** to shovel snow with teaspoon.

터무니없는 absurd

496. the president may use his **prerogative** to pardon a criminal.

특권 privilege

497. have a **presage** of danger 예감 omen

498. an instinctive **prescience** of the approach of danger. 예지 foresight

---

80) preeminent, pregnant, prelude, premature, premise, premonition, preposterous, prerogative, presage, prescience, prescribe, prestige, pretext, prevail

499. **prescribe** for the pain. 처방하다 order as medicine

500. a **prestige** school 명성이 있는 reputable

501. a **pretext** for not going to school. 프리텍스트, 핑계 excuse

502. reason **prevailed** over emotion. 우세하다 win

503. a **proclivity** of finding fault[81] 경향 tendency

504. it is not wise to **procrastinate**. 지체하다 delay

505. his **prodigal** lifestyle 낭비하는 lavish

506. a **prodigious** sum 거대한 huge

507. **proffer** a present 증정하다 render

508. **proficient** in surgery. 능숙한 skillful

509. **prognosticate** a rebellion. 예언하다 forecast

510. a **prolific** novelist 다산의 productive

511. the **prologue** of the play 서사 introduction

---

81) proclivity, procrastinate, prodigal, prodigious, proffer, proficient, prognosticate, prolific, prologue, prolong, prominent, promiscuous, promising, promulgate, propensity

512. **prolong** a sick person's life. 연장하다 lengthen

513. a **prominent** music critic 뛰어난 outstanding

514. a **promiscuous** heap of clothing. 뒤섞인 miscellaneous

515. a **promising** young writer 장래가 촉망되는 hopeful

516. the king **promulgated** a decree 공포하다 proclaim

517. a **propensity** for the lavish spending of money 성벽 proclivity

518. he **prophesied** that the war would come to an end before long.[82]
예언하다 predict

519. **propitious** benefits. 길조의 favorable

520. a starting salary **proportional** to her experience.
비례하는 commensurable

521. observe the **proprieties.** 예절 etiquette

522. **proscribe** fat from diet 금지하다 forbid

523. her teeth **protrude** too far. 튀어나오다 stick out

---

82) prophesy, propitious, proportional, propriety, proscribe, protrude, protocol, ransom, rebuke, recant, reciprocal, recline, recourse, recuperate

524. **protocol** demands that the queen meet him at the airport.
외교 의례 diplomacy

525. hold a person to **ransom** 몸값 the price demanded for release

526. **rebuke** a person for his carelessness. 비난하다 reprove

527. the critics of the government publicly **recanted** their errors.
취소하다 revoke

528. **reciprocal** help 상호의 mutual

529. **recline** against a wall 기대다 lean

530. by **recourse** to violence 의지 resort

531. **recuperate** after illness. 회복하다 recover

532. leap year **recurs** every four years.[83] 다시 일어나다 repeat

533. **redeem** mortgaged land 되찾다 regain

534. the kitchen was **redolent** of onions.
냄새가 나는 fragrant, 연상시키는 reminiscent

---

83) recur, redeem, redolent, redress, redundant, refute, regenerate, rehabilitate, reimburse, reiterate, rejuvenate, relegate, relevant, relinquish, reluctant

535. **redress** social evils. 고치다 correct

536. **redundant** population 과잉의 surplus

537. **refute** his allegation 반박하다 confute

538. lizards that **regenerate** lost tails 재생시키다 revive

539. **rehabilitate** patients 원상태로 돌리다 recover

540. **reimburse** the loss 변상하다 repay

541. the policeman **reiterated** his command. 반복하다 repeat

542. the long rest and new clothes have **rejuvenated** her.
다시 젊어지게 하다 refresh

543. **relegate** a person to an inferior post.
좌천시키다 put away to a lower position

544. matters **relevant** to the subject 관련된 proper

545. **relinquish** the throne to a person. 포기하다 abandon

546. I am **reluctant** to go out in very cold weather. 꺼리는 hesitant

547. a cloud **reminiscent** of a ship[84] 연상시키는 remindful

548. be **remiss** in one's duties. 태만한 neglectful

549. **remit** me the money at once. 송금하다 transmit

550. **remnant** of a banquet 나머지 rest

551. feel **remorse** for one's fault 후회 penitence

552. he is not a **renegade** Catholic. 변절자 traitor

553. **renounce** a demand 포기하다 abandon

554. Japanese **reparations** for the war 배상 compensation

555. be **replete** with every comfort and luxury 가득한 full

556. **repress** a rebellion 진압하다 suppress

557. they bombed the enemy village as a **reprisal**. 보복 revenge

558. **repudiate** a charge as untrue. 부인하다 reject

559. he is **resolute** to fight. 단호한 firm

---

84) reminiscent, remiss, remit, remnant, remorse, renegade, renounce, reparation, replete, repress, reprisal, repudiate, resolute, respire, restraint, restrict

560. **respire** irregularly. 호흡하다 breathe

561. lay **restraint** on one's emotion 억제 restriction

562. our membership is **restricted** to twenty. 제한하다 circumscribe

563. be **reticent** about the matter.[85] 말이 없는 silent

564. **retrench** school expenses 절약하다 curtail

565. **retrieve** freedom 되찾다 recover

566. pray with **reverence** 존경 respect

567. **revert** to the old system 되돌아가다 return

568. he **reviled** me with a stream of abuse. 비방하다 scold

569. **seclude** oneself from society 격리하다 isolate

570. **sedition** against the government 선동 coup

571. **seduce** a person into committing a crime 유혹하다 mislead

572. **segregate** the colored 인종차별하다 discriminate

---

85) reticent, retrench, retrieve, reverence, revert, revile, seclude, sedition, seduce, segregate, sever, sojourn, subjugate, subordinate, subscribe, subsequent

573. **sever** the rope with a knife 끊다 cut

574. **sojourn** many days in the desert 체류하다 live for a time in a place

575. ancient Rome **subjugated** most of Europe 정복하다 conquer

576. **subordinate** one's wishes to general good. 하위에 두다 subsidiary

577. **subscribe** one's name at the end of the will

    서명하다 sign, 기부하다 contribute, 동의하다 agree, 정기구독하다

578. **subsequent** events proved that he was right. 잇따른 later

579. the waves **subsided** when the wind stopped[86] 진정되다 abate

580. ask a **subsidiary** question 부가의 subordinate

581. a club cannot **subsist** without members. 존속하다 exist

582. **substantiate** one's claim in a court. 입증하다 verify

583. **subtract** 50 from 100 빼다 deduct

584. **succumb** to the temptation 굴복하다 yield

---

86) subside, subsidiary, subsist, substantiate, subtract, succumb, suffocate, suffrage, supplement, supplicate, susceptible, surfeit, surmise, unprecedented

585. be **suffocated** by heavy smoke 질식시키다 choke

586. grant **suffrage** to women 투표권 vote

587. **supplement** one's diet with vitamin ills. 보완하다 complement

588. **supplicate** the judge to pardon him. 애원하다 entreat

589. she is very **susceptible** to persuasion 영향 받기 쉬운 sensitive

590. a **surfeit** of food makes one sick. 과식 excess

591. his remarks were pure **surmise.** 추측 conjecture

592. **unprecedented** rainfall 전례 없는 unexampled

Part 3
시험 대비 단어

01 He _____ ownership of the dog.

    a. disclaim   b. proclaim   c. reclaim   d. prodigy

02 He was _____ in his thanks.

    a. profuse   b. effusive   c. suffuse   d. transfuse

03 They offered sacrifices to _____ the gods.

    a. prognosticate   b. agnostic   c. propitiate   d. protrude

04 He is always _____ing me to lend him money.

    a. importune   b. opportune   c. deport   d. deportment

05 Every male citizen is required to initiate military service within two years of graduation from high school, unless arrangements are made for a _____.

    a. preferment   b. preference   c. deference   d. deferment

06 I am _____ with cold.

    a. indisposed   b. abjure   c. conjure   d. depose

07 She _____ the tune but not the words of the song.

    a. detain   b. retain   c. obsequious   d. ingratiate

08 He tried to _____ himself with his superiors.

    a. ingratiate   b. conducive   c. ineluctable   d. decrepit

09 He was accused of _____ in the crime.

    a. epitome   b. abstemious   c. complicity   d. modish

10 I must say I feel pretty _____ about whether or not we go to France this year.

    a. ambivalent   b. regenerate   c. complimentary   d. condone

11 His conduct is _____ to his dignity.

   a. impose   b. depredation   c .derogatory   d. subsist

12 Education should _____ people of superstition.

   a. perspicacious   b. despondent   c. disabuse   d. discomfit

13 Until recently, very little _____ work had been done, aside from Mil gram's initial experiment.

   a. enjoin   b. empirical   c. mendacious   d. expiate

14 _____ gossip

   a. immolate   b. recapitulate   c. salacious   d. restitution

15 _____ events showed that I was right.

   a. subordinate   b. subsequent   c. subservient   d. respire

16 The trouble with your studying is that you spend too much time on

_____ details.

a. luscious   b. inflate   c. picayune   d. frail

17 My brother's _____ over getting into college ended when he

received word that he had been accepted.

a. default   b. remiss   c. solicitude   d. domicile

18 My sister _____ over the dishes, Mother gets them done without wast

ing time.

a. infraction   b. defer   c. dawdle   d. protract

19 The witness _____ the Fifth Amendment.

a. bipartisan   b. evoke   c. invoke   d. incarcerate

20 A superior officer has the power to _____ orders issued by a

subordinate.

a. contravene   b. countermand   c. incontrovertible   d. intermediary

21 Kim was _____ in the early grades, not because of poor intelligence, but because he couldn't speak English.

a. maladjust   b. dispassionate   c. circumscribed   d. collusion

22 Today's rain has completely _____ yesterday's snow.

a. obliterate   b. obsess   c. obstruct   d. preclude

23 The _____ strength of the allies.

a. enamor   b. animus   c. aggregate   d. luminous

24 The alumni association is not under the control of the school. It is a completely _____ group.

a. autonomous   b. kleptomania   c. anonymous   d. genuine

25 Bob meant it when he said he was quitting the team. He was not being _____.

a. contend   b. content   c. facetious   d. fictitious

26 He _____ the king for mercy.

a. engraft   b. entreat   c. forbear   d. forgive

27 She was _____ in a man's clothes.

a. overthrow   b. postmortem   c. disguise   d. intermingle

28 The picture is _____, so I must correct it.

a. pernicious   b. oblique   c. precarious   d. preposterous

29 As she was _____ woman, you'd better be careful.

a. captious   b. cloister   c. corpulent   d. miscreant

30 If the problem happens, you should _____ my opinion.

a. excurse   b. vindicate   c. condone   d. subdue

31 When you criticize others, you had better use an _____ expression.

    a. diaphanous   b. euphemistic   c. florescent   d. fecund

32 Through _____, girls become completely mature.

    a. matrimony   b. expatriate   c. eject   d. commensuration

33 My heart _____ with inexpressible joy when I received in first prize.

    a. collate   b. dilate   c. immunize   d. remiss

34 Please _____ if you want to do it clearly.

    a. cerebrate   b. deprecate   c. depose   d. impound

35 The teacher _____ Ted to take charge of the class while he was away.

    a. reprobate   b. depute   c. perquisite   d. derogate

36 They didn't lose their _____ even in the temptation.

    a. rectitude   b. subscription   c. execration   d. speculation

37 We must destroy such _____ publications.

    a. theocracy   b. invalidate   c. erupt   d. subversive

1. disclaim, proclaim, reclaim 의 의미 차이는 접두어 dis, pro, re 의 차이이다.
claim 은 요구, dis 는 부정, pro 는 앞, re 는 다시[87]

   1. He **disclaimed** ownership of the dog. 그는 그 개의 소유를 부인했다.
   2. His manners **proclaims** him a gentleman.
      그의 예의범절은 그가 신사라는 것을 선언한다.
   3. Her mission was to **reclaim** former criminals.
      그의 임무는 전과자를 갱생하는 것이다.

2. prodigy 는 자연에 대한 찬사나 경의와 인간에 대한 천재의 의미가 있다.[88]

   4. An eclipse of the sun seemed a **prodigy** to early man.
      일식은 원시인에게는 자연의 경이였다.
      a **prodigy** of learning. 학문의 천재
      An infant **prodigy.** 유아 천재 * child genius

144

3. officiate 는 사회보다. officious 는 주제넘게 나서는[89]

   5. **officiate** at a marriage. 결혼식 사회를 보다.
   6. an **officious** manner. 주제넘게 나서는 태도

4. profuse 풍부한, effusive 방출하는, suffuse 뒤덮다, transfuse 수혈하다.[90]

   7. He was **profuse** in his thanks. 그는 무척 감사했다.

---

87) 1. disclaim, proclaim, reclaim
88) 2. prodigy
89) 3. officiate, officious
90) 4. profuse, effusive, suffuse, transfuse

be **profuse** with money. 돈이 많다.

8. be **effusive** in one's gratitude. 감사를 표하다.

9. The sky was **suffused** with sunlight. 하늘은 햇살로 뒤 덮였다.

10. **transfuse** = transfer blood. 수혈하다

5. prognosticate 예시하다, agnostic 불가지론자에서 gno 는 know 의미, pro는 미리, a 는 not 의 의미이다.[91]

11. The clouds **prognosticate** a storm. 구름은 폭풍우를 예시하다

12. **agnostic** = can not know 불가지론의

13. **propitiate** = gain the good will of 비위를 맞추다.
    They offered sacrifices to **propitiate** the gods.
    그들은 신을 달래기 위해 제물을 바쳤다.

145

6. protrude 돌출하다, obtrude 참견하다. 에서 trude 는 내밀다[92]

14. The bone did not **protrude** through the skin.
    뼈는 피부를 통하여 삐져나오지 않았다.

15. **obtrude** on someone's privacy. 다른 사람의 프라이버시에 참견하다.

7. voke 부르다. 에서 convoke 소집하다, invoke 호소하다, revoke 취소하다[93]

16. Parliament was **convoked** in April. 의회는 4월에 소집된다.

17. **invoke** God's blessing 하나님의 축복을 기원하다.
    invoke the protection of the law 법의 보호를 호소하다

---

91) 5. prognosticate, agnostic, propitiate
92) 6. protrude, obtrude
93) 7. convoke, invoke, revoke

18. **revoke** a license 자격증을 취소하다

8. importune 조르다, opportune 적합한, deport 추방하다, deportment 행동, deportation 추방, disport 즐기다, purport 목적[94]

19. He is always **importuning** me to lend him money. 그는 항상 나에게 돈을 빌려달라고 조른다. * importune(임퍼츈) to make persistent and usually annoying requests of someone.

20. He appeared at a most **opportune** moment.
    그는 가장 적합한 순간에 나타났다.

21. a **deportation** order 추방령

22. a model of good **deportment** 선행의 모델

23. We **disported** ourselves on the beach. 우리는 해변에서 즐겼다.
    * disport 즐기다 to indulge (oneself) in lively amusement

24. W wished to know the **purport** of H's thesis.
    W는 H의 논문의 주제를 알기를 원했다.

9. preferment 승진, preference 선호도, deference 복종, deferment 연기[95]

25. **preferment** = moving up to a higher rank, promotion 승진

26. A teacher should not show **preference** for anyone of his pupils.
    선생님은 그의 학생들 중 어느 누구에 대한 선호를 보여서는 안 된다.

27. blind **deference** 맹종 * deference 복종, 경의 willingness to consider or respect the wishes, etc of others.
    in deference to someone's wishes
    어느 누구의 희망에 복종하여 (데페런스)

---

94) 8. importune, opportune, deportation, deportment, deportation, disport, purport

95) 9. preferment, preference, deference, deferment

He treats his mother with as much **deference** as if she were the Queen.

그는 자기 어머니를 마치 여왕인 것처럼 최대의 존경을 다해 대했다.

28. deferment = put off, postpone 연기하다

Every male citizen is required to initiate military service within two years of graduation from high school, unless arrangements are made for a deferment. 남자들은 징집 연기를 한 경우를 제외하고는 누구나 고등학교 졸업 이후 2년 내로 군 복무를 시작해야 한다.

10. rog 는 ask 묻다 에서 surrogate 대리, derogate 강등시키다, abrogate 취소하다.[96]

29. **surrogate** mother 대리모

30. **derogate** from one's authority. 권위를 떨어뜨리다

31. **abrogate** a treaty 조약을 취소하다 * abrogate (애브로게잇) 폐기하다

to cancel (a law, agreement, etc) formally or officially

11. convalesce 회복하다, perfidious 배반하는, indispose -하기 쉽다.[97]

32. The patient is **convalescing** slowly. 환자는 회복이 더디다.

33. a **perfidious** friend 배반하는 친구

34. indispose 는 마음이 내키지 않다 와 - 하기 쉽다 의 의미

I am **indisposed** with cold. 나는 감기에 걸리기 쉽다.

* indispose 가벼운 병에 걸리기 쉽다. slightly ill.

He is **indisposed** to help us. 그는 우리를 도울 마음이 내키지 않는다.

---

96) 10. surrogate, derogate, abrogate

97) 11. convalesce, perfidious, indispose

12. abjure 포기하다, conjure 불러내다, depose 는 면직시키다, 선서증언하다[98]

    35. **abjure** one's religion 자신의 종교를 포기하다

    36. **conjure** up a devil 악령을 불러내다 * conjure(칸저) to perform magic tricks, especially ones which deceive the eye or seem to defy nature.

    conjure a pigeon out of an empty hat 비둘기를 빈 모자로부터 불러내다.

    37. depose 는 면직시키다, 선서증언하다

    depose someone from office. 사무실에서 면직시키다.

    He **deposed** that he had seen the prisoner on that day.

    그는 그가 그 날 그 죄수를 보았다고 선서 증언하였다.

13. detain 잡아두다, retain 보유하다[99]

    38. be **detained** by business 사업에 얽매이다.

    detain a suspect for further examination

    더 조사하기 위해 용의자를 억류하다.

    39. **retain** an old custom 오랜 관습을 보유하다.

    She **retained** the tune but not the words of the song.

    그녀는 그 음은 기억하나 그 노래의 가사는 기억하지 못한다.

    soils **retentive** of moisture 습기를 간직하고 있는 토양

    She has a very **retentive** memory 그녀는 아주 기억력이 좋다.

14. obsequious 아부하는, ingratiate 아부하다[100]

    40. She is almost embarrassingly **obsequious** to anyone in authority.

    그녀는 권력자라면 아무한테나 거의 당황스러울 정도로 굽실거린다.

---

98) 12. abjure, conjure, depose
99) 13. detain, retain
100) 14. obsequious, ingratiate

41. He tried to **ingratiate** himself with his superiors.

그는 그의 상관에게 아부하기 위해 노력했다.

15. conducive 공헌하는, ineluctable 피할 수 없는, decrepit 노쇠한, invidious 사악한, incubus 악몽[101]

42. Fresh air is **conducive** to health. 신선한 공기는 건강에 공헌한다.

43. ineluctable = inevitable 피할 수 없는

ineluctable logic 당연한 논리

44. a **decrepit** man 노인

45. **invidious** remarks 사악한 말

46. The examination will be an **incubus** until I have passed it.

그 시험은 내가 통과할 때까지 악몽이었다.

149

16. epitome 전형, abstemious 절제하는, complicity 공범, modish 유행하는, adumbrate 개략설명하다[102]

47. the **epitome** of a perfect soldier 완전한 군인의 전형

48. **abstemious** in the use of tobacco. 담배의 사용을 절제하는 * austere

(반의어는 self-indulgent) ascetic, self-denying

49. He was **accused** of complicity in the crime.

그는 그 범죄의 공범으로 기소되었다.

50. a **modish** hat 유행하는 모자

51. **adumbrate** the plan 그 계획을 개략설명하다

---

17. exhort 훈계하다, contiguous 인접하는, aggrieve 슬프다, petite 작은[103]

52. I **exhort** you not to go. 나는 너에게 가지 말라고 훈계한다.

53. two **contiguous** properties 두 개의 인접하는 재산들

54. He was very much **aggrieved** at the insult from his friend.
그는 그의 친구로부터 모욕에 매우 슬펐다.

55. **petite** ⟨ regular ⟨ tall 작은

18. condole 조문하다, compendium 요약, aspiring 열망하는, insidious 잠행성의[104]

56. I **condoled** with him on the loss of his wife.
나는 그의 처의 상실에 대하여 그에게 조문했다.

57. a **compendium** of modern medicine. 현대 의학의 요약본
compendious = concise 요약, 간결한

58. **aspiring** doctor 인턴 의사
aspiring lawyer 고시생

59. an **insidious** disease 잠행성의 질병

19. ambivalent 반대감정이 양립하는, regenerate 재생하다, complimentary 무료의, condone 용서하다[105]

60. ambivalent = having opposite and conflicting feelings. Love and hate to ward
the some object. 반대감정이 양립하는
I must say I feel pretty **ambivalent** about whether or not we go to
France this year. 올해에 우리가 프랑스에 갈지 안 갈지에 대해서 나는 감정이 꽤나

---

103) 17. exhort, contiguous, aggrieve, petite

104) 18. condole, compendium, aspiring, insidious

105) 19. ambivalent, regenerate, complimentary, condone

오락가락한다고 말해야겠다.

61. Certain animals are able to **regenerate** lost parts of the body.

   어떤 동물들은 신체의 상실된 부분을 재생할 수 있다.

62. **complimentary** ticket 무료 표

63. **condone** someone's faults 잘못을 용서하다

20. confer 주다, constrain 강요하다, contrite 후회하는, emolument 보수[106]

64. <u>confer</u> a gift 선물을 주다

   <u>confer with</u> someone about something. 상의하다

65. He <u>constrained</u> me to go. 그는 나에게 가라고 강요했다.

   <u>constrained</u> confession 강요된 자백

66. shed <u>contrite</u> tears 후회의 눈물을 흘리다.

67. Her <u>emoluments</u> amounted to very little.

   그녀의 급료는 극히 얼마 안 되었다.

(151)

21. impose 부과하다, depredation 약탈, derogatory 경멸적인, subsist 생존하다[107]

68. Duties are **imposed** on wines. 세금이 와인에 부과되다.

69. the **depredations** of the invaders. 습격 자들의 약탈

70. His conduct is **derogatory** to his dignity.

   그의 행동은 그의 인격에 대한 경멸이다.

71. We are unable to **subsist** without air and water.

   우리는 공기와 물 없이는 생존할 수 없다.

---

106) 20. confer, constrain, contrite, emolument
107) 21. impose, depredation, derogatory, subsist

22. perspicacious 총명한, despondent 낙담한, disabuse 잘못을 깨우치다, discomfit 당황하다[108]

> 72. a **perspicacious** mind. 총명한 생각
>
> 73. despondent = discouraged 낙담한
>
> She's **despondent** about losing her bracelet.
>
> 그녀는 팔찌를 잃어버린 데 대해 낙담했다.
>
> 74. Education should **disabuse** people of superstition.
>
> 교육은 사람들로부터 미신의 잘못을 깨우쳐야만 한다.
>
> * disabuse 오해를 풀어 주다.
>
> to rid them of a mistaken idea or impression.
>
> 75. be <u>discomfited</u> by a question. 질문에 당황하다

23. discretion 자유재량, disentangle 풀다, disincline 마음이 내키지 않다, recline 기대다, discordant 불협화음의[109]

> 76. It is within your **discretion** to do it.
>
> 그것을 하는 것은 당신의 자유재량 내에 있다.
>
> 77. **disentangle** a complicated knot 복잡한 매듭을 풀다
>
> 78. I am **disinclined** to accept it.
>
> 나는 그것을 승인할 마음이 내키지 않는다.
>
> 79. **recline** one's head on the pillow 머리를 베개에 기대다
>
> 80. a **discordant** sound 조화롭지 않은 소리

---

108) 22. perspicacious, despondent, disabuse, discomfit

109) 23. discretion, disentangle, disincline, recline, discordant

24. disparagement 멸시, asperse 중상하다, perverse 고집 센, perversion 왜곡[110]

> 81. Poverty is no **disparagement** to greatness.
>
> 가난은 위대함에 대한 멸시가 아니다.
>
> 82. **asperse** someone's good name 좋은 평가를 중상모략하다
>
> 83. The **perverse** man continued to smoke against his doctor's orders.
>
> 고집쟁이는 의사의 명령에 반대하여 계속 담배를 피웠다.
>
> The statement is an audacious **perversion** of the truth.
>
> 그 말은 진실의 담대한 왜곡이다.

25. enjoin 명령/금지하다, empirical 경험적인, mendacious 거짓의, expiate 속죄하다[111]

> 84. **enjoin** silence on the children 어린이들에게 침묵을 명령하다.
>
> **enjoin** someone from infringing a right 권리를 침범하는 것을 금지하다.
>
> 85. Until recently, very little **empirical** work had been done, aside from Mil
>
> gram's initial experiment. 최근까지도 밀그램의 초기 실험을 제외하고는
>
> 실증 실험이 거의 이루어지지 않았다.
>
> 86. a **mendacious** report 거짓 보고
>
> 87. The thief **expiated** his theft. 도둑은 도둑질을 속죄했다.

26. expurgate 불온부분을 삭제하다, extortionate 터무니없는, extricate 구출하다, evanescent 덧없는, effete 쇠퇴한[112]

> 88. an **expurgated** edition of a novel 소설의 삭제 판
>
> 89. an **extortionate** price 터무니없는 가격

---

110) 24. disparagement, asperse, perverse, perversion

111) 25. enjoin, empirical, mendacious, expiate

112) 26. expurgate, extortionate, extricate, evanescent, effete

90. Tom **extricated** the bird from the net.

톰은 그 새를 그물에서 구출했다.

91. The joys of life is **evanescent**. 삶의 즐거움은 덧없다.

92. an **effete** civilization. 쇠퇴한 문명

27. immolate 제물로 바치다, recapitulate 요약하다, salacious 외설스러운, restitution 보상, submissive 복종하는[113]

93. I'm **immolated** my live to make my daughter a pianist. 나의 삶을 딸이 피아니스트 되는 데에 바치다. * immolate (이믈레잇) 제물로 바치다. to kill or offer as a sacrifice.

94. After listening to the speakers, he **recapitulated** their main argument.

연사의 말을 들은 후, 그는 그의 요점을 요약했다.

95. **salacious** gossip 음담패설

96. We should make restitution for the harm we have done.

우리는 우리가 행한 해에 대한 보상을 해야 한다.

97. a **submissive** gesture

순종적인 몸짓

28. subordinate 하위의, subsequent 후의, subservient 복종하는, respire 숨 쉬다[114]

98. Pleasure should be **subordinate** to duty.

노는 것은 일하는 것의 하위가 되어야 한다.

99. **Subsequent** events showed that I was right.

후의 사건들이 내가 옳았다는 것을 보여주었다.

100. Everything else is **subservient** to the child's welfare.

---

113) 27. immolate, recapitulate, salacious, restitution, submissive

114) 28. subordinate, subsequent, subservient, respire

다른 모든 것은 그 아이의 복지보다 부차적이다.

101. Some reptiles **respire** through their skin.

일부 파충류는 피부로 호흡한다.

29. opulence 풍요, indigence 가난, sumptuous 사치스런, apprehensive 염려하는, intimidate 위협하다, devour 게걸스럽게 먹다.[115]

102. Dickens contrasts the **opulence** of France's nobility with the indigence of her peasants.

디킨스는 프랑스 귀족의 부와 소작인의 가난을 대비한다.

103. beautiful but a bit **sumptuous.** 아름다우나 약간 사치스런

104. several **apprehensive** parents. 여러 염려하는 부모들

105. If the older boys hadn't **intimidated** them,

만약에 나이든 소년들이 그들을 위협하지 않았다면,

106. **devoured** the hamburgers. 햄버거를 게걸스럽게 먹다

30. luscious 맛좋은, inflate 공기를 불어넣다, picayune 사소한, frail 허약한, cogent 설득력이 있는[116]

107. The watermelon was very **luscious**. 그 수박은 매우 맛이 좋았다.

108. Since the football has lost air, we shall need a pump to **inflate.**

그 축구공이 공기가 빠졌기 때문에 우리는 공기를 불어넣기 위해 펌프가 필요할 것이다.

109. The trouble with your studying is that you spend too much time on **picayune** details. 너의 공부와 관련된 어려운 점은 네가 사소한 세부사항에 너무 많은 시간을 소비한다는 것이다.

110. It is not an occupation for a **frail** person.

---

115) 29. opulence, indigence, sumptuous, apprehensive, intimidate, devour

116) 30. luscious, inflate, picayune, frail, cogent

그 것은 허약한 사람을 위한 직업이 아니다.

111. Others are more <u>cogent,</u> such as a physician's note.

다른 사람들은 의사의 진단서와 같이 조금 더 설득력이 있었다.

31. tenacious 고집 센, default 궐석, remiss 태만한, solicitude 염려, domicile 주소지[117]

112. After the dog got the ball, I tried to **dislodge** it from her tenacious jaws.

개가그 공을 얻은 후 나는 그 개의 고집 센 턱으로부터 그 공을 빼앗으려고 노력했다.

113. If they do not appear, they will lose the game by **default**.

그들이 나타나지 아니한다면, 그들은 불출석으로 인해 경기를 패할 것이다.

114. The owner of the stolen car was himself **remiss**.

도난당한 차의 소유자는 그 자신이 태만했다.

115. My brother's **solicitude** over getting into college ended when he received word that he had been accepted. 대학을 들어가는 것에 대한 나의 형제의 근심은 그가 받아들여졌다는 말을 들었을 때 끝났다.

116. The Coopers have moved and invite you to visit them at their new <u>domicile</u>. 쿠퍼 가족이 이사 와서 그들의 새로운 주소지에서 그들을 방문하라고 너를 초대한다.

32. infraction 위반, defer 복종하다, dawdle 빈둥거리다.[118]

117. Motorists committing this **infraction** are heavily fined.

이러한 위반을 자행하는 운전자는 무겁게 벌금을 받는다.

118. Husbands as a rule do not decide on the colors of home furnishings but **defer to** their wives. 대체로 남편들은 집 가구의 색깔에 대하여 결정하지 아니하고 처에 복종한다.

---

117) 31. tenacious, default, remiss, solicitude, domicile
118) 32. infraction, defer, dawdle

119. My sister **dawdles over** the dishes, Mother gets them done without wasting time.

나의 누이는 설거지를 하지 아니하고 빈둥거리지만 빈둥거리다

33. protract 연장하다, foreboding 예감, arbitrate 중재시키다.[119]

120. We **protracted** our visit until after dinner.

우리는 저녁 후까지 우리의 방문을 연장했다.

121. The hero had a **foreboding** that he might not return.

그 영웅은 그가 돌아오지 못할 지도 모른다고 불길한 예감을 가졌다.

122. **arbitrate** their dispute because they consider him unbiased.

그들은 그가 공평무사하다고 생각했기 때문에 그들의 분쟁을 중재 시켰다.

]

34. undeceive 잘못을 깨우치다, recuperate 회복하다, adjacent 인접한[120]

123. Let me underceive you I have no influence with him.

나는 그에게 영향을 가지지 못한다는 것을 너에게 깨우쳐 주고 싶다.

124. While the star is **recuperating** from her illness, her role will be played by her understudy. 그 스타가 그녀의 병으로부터 회복하는 동안 그녀의 역할은 그녀의 대역에 의해 연기될 것이다.

125. The island of Cuba is **adjacent** to Florida.

쿠바 섬은 플로리다와 인접해 있다.

---

119) 33. protract, foreboding, arbitrate

120) 34. undeceive, recuperate, adjacent

35. bipartisan 초당적인, evoke 불러일으키다, invoke 호소하다[121]

126. Our foreign policy is **bipartisan**. 우리의 외교 정책은 초당적이다.

127. Proposals to increase taxes usually **evoke** strong resistance.
세금을 인상하는 제안은 주로 강한 저항을 불러일으키다.

128. The witness **invoked** the Fifth Amendment.
그 증인은 수정헌법 제5조에 호소했다.

36. incarcerate 투옥하다, contravene 위반하다, countermand 철회하다[122]

129. freed the prisoners **incarcerated** in the Bastille.
베르사이유 감옥에 투옥된 죄수들을 석방했다.

130. The dictator **contravened** his earlier pledge to guarantee its indepen dence.
그 독재자는 그것의 독립을 보장하겠다는 그의 초기 서약을 위반했다.

131. A superior officer has the power to **countermand** orders issued by a subordinate.
그 고위층은 부하에 의하여 시행된 명령을 철회하는 권력을 가졌다.

37. incontrovertible 다툴 수 없는, intermediary 중재자, immaculate 결점이 없는[123]

132. A person's birth certificate is **incontrovertible** proof of his age.
한 사람의 출생증명서는 그의 나이의 다툴 수 없는 증거이다.

133. Though he has been asked repeatedly to be an **intermediary**
in the labor dispute, -비록 그가 반복적으로 그 노동 분쟁에 있어서 중재자로 되어 달라고 요청받았음에도 불구하고, -

---

121) 35. bipartisan, evoke, invoke
122) 36. incarcerate, contravene, countermand
123) 37. incontrovertible, intermediary, immaculate

134. Nearly every soap manufacturer claims his product will make dirty linens **immaculate**. 거의 모든 비누 제조업자는 그의 생산품이 더러운 침대보를 깨끗하게 만든다고 주장한다.

38. ingratitude 몰염치, irrevocable 돌이킬 수 없는, maladjust 적응하지 못하다.[124]

135. Did you ever hear of such **ingratitude**?
당신은 그런 몰염치에 관하여 들어 본 적이 있느냐?

136. When the empire says you are out, it is useless to argue because his decision is **irrevocable**. 심판이 당신이 아웃이라고 말하면, 그의 결정은 돌이킬 수 없기 때문에 논쟁하는 것은 무의미하다.

137. C was **maladjusted** in the early grades, not because of poor intelligence, but because he couldn't speak English. C 는 그의 초기 학년에 적응하지 못했다. 지능이 낮아서가 아니고 그가 영어를 말하지 못했기 때문이다.

39. dispassionate 공평한, circumscribed 한정된, collusion 공모[125]

138. For a **dispassionate** account of how the fight started, ask a neutral observer.
어떻게 그 싸움이 시작했느냐에 관한 공평한 설명을 위해 중간 관찰자에게 물어봐라.

139. The patient was placed on a very **circumscribed** diet.
그 환자는 아주 한정된 음식에 놓여졌다.

140. Those who work in **collusion** are seeking to commit fraud.
공모한 자들은 사기를 범하려고 하고 있다.

159

---

124) 38. ingratitude, irrevocable, maladjust
125) 39. dispassionate, circumscribed, collusion

40. congenital 선천적인, obliterate 말소하다, obsess 망상으로 사로잡다.[126]

141. were not **congenital** defects but were acquired after birth.
선천적이 결점이 아니고 출생 후에 얻어진 결점

142. Today's rain has completely **obliterated** yesterday's snow.
오늘 내린 눈이 어제 내린 눈을 완전히 말소했다.

143. The notion that she had forgotten to lock the front door **obsessed**
mother all through the movie. 그녀가 앞문을 잠그는 것을 잊어버렸다는 생각
이 그 영화 내내 어머니를 괴롭혔다.

41. obstruct 막다, preclude 방해하다, preconceived 미리 생각한[127]

144. **obstruct** the entrance 입장을 막다.

145. J's numerous absences **preclude** his passing for the first quarter.
J 의 빈번한 결석은 첫 분기의 그의 통과를 방해했다.

146. My **preconceived** dislike for the book disappeared when I read a few
chapters. 나의 그 책에 대한 선입적인 싫어함은 내가 약간의 장을 읽었을 때 사라졌다.

42. amicable 우호적인, enamor 매혹하다, animus 적의[128]

147. Let us try to settle our differences in an **amicable** manner.
우리의 차이점을 우호적인 방법으로 해결하자.

148. became **enamored** of the Indian princess. 인디언 공주에 반하다.

149. Though Howard defeated me in the election I bear no **animus** toward
him, we are good friends. 비록 하워드가 선거에서 나를 이겼지만
나는 그에게 어떠한 반감도 가지고 있지 않다. 우리는 좋은 친구이다.

---

126) 40. congenital, obliterate, obsess
127) 41. obstruct, preclude, preconceived
128) 42. amicable, enamor, animus

43. aggregate 총체의, luminous 빛나는, append 첨부하다[129]

150. The **aggregate** strength of the allies. 모아진 연합군의 힘

151. **Luminous** paint is used for road signs so that they may be visible to night drivers. 야광 페인트는 야간 운전자들이 볼 수 있도록 하기 위해 도로 표지로 사용된다.

152. **append** a note explaining the reason for the delay. 늦은 이유를 설명하는 노트를 첨부하다.

44. simile 직유, verify 증명하다, autonomous 자치적인[130]

153. Did you know you were using a **simile** when you said I was as sly as a fox? 당신이 내가 여우같이 교활하다고 말했을 때 당신은 직유법을 사용하고 있다는 것을 아느냐?

154. So far, the charges have been neither disproved nor **verified**. 지금까지, 그 혐의는 부인되지도 증명되지도 아니했다.

161

155. The alumni association is not under the control of the school. It is a completely **autonomous** group. 그 동창회는 학교의 통제 하에 있는 것이 아니라 완전히 자치 그룹이다.

45. kleptomania 병적 도벽 증, anonymous 익명의, genuine 진짜의[131]

156. The millionaire who was caught shoplifting was found to be suffering from **kleptomania**. 좀도둑질로 잡힌 그 백만장자는 병적 도벽 증으로 고통 받고 있다고 알려졌다.

157. the **anonymous** test paper 익명의 시험지

---

129) 43. aggregate, luminous, append
130) 44. simile, verify, autonomous
131) 45. kleptomania , anonymous , genuine

158. Everyone thought it was made of **genuine** leopard skin.
모든 사람은 그것이 진짜 표범 가죽으로 만들어 졌다고 생각했다.

46. inter 매장하다, commend 칭찬하다, relinquish 양도하다[132]

159. Many American heroes are **interred** in Arlington National Cemetery.
많은 미국 영웅들은 웰링턴 국립묘지에 묻혀있다.

160. Our class was **commended** for having the best attendance for January.
우리 학급은 1월에 가장 좋은 출석률로 칭찬받았다.

161. **relinquished** his seat to her. 그의 자리를 그녀에게 양보했다.

47. contend 경쟁하다, content 만족한, facetious 농담의[133]

162. try to predict the two teams that will **contend** in the next World Series.
내년 월드 시리즈에서 경쟁할 두 팀을 예상하도록 노력하다.

163. If you are not **content** with the merchandise,
당신이 그 상품에 만족하지 못한다면,

164. Bob meant it when he said he was quitting the team. He was not being **facetious.** 밥이 그가 팀을 그만둔다고 말했을 때 그는 농담이 아니었다.

48. fictitious 가공의, beguile 속이다, bequeath 유증하다[134]

165. There are **fictitious** characters. 가공인물들이 있다.

166. He **beguiled** an old woman. 그는 노파를 속였다.

167. My father **bequeathed** a little some of money to me.

---

132) 46. inter, commend, relinquish
133) 47. contend, content, facetious
134) 48. fictitious, beguile, bequeath

나의 아버지는 나에게 약간의 돈을 유증했다.

49. betroth 약혼시키다, engraft 접목하다, entreat 간청하다.[135]

168. He **betrothed** his daughter to a rich.
그는 그의 딸을 부자에게 약혼시켰다.

169. Invaders **engrafted** their customs on the new colony.
침입자들은 그 새로운 식민지에 그들의 관습을 이식했다.

170. He <u>entreated</u> the king for mercy. 그는 왕에게 자비를 간청했다.

50. forbear 참다, forgive 용서하다, forestall 미리 막다.[136]

171. I wanted to punch him but I **forbore**.
나는 그에게 펀치를 날리고 싶었지만 참았다.

172. The little boy was **forgiven** for stealing the money.
그 작은 소년은 그 돈을 훔친 것에 대하여 용서 받았다.

173. You should **forestall** your contestants in the game.
당신은 그 게임에서 당신의 경쟁자들을 미리 막아야 한다.

51. overthrow 뒤집어엎다, postmortem 사체검시, disguise 가장하다.[137]

174. The revolutionary soldiers attempt to **overthrow** the government.
그 혁명군들은 그 정부를 전복하기 위해 시도했다.

175. His corpse was carried to the police for **postmortem**.
그의 시체는 사체검시를 위해 경찰로 이동되었다.

---

135) 49. betroth, engraft, entreat
136) 50. forbear, forgive, forestall
137) 51. overthrow, postmortem, disguise

176. She was **<u>disguised</u>** in a man's clothes.

그녀는 그 남자의 옷으로 가장했다.

52. intermingle 섞다, pernicious 해로운, oblique 비스듬한[138]

177. Please **<u>intermingle</u>** this medicines with that one.

이 약을 저 것과 섞으시오.

178. That is a manner **<u>pernicious</u>** to others.

저것은 다른 사람들에게 해로운 방식이다.

179. The picture is **<u>oblique</u>**, so I must correct it.

그 그림은 비스듬해서 나는 바로잡았다.

53. precarious 불안한, preposterous 앞뒤가 뒤바뀐, sequestrate 몰수하다[139]

180. The refuges make **<u>precarious</u>** living.

그 난민들은 불안한 삶을 영위했다.

181. Your explanation is **<u>preposterous</u>**. 너의 설명은 앞뒤가 맞지 않는다.

182. Your property shall be **<u>sequestrated</u>** in case of your malfeasance.

당신의 재산은 비행의 경우 몰수될 것이다.

54. delinquency 비행, intransigent 비타협적인, enamor 매혹하다[140]

183. Juvenile **<u>delinquency</u>** is the most exigent problem facing us today.

청소년 비행은 오늘날 우리가 직면하는 가장 시급한 문제이다.

184. The party is always **<u>intransigent</u>** in the incumbent government.

---

138) 52. intermingle, pernicious, oblique

139) 53. precarious, preposterous, sequestrate

140) 54. delinquency, intransigent, enamor

그 정당은 항상 현 정부에 비타협적이다.

185. He **enamored** the innocent virgin by means of his fluent speech.

    그는 그 순진한 처녀를 그의 유창한 언어를 수단으로 매혹했다.

55. animadvert 비난하다, pusillanimous 겁 많은, captious 헐뜯는[141]

186. I'm not going to **animadvert** your plain manner but your rude behavior.

    나는 너의 평범한 방식이 아니라 무례한 행동을 비난하려는 것이다.

187. His only weakness is that he is **pusillanimous.**

    그의 단하나의 약점은 그가 소심하다는 것이다.

188. As she was **captious** woman, you'd better be careful.

    그녀는 고약한 여자이기 때문에 너는 조심하는 편이 더 낫다.

56. cloister 격리시키다, corpulent 뚱뚱한, miscreant 악한의[142]

189. He had led a **cloistered** life in one of unknown islands.

    그는 격리된 삶을 영위했다. 알려지지 않은 섬 중의 하나에서

190. The man is excessively **corpulent**, so he needs to diet.

    그 남자는 과도하게 뚱뚱하다, 그래서 그는 다이어트를 필요로 한다.

191. I couldn't endure such a **miscreant** behavior.

    나는 그런 악행을 참을 수 없다.

57. excurse 소풍가다, vindicate 변호하다, condone 용서하다[143]

192. Our school has a plan to **excurse** to the old temple in October.

우리 학교는 10월에 오래된 사찰로 소풍가는 계획을 가지고 있다.

193. If the problem happens, you should **vindicate** my opinion.
그 문제가 발생한다면, 당신은 나의 의견을 지지해야 한다.

194. He would **condone** my mistake. 그는 나의 실수를 용서하곤 했다.

58. subdue 정복하다, diaphanous 투명한, euphemistic 완곡어법의[144]

195. The nation without arms for defense is easily **subdued** by enemies.
방어의 무기가 없는 나라는 쉽게 적에 의해 정복당한다.

196. The water of this lake is highly **diaphanous**.
이 호수의 물은 아주 투명하다.

197. When you criticize others, you had better use an **euphemistic** expres
sion. 당신의 다른 사람들을 비판할 때, 당신은 완곡 표현을 사용하는 것이 더 낫다.

59. florescent 개화기의, fecund 비옥한, docile 유순한[145]

198. All men like flowers have their **florescent** time.
꽃과 같이 모든 사람들은 그들의 개화기를 가지고 있다.

199. He made a steady effort and the land a **fecund** one.
그는 꾸준히 노력했고 그 땅은 비옥하게 되었다.

200. The animal is not **docile** because it is feral.
그 동물은 야성이기 때문에 유순하지 않다.

---

144) 58. subdue, diaphanous, euphemistic
145) 59. florescent, fecund, docile

60. afferent 구심성의, disgorge 분출하다, obfuscate 당황하게 하다[146]

> 201. The nerve cells of our body are **afferent** to our brain.
>
> 우리 신체의 신경 세포들은 우리 뇌로 모아진다. (* efferent 원심성의)
>
> 202. Then the volcano regarded as **dormant** began to disgorge fire.
>
> 그 때 휴화산으로 간주된 화산이 불을 뿜어내기 시작했다.
>
> 203. His sad story **obfuscated** my mind on a sudden.
>
> 그의 슬픈 이야기는 갑자기 나의 마음을 당황하게 했다.

61. lenity 아량, exhume 발굴하다, hortation 충고[147]

> 204. Her **lenity** made her more attractive.
>
> 그녀의 아량은 그녀를 더욱 매혹적으로 만들었다.
>
> 205. They are going to **exhume** the old grave.
>
> 그들은 그 오래된 무덤을 발굴하려고 한다.
>
> 206. He would not follow your **hortation.**
>
> 그는 너의 충고를 따르려고 하지 않았다.

62. matrimony 결혼, expatriate 추방하다, eject 내쫓다[148]

> 207. Through **matrimony,** girls become completely mature.
>
> 결혼을 통해 소녀들은 완전히 성숙한다.
>
> 208. The court decided that he would be **expatriated.**
>
> 그 법원은 그가 추방되도록 결정했다.
>
> 209. The librarian was forced to **eject** the student who refused to be quiet.
>
> 그 도서관 사서는 조용하기를 거부하는 그 학생을 내쫓도록 강요했다.

---

146) 60. afferent, disgorge, obfuscate

147) 61. lenity, exhume, hortation

148) 62. matrimony, expatriate, eject

63. commensurate 비례하는, collate 대조하다, dilate 팽창하다[149]

210. You will get your rewards **commensurate** your endeavor.
당신은 노력에 비례하는 보수를 받을 것이다.

211. I'm going to **collate** this new book with an earlier one to see what changes have been made. 나는 어떤 변화가 있었는지 알아보기 위해 초기 책과 새로운 책을 비교하려고 한다.

212. My heart **dilated** with inexpressible joy when I received in first prize.
나의 가슴은 내가 일등상을 받았을 때 표현하기 힘든 기쁨으로 팽창되었다.

64. immunize 예방하다, remiss 태만한, impediment 곤경[150]

213. This vaccine will **immunize** the disease.
그 백신은 그 질병을 예방할 것이다.

214. Children at camp are **remiss** in their obligation to write home regularly.
캠프의 어린이들은 집에 규칙적으로 편지를 쓰는 그들의 의무에 태만하다.

215. The **impediment** of our country should be abolished as soon as possible. (임패더먼트) 우리나라의 곤경은 가능한 한 빨리 없어져야 한다.

65. cerebrate 생각하다, deprecate 비난하다, depose 선서증언하다[151]

216. Please **cerebrate** if you want to do it clearly.
네가 그것을 명확하게 하기를 원한다면 숙고해라.

217. He **deprecated** such an extreme measure.
그는 그런 극단적인 조치를 비난했다.

218. He **deposed** that he never saw the accused before.

---

149) 63. commensurate, collate, dilate
150) 64. immunize, remiss, impediment
151) 65. cerebrate, deprecate, depose

그는 그가 결코 전에 그 범인을 본 적이 없다고 증언했다.

66. impound 감금하다, reprobate 타락자, depute 대리자로 삼다.[152]

219. The ferocious dog was **impounded** by us.
그 사나운 개는 우리에 의해 감금되었다.

220. He is an old **reprobate** who spends all his money on beer.
그는 맥주의 모든 그의 돈을 소비하는 늙은 타락자 이다.

221. The teacher deputed Ted to take charge of the class while he was away.
(디퓨릿) 선생님은 그가 없는 사이 그 학급의 책임을 테드에게 대리했다.

67. perquisite 팁, derogate 평판을 떨어뜨리다, rectitude 정직[153]

222. The maid's **perquisites** include the old dresses of her mistress.
그 하인의 팁은 그녀의 주인의 낡은 옷들을 포함한다.

223. Such a mean attitude **derogated** your character.
그런 비열한 태도는 너의 인격에 대한 평판을 떨어뜨렸다

224. They didn't lose their **rectitude** even in the temptation.
그들은 유혹에도 불구하고 그들의 정직을 잃지 않았다.

68. subscribe 기부하다, execrate 저주하다, speculate 투자하다[154]

225. He **subscribed** a large sum to charities.
그는 많은 금원을 자선에 기부했다.

226. Don't **execrate** your enemy. 너의 적을 저주하지 말라.

---

152) 66. impound, reprobate, depute
153) 67. perquisite, derogate, rectitude
154) 68. subscribe, execrate, speculate

227. He **speculated** in shares but he failed to earn much money.

그는 주식에 투자했지만 많은 돈을 버는 것에 실패했다.

69. perspicacious 총명한, suspire 한숨 쉬다, subsist 살아가다[155]

228. The little boy was so **perspicacious** that he could save all men.

그 작은 소년은 너무나 총명해서 모든 사람들을 구할 수 있었다.

229. When he heard of the failure, he **suspired** with despair.

그가 그 실패를 들었을 때, 그는 체념의 한숨을 쉬었다.

230. In the event of hard time, you had to **subsist** by begging.

어려운 시기에 당신은 구걸로서 살아가야만 한다.

70. tenable 방어할 수 있는, detain 억류하다, distend 넓히다[156]

231. I think that is **tenable** assertion.

나는 그것이 유지 가능한 주장이라고 생각한다.

232. I was detained by traffic jam. 나는 교통체증으로 지체했다.

233. They had to **distend** this narrow road.

그들은 이 좁은 도로를 확장해야 했다.

71. extenuate 작량감경하다, theocracy 신권정치, invalidate 무효로 하다.[157]

234. The judge **extenuated** the criminal because of his incurable disease.

그 판사는 그 범인의 치유할 수 없는 질병으로 인하여 작량 감경했다.

235. Under **theocracy**, all men are subject to God.

155) 69. perspicacious, suspire, subsist
156) 70. tenable, detain, distend
157) 71. extenuate, theocracy, invalidate

신권정치 아래, 모든 사람은 신의 지배를 받는다.

236. We should **invalidate** our prior engagement.

우리는 우리의 전의 약혼을 무효로 하여야만 한다.

72. pervert 왜곡하다, subversive 전복적인, [158]

237. Don't **pervert** other's real belief. 다른 사람의 신념을 왜곡하지 말라.

238. We must destroy such **subversive** publications.

우리는 그런 전복적인 출판물을 없애야 한다.

---

158) 72. pervert, subversive

01 After much discussion, the committee decided to _____ the new budget.

a. blunder b. arduous c. inordinate d. endorse

02 When one is unfamiliar with the customs, it is easy to make a _____.

a. relinquish b. blunder c. ephemera d. defunct

03 My friend sent me a few _____ tickets for the concert.

a. assess b. precarious c. propitious d. complimentary

04 The government agreed to _____ the country's economy.

a. infallible b. impartial c. overhaul d. anonymous

05 El Nino is a _____ of the ocean-atmosphere system in the tropical Pacific having important consequences for weather around the globe.

a. intrepid b. disruption c. disentangle d. pious

06 He seemed to contradict merely to_____ me.

a. malign b. pecuniary c. alternative d. aggravate

07 I did not know how to _____ his statement.

a. conviction b. docile c. construe d. impute

08 I hope you don't bear me any _____.

a. grudge b. audacious c. circumvent d. chronic

09 It would be _____ing to find myself ten francs short and be obliged to borrow from my guest.

a. mortify b. erudite c. curse d. exonerate

10 The treasurer _____ with the company funds.

a. mandatory b. abscond c. landmark d. allocate

11 They made a fortune from the _____ arms deal.

a. lucrative b. abstruse c. erudite d. indolent

12 She, a novice, had the _____ to challenge the champion

a. temerity b. turbulent c. obese d. eruption

13 Because gymnasts exercise regularly, they have _____ bodies.

a. evanescent b. forestall c. supple d. trigger

14 Throughout the first two decades of the century the diagnosis of _____ anemia was almost equivalent to a death sentence.

a. indigenous b. extricate c. pernicious d. pugnacious

1. revoke, arduous, inordinate, endorse, relinquish[159]

   1. The authorities have **revoked** their original decision. =withdrawn
   2. It has become an **arduous** climb. =difficult.
   3. He always spent an **inordinate** length of time on the bathroom.
     =excessive
   4. After much discussion, the committee decided to <u>endorse</u> the new bud get. =approve.
   5. **relinquish** his seat. =give up

2. blunder, ephemeral, defunct, assess, precarious[160]

   6. When one is unfamiliar with the customs, it is easy to make a **blunder**.
     =mistake
   7. Her success as a singer was **ephemeral.** =transitory.
   8. three **defunct** New York City newspaper. =extinct.
   9. **assess** the damage. =appraise.
   10. Life for poor people will be more **precarious** in the future than it is now.
     =insecure.

3. propitious, complimentary, irreversible, capitulate, perjury[161]

   11. The **propitious** weather gave the farmers assurance of a good crop.
     =auspicious.
   12. My friend sent me a few **complimentary** tickets for the concert.
     =free.

---

159) 1. revoke, arduous, inordinate, endorse, relinquish
160) 2. blunder, ephemeral, defunct, assess, precarious
161) 3. propitious, complimentary, irreversible, capitulate, perjury

13. Life is an **irreversible** process to everyone. =unalterable.

14. I begged Mom to stay in her room until we'd found him, and she **capitu lated** readily. =give in.

15. Perjury in a serious court case can result in life imprisonment. =lying under oath.

4. infallible, impartial, overhaul, anonymous, deluge[162]

16. It would be nice to pretend that The Times is **infallible**. =faultless.

17. an **impartial** view =unbiased.

18. The government agreed to **overhaul** the country's economy. =boost rapidly

19. The poem was composed by an **anonymous** author =unknown.

20. Every day they have to deal with a **deluge** of information. =flood.

5. intrepid, disruption, disentangle, pious, malign[163]

21. He is the most **intrepid** explorer in the present century. =fearless

22. El Nino is a **disruption** of the ocean-atmosphere system in the tropical Pa cific having important consequences for weather around the globe. =sev-erance.

23. The phenomena we encounter in our individual experience are so vari ous, so complicated and contradictory that we can scarcely **disentangle** them. =unravel

24. He was a very **pious** man and devoted his whole life to Christian mission work. = devout.

---

162) 4. infallible, impartial, overhaul, anonymous, deluge
163) 5. intrepid, disruption, disentangle, pious, malign

25. This leaves his speeches open to all sorts of **malign** interpretation.
    =evil

6. pecuniary, alternative, aggravate, conviction, docile[164]

26. Every physician treats some patients from whom he expects no pecuniary reward. =financial.

27. Although I didn't want to, I took the job because there was no alternative.
    =other choice.

28. He seemed to contradict merely to **aggravate** me. = make angry.

29. He held the **conviction** that his country would win the war in the end.
    =strong belief.

30. Unless something is done to anger them, camels are usually quite **docile**.=obedient.

(177)

7. construe, impute, grudge, audacious, circumvent[165]

31. I did not know how to **construe** his statement. =interpret.

32. Ancient physicians **imputed** many diseases to the planets. =attributed.

33. I hope you don't bear me any **grudge.** =unfriendly feelings.

34. Many of these pioneers in wisdom were **audacious** radicals. =bold.

35. The politician **circumvented** the problem. =avoided.

---

164) 6. pecuniary, alternative, aggravate, conviction, docile
165) 7. construe, impute, grudge, audacious, circumvent

8. chronic, biennially, mortify, erudite, malediction[166]

36. Experiments with wild rats show that lower animals can also become really ill and even die under **chronic** stress.=persistent.
37. They imported 500 million tons of crude oil **biennially.**=every other year.
38. It would be **mortifying** to find myself ten francs short and be obliged to borrow from my guest.=humiliating.
39. There has been much **erudite** discussion about the origin of names. =scholarly
40. The king, facing his enemies, uttered a **malediction** upon them.=curse

9. exonerate, gingerly, mandatory, abscond, landmark[167]

41. The confession of one prisoner **exonerated** the other suspects. =acquitted.
42. Laboratory technicians must be trained to handle delicate instruments **gingerly.**=cautiously.
43. a **mandatory** subject=required
44. The treasurer **absconded** with the company funds. =departed suddenly.
45. The judge made two **landmark** decisions.=important.

10. allocate, lucrative, abstruse, prerogative, indolence[168]

46. All important resources were **allocated** by the government = distributed.

---

166) 8. chronic, biennially, mortify, erudite, malediction
167) 9. exonerate, gingerly, mandatory, abscond, landmark
168) 10. allocate, lucrative, abstruse, prerogative, indolence

47. They made a fortune from the **lucrative** arms deal.=profitable

48. Mr. Kim remained confounded on account of the **abstruse** expression of words.=difficult.

49. It's a woman's **prerogative** to bear children.=special privilege.

50. The sultry weather in the tropics encourages a life of **indolence.** =laziness

11. temerity, turbulent, obese, erupt, evanescent[169]

51. She, a novice, had the **temerity** to challenge the champion.=boldness

52. On my way to Seoul, I met a **turbulent** storm.=violent.

53. He had an extremely **obese** friend whose mind was constantly occupied with the thought of delicacies.=corpulent.

54. Mount St. Helens **erupted** in March 1980 after one hundred twenty-three years of silence.=exploded.

55. The culture is **evanescent**.=fleeting

12. forestall, supple, trigger, gorgeous, indigenous[170]

56. Strict sanitary procedures help to **forestall** outbreaks of disease. =prevent.

57. Because gymnasts exercise regularly, they have **supple** bodies. =flexible

58. Their small protest **triggered** a mass demonstration.=set off

59. Everyone agreed that the woman in the photo was **gorgeous.** =beautiful

---

169) 11. temerity, turbulent, obese, erupt, evanescent

170) 12. forestall, supple, trigger, gorgeous, indigenous

60. the **indigenous** plants = native

13. extricate, pernicious, pugnacious[171]

61. I have **extricated** myself from the temporary difficulty.=free
62. Throughout the first two decades of the century the diagnosis of **pernicious** anemia was almost equivalent to a death sentence.=deadly
63. **pugnacious** people=quarrelsome

---

171) 13. extricate, pernicious, pugnacious

01 These rubber boots are not _____ to water.

   a. perverse   b. pervious   c. preclude   d. precocious

02 Should _____ building be the chief aim of education?

   a. precursor   b. primordial   c. proclivity   d. prodigious

03 AIDS can be resulted from a _____ sexual intercourse.

   a. progenitor   b. prognosis   c. promiscuous   d. propound

04 Our firm doesn't have a _____ fund for the staff.

   a. protrude   b. provident   c. provocation   d. purgatory

05 This mountain erupted all of a sudden after remaining _____ for twenty years.

   a. quiescent   b. rarefied   c. recapitulate   d. recuperate

06 He already has a house _____ with every modern convenience.

a. reminiscence   b. replete   c. ruminate   d. solvent

07 The _____ newspapers in India is pressed by the various languages of India.

a. subsidiary   b. vernacular   c. vivacious   d. wheedle

08 The baby was _____; he did not cry all day long.

a. bungle   b. captious   c. chide   d. compliant

09 The _____ lady was liked by all who met her, including the members of the opponent.

a. consecrate   b. corpulent   c. debonair   d. delude

10 His erudite writing is so _____ that no one can understand it.

a. deviate   b. enrapture   c. abstruse   d. espionage

11 His body was _____ so that the autopsy might be performed.

a. exculpate   b. exhume   c. exorbitant   d. expatiate

12 It is easier for us to _____ our faults than those of others.

a. expedite   b. expiate   c. expurgate   d. extenuate

13 Many of the incidents are _____ in that book.

a. extricate   b. fictitious   c. fractious   d. grapple

14 I prefer to shop in a store that has one price policy, because I don't like to

_____ with the shop-keeper.

a. guileless   b. haggle   c. humdrum   d. ignominious

15 The old teacher tried to _____ the young students the duty of loyalty.

a. inculcate   b. indolence   c. insolent   d. instigate

16 He has an _____ prejudice against the black.

a. intuition   b. inveterate   c. irrevocable·   d. judicious

17 She called him a _____ because he stayed single through his life.

a. misogynist   b. neophyte   c. nexus   d. obdurate

18 You always _____ your opinion into matters of no concern to you.

a. obese   b. obliterate   c. obsession   d. obtrude

19 His _____ wisdom and sagacity can solve that complicated situation.

a. obviate   b. parasite   c. perfidious   d. perspicacious

1. Your **perverse** attitudes probably come from your inferiority. [172]

   너의 비뚤어진 태도는 아마도 너의 열등감으로부터 온 것이다.

   perverse 외고집의 deliberately departing from what is normal and reasonable.

2. These rubber boots are not **pervious** to water.

   이 고무 부츠들은 방수가 아니다. pervious 침투시키는

3. This money must not **preclude** my intention to make him go to jail.

   이 돈이 그를 감옥으로 보내려는 나의 의도를 미리 막을 수는 없다.

4. The **precocious** child already reads well at the age of three.

   그 조숙한 아이는 이미 3살 때 잘 읽는다.

5. All the **precursors** of social reform or cultural movement are subject to perse

   cution.

   모든 사회적인 개혁이나 문화적인 운동의 선구자들은 박해 당한다.

6. The **primordial** plan was better than the plan we followed.

   최초의 계획이 우리가 추구했던 계획보다 더 낫다.

   primordial 원래의 existing from the beginning; formed earliest.

7. Should **proclivity** building be the chief aim of education?

   성격형성이 교육의 주요한 목표인가?

   proclivity 성향 a tendency, liking or preference

185

---

172) perverse, pervious, preclude, precocious, precursor, primordial, proclivity, prodigious, progenitor

8. He inherited a **prodigious** sum of money.

그는 아주 많은 돈을 상속받았다.

9. The ritual means the worship of their **progenitors** as spirits or gods.

그 의식은 그들의 조상들을 정신이나 신으로 숭배함을 의미한다.

progenitor 조상 an ancestor, forebear or forefather.

10. The old doctor concealed the **prognosis** of the disease of their fathe r not to frighten them.[173] 그 늙은 의사는 그들의 아버지의 병의 진단을 그들을 겁주지 않기 위해 숨겼다.

11. AIDS can be resulted from a **promiscuous** sexual intercourse.

에이즈는 난잡한 성교에 의해 올 수 있다.

12. The motion **propounded** by John Henry was agreed unanimously.

존 헨리에 의해 제안된 동의안은 만장일치로 승인되었다.

propound 제안하다 to put forward (an idea or theory, etc) for consideration or discussion.

13. He fixed the shelf that **protruded** from the wall.

그는 벽에서 튀어나온 선반을 고정했다.

protrude 돌출하다 to project; to stick out.

14. Our firm doesn't have a **provident** fund for the staff.

우리 회사는 그 직원들을 위한 현명한 자금을 가지고 있지 않다.

provident 장래를 대비하는, 현명한

---

173) prognosis, promiscuous, propound, protrude, provident, provocation, purgato

15. He was ready to draw his gun at the slightest **provocation.**

   그는 아주 작은 도발에도 그의 총을 꺼낼 준비가 되어 있었다.

   provocation 도발, 자극, 화낼 이유 the act of provoking or state of being pro-
   voked; incitement.

16. The dead soul must be purified at the **purgatory** in preparation for
   heaven.

   죽은 영혼은 천국의 준비로서 연옥에서 정화되어야 한다.

   purgatory 연옥 a place or state into which the soul passes after death,
   where it is cleansed of pardonable sins before going to heaven.

17. This mountain erupted all of a sudden after remaining **quiescent** for
   twenty years.[174] 이 산은 20년의 침묵 후에 갑사기 분출했다.

   quiescent 조용한 quiet, silent, at rest or in an inactive state, usually tempo-
   rarily.

18. The **rarefied** air of the mountain tops make me hold my breath.

   그 산 정상의 희박한 공기는 내가 숨을 못 쉬게 만든다.

19. Jefferson **recapitulated** his ideas about democracy.

   제퍼슨은 민주주의에 관한 그의 생각들을 요약했다.

20. He went to the seaside to **recuperate** his health before he died.

   그는 죽기 전에 그의 병을 회복하기 위해 해변으로 갔다.

187

---

174) quiescent, rarefy, recapitulate, recuperate, reminiscence, replete, ruminate, solvent, subsidiary

21. There is a **reminiscence** of his father in the way he talks.

그가 이야기하는 방식에는 그의 아버지의 회상이 있다. (레머니쓴스)

22. He already has a house **replete** with every modern convenience.

그는 이미 모든 현대 편의시설이 가득찬 집을 가지고 있다.

23. He **ruminated** on his misfortunes.

그는 그의 불운에 대해 곰곰이 생각했다.

ruminate 반추하다. to chew the cud (되새김질 거리)

24. The boss was **solvent** and avoided bankruptcy proceedings by the help of his cousin.

그 사장은 지불능력이 있고 조카의 도움으로 도산 절차를 피했다.

25. The **subsidiary** company is always controlled by a larger one.

자회사는 항상 더 큰 회사에 의해 통제받는다.

subsidiary 보조의 of secondary importance; subordinate.

26. The **vernacular** newspapers in India is pressed by the various languages of India.[175] 인도의 지방 신문들은 인도의 여러 언어로 출판된다.

vernacular 토속의 the native language of a country or people, as opposed to a foreign language that is also in use.

27. He felt alone among the **vivacious** conversations.

그는 그 활기찬 대화 속에서 고독을 느꼈다.

---

175) vernacular, vivacious, wheedle, baffle, bungle, captious, chide, compliant

28. The girl **wheedled** her father into buying a bicycle.

그 소녀는 그의 아버지를 감언이설로 꼬여 자전거를 사게 만들었다.

wheedle (위를) 감언이설로 꼬이다. to coax or cajole someone; to persuade them by flattery

29. One of the examination questions **baffled** me completely.

시험 문제 중의 하나가 나를 완전히 당황하게 만들었다.

30. He **bungled** the work of his father by lack of skill.

그는 기술이 없어 그의 아버지의 작품을 망쳤다.

31. John's **captious** and frivolous criticisms always spoil the atmosphere.

존의 헐뜯는 사소한 비평들은 항상 분위기를 망친다.

32. Father did not **chide** Washington for his cutting out the tree.

아버지는 워싱턴이 그 나무를 잘랐다고 나무라지 않았다.

33. The baby was **compliant** ; he did not cry all day long.

그 아이는 유순했다. 그는 하루 종일 울지 않았다.

34. The nation **confiscated** all the metals available except for necessities.

그 나라는 필수품을 제외하고 모든 가능한 금속을 몰수했다.

35. They shall **consecrate** their lives to the honor of their family.[176]

그들은 그들의 가족의 명예에 그들의 삶을 성화할 것이다.

consecrate 신성한 to make sacred; to dedicate something to God.

176) consecrate, corpulent, debonair, delude, deviate, enrapture, erudite, espionage, eulogistic, evanescent

36. The **corpulent** woman decided not to eat anything for 3 days.

그 뚱뚱한 여자는 3일 동안 아무것도 먹지 않을 것을 결심했다.

37. The **debonair** lady was liked by all who met her, including the members of the opponent. 그 상냥한 여자는 그녀를 만난 모든 사람들에 의해 사랑받는다. 적들도 포함하여 debonair 상냥한 cheerful, charming and of elegant appearance and good manners.

38. Do not **delude** her into falling a prey on the plan.

그녀를 속여 그 계획의 먹이로 떨어지도록 하지 마라.

39. He sometimes **deviates** from the main topic.

그는 때때로 주제로부터 벗어난다.

40. The audience was **enraptured** by the sweet sound of her piano.

그 청중은 그녀의 피아노의 달콤한 소리에 의해 매혹되었다.

41. His **erudite** writing is so abstruse that no one can understand it.

그의 박식한 작품은 너무나 어려워서 아무도 그것을 이해할 수 없다.

42. To obtain the secret of the plan, government developed a system of **espionage**. 그 계획의 비밀을 얻기 위해 정부는 스파이 체계를 발전시켰다.

43. To my surprise, the speech was very **eulogistic** and full of praise

놀랍게도 그 연설은 아주 칭송 적이고 칭찬으로 가득 찼다.

44. **Evanescent** political triumph soon faded away from the memory of

the people. 일시적인 정치적 승리는 곧 사람들의 기억에서 사라졌다.

45. The judge **exculpated** him from a charge of rape. [177]

그 판사는 그를 강간의 혐의로부터 벗어나게 해 주었다.

46. His body was **exhumed** so that the autopsy might be performed.

그의 시체는 발굴되어 검시가 수행되었다.

47. Monopoly can cause **exorbitant** price to the consumers.

독점은 고객에게 아주 엄청난 가격의 원인이 될 수 있다.

48. You must **expatiate** the situation to disentangle yourself from this case.

당신은 그 사건으로부터 빗어나기 위해 그 상황을 설명해야만 한다.

expatiate (익스뻬이쉬에잇) 자세히 설명하다 to talk or write at length or in detail

49. A little more rain can **expedite** the growth of plant.

약간의 비가 식물 성장을 촉진할 수 있다.

50. He tried to **expiate** his crimes by praying for her.

그는 그녀를 위해 기도함으로써 그의 범죄를 속죄하려고 노력했다.

51. The editor insists on **expurgating** some pages to pass the censorship

편집자는 검열을 통과하기 위해 약간의 페이지를 제거하기를 주장한다.

52. It is easier for us to **extenuate** our faults than those of others.

---

177) exculpate, exhume, exorbitant, expatiate, expedite, expiate, expurgate, extenuate, extricate

우리가 다른 사람의 잘못보다 우리의 잘못을 작량 감경하는 것은 쉽다.
extenuate 정상참작하다.

53. She found the way to **extricate** herself from the false marriage.

그녀는 잘못된 결혼으로부터 구출하는 방법을 발견했다.

54. Many of the incidents are **fictitious** in that book.[178]

그 사고의 많은 부분이 그 책에서는 허구이다.

55. The **fractious** woman grumbled at the low pay offered to her.

그 성깔 있는 여자는 그녀에게 제공된 낮은 봉급에 불평했다.

fractious 화 잘 내는 quarrelsome; inclined to quarrel and complain.

56. The wrestlers **grappled** together on the ground.

레슬링 선수들은 땅에서 서로 싸웠다.

57. He is not such a **guileless** man as to believe your lying.

그는 너의 거짓말을 믿을 정도로 그렇게 순진한 남자가 아니다.

58. I prefer to shop in a store that has one price policy, because I don't like to **haggle** with the shop-keeper. 나는 한 가지 가격 정책을 가지고 있는 상점에서 쇼핑하고 싶다. 왜냐하면 나는 상점 주인과 가격협상을 하기를 원하지 않기 때문이다. haggle 가격 흥정하다 to bargain over or argue about (a price, etc)

59. After the great war, they returned to the **humdrum** existence.

그 큰 전쟁 후에 그들은 단조로운 일상으로 되돌아갔다.

178) fictitious, fractious, grapple, guileless, haggle, humdrum, ignominious, inc

humdrum 단조로운 dull or monotonous; ordinary.

60. The country regarded the defeat as truly **ignominious** and dreamed the day of victory. 그 나라는 그 패배를 아주 수치스럽게 간주했고 승리의 날을 꿈꾸었다.

61. The old teacher tried to **inculcate** the young students the duty of loyalty. 그 늙은 스승은 젊은 학생들에게 충성의 의무를 주입시키려고 노력했다. inculcate 주입하다 to teach or fix (ideas, habits, a warning, etc) firmly in their mind by constant repetition

62. The sultry weather in the tropics encourages a life of **indolence**.[179)] 적도의 무더운 날씨는 게으름의 삶을 격려한다.

63. She resented your **insolent** manner

그녀는 당신의 오만한 태도에 분개한다. insolent 오만한 rude or insulting; showing a lack of respect.

64. Socialists **instigated** workers to down tools.

사회주의자들은 노동자들에게 도구를 내려놓으라고 충동한다.

instigate 부추기다 to urge someone on or incite them, especially to do something wrong or evil.

65. She thought that she could know everything by **intuition**.

그녀는 그녀가 직관에 의해 모든 것을 알 수 있다고 생각했다.

179) indolence, insolent, instigate, intuition, inveterate, irrevocable, judicious, mellifluous, misogynist

66. He has an **inveterate** prejudice against the black.

그는 흑인에 대해 몸에 밴 편견을 가지고 있다.

inveterate 뿌리 깊은 firmly established

67. Let us not complain about the **irrevocable** judgment of that case.

그 사건의 되돌릴 수 없는 판단에 대해서 불평하지 말자.

68. I guess that this scheme is not **judicious** ; it is rather risky.

이 계획은 현명하지 못하고 오히려 위험하다고 생각한다.

judicious 분별력 있는 shrewd, sensible, wise or tactful.

69. French is a **mellifluous** language especially in bed.

프랑스어는 특히 침대에서 감미로운 언어이다.

70. She called him a **misogynist** because he stayed single through his life.

그녀는 그가 일생을 혼자서 보냈기 때문에 그를 여성혐오자로 불렀다.

misogynist (미싸저니스트) 여성 혐오 자

71. Experts as well as **neophytes** must be cautious about handling that situation.[180] 초보자뿐만 아니라 전문가도 이 상황을 다루는 데에 있어서 주의해야만 한다.

72. I failed to discover the **nexus** which connects these two widely sepa rated events. 나는 이 두 개의 광범위하게 분리된 사건들을 연결하는 유대를 발견하는 데에 실패했다.

---

180) neophyte, nexus, obdurately, obeisance, obese, obliterate, obsession, obtrude, obviate

73. He refused **obdurately** to listen to her excuse.

그는 그녀의 핑계를 듣는 것에 대하여 고집스럽게 거절했다.

74. He made a hearty **obeisance** when the King and Queen entered the room. 그는 왕과 여왕이 들어왔을 때 마음에서 우러나오는 복종을 하였다.

75. The **obese** woman tried to lose weight in vain.

그 뚱뚱한 여인은 체중을 줄이려고 노력하였으나 실패했다.

76. The character on the stone was **obliterated** by someone.

그 돌의 개성이 누군가에 의해 말소되었다.

77. These **obsession** of the superstition have made him unpopular with his neighbors. 이 미신의 망상으로 인해 그는 이웃과 잘 지내지 못했다.

78. You always **obtrude** your opinion into matters of no concern to you.

너는 항상 너의 의견을 너와 관련이 없는 문제들에 개입한다.

obtrude 주제넘게 나서다

79. This contribution will **obviate** any need for further collections of funds. 이 기부가 자금의 더 많은 모음을 필요 없게 만들 것이다.

obviate 미연에 방지하다. to remove a problem or the need for something.

80. He lived like a **parasite** supported by other people and giving them nothing in return.[181] 그는 다른 사람의 도움에 의해 살면서도 아무 것도 되돌려 주지 않는 기생충 삶을 살았다. parasite (패러싸잇) 기생충 a small animal or

---

181) parasite, perfidious, perspicacious

plant that lives on or inside another animal or plant and gets its food from it

81. **When we learned of his <u>perfidious</u> acts, we were all shocked and dismayed.** 우리가 그의 배반하는 행동을 알았을 때 우리는 모두 놀랐고 당혹했다.

82. **His <u>perspicacious</u> wisdom and sagacity can solve that complicated situation.** 그의 현명한 지혜와 명석함은 그 복잡한 상황을 풀 수 있을 것이다. perspicacious 선경지명이 있는 able to understand sb/sth quickly and accurately

Part 4
접두어

01 He was _____ by four gunmen.

a. abdicate   b. abduct   c. abhor   d. abject

02 He was arraigned on charges of aiding and _____ing terrorists.

a. abet   b. abridge   c. accede   d. accomplice

03 The scheme was designed as an _____ to existing health care facilities.

a. adjacent   b. adjourn   c. adjunct   d. admonish

04 The play opens with a fierce storm which _____ the violence to follow.

a. adulterate   b. adumbrate   c. advent   d. adverse

05 There is an _____ between the two languages.

a. affable   b. affiance   c. affiliate   d. affinity

06 The drugs did nothing to _____ her pain.

a. aggravate   b. aggregate   c. alleviate   d. allocate

07 I had an expert _____ the house beforehand.

a. append   b. apposite   c. appraise   d. apprehend

08 Although he was born a Catholic, he was an _____ for most of his adult life.

a. agnostic   b. amnesty   c. amorphous   d. anarchy

09 She was _____ed of her parents by a traffic accident.

a. belate   b. belie   c. belittle   d. bereave

10 The wicked fairy _____ the prince and turned him into a frog.

a. behold   b. beseech   c. betroth   d. bewitch

11 Ships were registered abroad to _____ employment and safety regulations.

a. circumlocution   b. circumscribe   c. circumspect   d. circumvent

12 He _____ a surprisingly tasty supper of pasta and vegetables.

a. concoct   b. condescend   c. condole   d. condone

13 I do wish he wouldn't _____ to the junior staff in his department.

a. condescend   b. condole   c. condone   d. confine

14 With her he would lead a life of _____ happiness.

a. console   b. conspire   c. construe   d. consummate

15 Her behavior _____ from the rules.

a. despise   b. destitute   c. deviate   d. devour

16 They hanged the dictator in _____.

    a. eccentric   b. efface   c. effigy   d. elucidation

17 An _____ from her new thriller will appear in this weekend's magazine.

    a. excerpt   b. exempt   c. exhort   d. exile

18 The government plans to _____ the emergency relief plan.

    a. expedient   b. expedite   c. expend   d. expire

19 It's an admirably objective and _____ report.

    a. illiterate   b. immaculate   c. immortal   d. impartial

20 Jealousy is _____.

    a. inmate   b. innate   c. inscribe   d. insidious

21 In the face of public _____, he was forced to resign.

    a. obliterate   b. oblivion   c. obloquy   d. obscene

22 A peaceful solution would _____ the need to send a UN military force.

    a. obstruct   b. obtrude   c. obviate   d. opponent

23 Jim Boren is representative of another kind of _____ presidential candidate.

    a. peremptory   b. perennial   c. perfidy   d. persecute

24 Financial constraints _____ excavation of more than part of the site.

    a. preclude   b. precursor   c. predilection   d. pregnant

25 The government sank _____ amounts of public money into the scheme.

    a. prodigal   b. prodigious   c. profane   d. proficient

26 The two superpowers agreed to _____ reduction of nuclear weapons.

    a. reciprocal   b. recompense   c. recondite   d. recuperate

27 He _____ mainly on vegetables and fruit.

    a. subside   b. subsidiary   c. subsist   d. subtract

1. 접두어 AB[182]

영어에서 접두어 공부는 필수적으로 필요한데, 우리가 이미 알고 있는 단어를 유추하여 어렵다고 여기는 중요 단어를 아주 쉽게 숙지할 수 있기 때문이다. 접두어 'AB-"는 <u>분리, 이탈 (away)의 의미</u>를 지닌다.

1. **Abdicate**

퇴위하다, 사임하다. Ab는 멀리, dic은 말(dictionary는 말을 모아 놓은 것)에서 <u>말을 하고 멀리가다</u> 라는 의미이다.

abdicate from the crown 왕위에서 물러나다.

This government will not **abdicate its responsibility** to beat inflation.
본 정부는 인플레이션을 타개하는 책임을 회피하지 않을 것입니다.

2. **Abduct**

납치하다(kidnap). to take someone away illegally by force or deception
Ab 멀리, duct 은 <u>끌고 가다</u>라는 의미이다. 유괴와 관련하여서는 ransom (몸값)과 hostage (인질)도 중요단어이다.

He was **abducted** by four gunmen.
그는 4명의 권총 강도에 의해 납치되었다.

3. **Abhor**

몹시 싫어하다 to hate or dislike
ab 멀리, hor 는 shudder (떨다, horrible 무서운, horrify 무섭게 하다)
<u>몸서리치면서 멀리할 정도로 싫은 의미</u>.
(abominate, detest, loathe 혐오하다 중 시험에 단골로 나오는 단어임으로 중요!)

---

182) 1. Abdicate 2. Abduct 3. Abhor 4. Abject 5. Aboriginal 6. Abortive 7. Abrogate 8. Abscond 9. Absolve 10. Abstain 11. Abstruse

abhor a snake 뱀을 몹시 싫어하다.

4. Abject

1. 비참한. miserable, Ab멀리, ject는 던지다. <u>인간은 엄마 뱃속에서 세상으로 멀리</u>
던져 진 순간부터 비참한 인생을 시작하는 것이다.
   They live in abject poverty. 그들은 극심한 가난 속에 산다.

2. 비열한, 야비한, 천한 노예근성의, 비굴한(slavish). showing lack of courage or
pride, submissive
   an abject liar 비열한 거짓말쟁이,
   an abject means 야비한 수단.

5. Aboriginal

1. 원시의, (민족·동시물이) 토착의. indigenous.
   ab(from 로부터), ori(기원, originate 생기다. Origin 기원) 여기서 ab는 off멀
   리의 개념이 아닌, from-로부터의 개념인 점에 유의하여야 한다. **aboriginal**
   people 토착민.

2. (A-) 호주 원주민의.

6. Abortive

1. 발육 부전의. Ab멀리, ori 기원, <u>발생하는 것을 멀리하다</u>에서 실패한(특히 조기에),
   abortion은 낙태(the act of removing an embryo) 동의어 futile 은 시험에 잘
   나온다.
   an abortive flower 열매를 맺지 않는 꽃.

2. 실패한, 수포로 돌아간, 성공하지 못한. unsuccessful.
   an abortive mission 성공하지 못한 임무

7. **Abrogate**

폐지하다 to cancel (a law, agreement, etc) formally or officially

ab 멀리, rog요청 (ask, rogation입법요청, prerogative 특권) 동의어 annul, nullify, revoke 에 유의!

abrogate a law 법을 폐지하다.

8. **Abscond**

(나쁜 짓을 하고) 자취를 감추다, to depart or leave quickly and usually secretly, especially because one has done something wrong and wants to avoid punishment or arrest

Ab 멀리, cond (hide 숨다, recondite 어려운)

시험에는 He **absconded** with her jewels. 형태로 나온다.

He **absconded** from police custody on the way to court.

그는 법정으로 가는 길에 탈주했다.

9. **Absolve**

용서하다. to release them or pronounce them free from a promise, duty, blame, etc.

ab(from로부터), solve (해결하다. Insolvent 지급불능의)

비난 등으로부터 멀어지도록 해결하다. 동의어로 acquit (무죄방면하다. 재판을 통해 해결하다), exonerate, exculpate, condone에 유의!

absolve a person from an obligation 남의 책임을 해제하다

absolve a person **of** his sin 남의 죄를 사면하다.

10. **Abstain**

절제하다. to choose not to take, have, do or undertake it.

Abs (from), tain (hold 잡다, detain 억류하다, pertain 적절하다.)

어떤 것으로부터 거리를 유지하다.

You should **<u>abstain</u>** from smoking in the office. 사무실에서는 금연이다.

He took a vow to **<u>abstain</u>** from alcohol. 그는 술을 끊기로 서약했다.

11. **Abstruse**

난해한 hard to understand

Abs (멀리), truse (thrust 밀다, extrude 밀어내다)

<u>쉬운 것으로부터 멀리 밀어붙인,</u>

an **abstruse** creed 심오한 교리.

I found her argument very **abstruse.**

나는 그녀의 주장이 매우 난해하다고 생각했다.

2. 접두어 AD[183]

접두어 Ad- 는 Ab와는 반대 개념으로 Ab가 원심력 적인 구조를 가졌다면, Ad- 는 구심력적인, 순응적인 구조를 가지고 있는 접두어 이다. 구심점으로의 접근성이 강조되는데, <u>to, toward</u>, intense(강조) 기능에 유의하자. 또한, 접두어 Ad-는 가장 중요하고 방대한 접두어로서, 변화무쌍한 철자 변화의 과정을 거친다. 우리나라의 신라가 실라로 발음되듯이, 발음 편의의 <u>euphony 현상</u>으로서 aff, agg, all, ann, app, arr, ass, att 등 변화된 형태의 스펠링을 가진다.

---

183) 12. Abase 13. Abate 14. Abbreviate 15. Abet 16. Abridge 17. Accede 18. Accomplice 19. Accost 20. Acquiesce 21. Addict 22. Adjacent 23. Adjourn 24. Adjunct 25. Admonish 26. Adore 27. Adulterate 28. Adumbrate 29. Advent 30. Adverse 31. Advert 32. Advocate 33. Affable 34. Affiance 35. Affiliate 36. Affinity 37. Affluent 38. Affront 39. Aggravate 40. Aggregate41. Alleviate 42. Allocate 43. Allude 44. Allure 45. Alluvial 46. Annex 47. Annihilate 48. Aplomb 49. Appall 50. Apparition 51. Append 52. Apposite 53. Appraise 54. Apprehend 55. Apprentice 56. Approbation 57. Arbitrary 58. Arrogant 59. Ascribe 60. Asperse 61. Aspire 62. Assent 63. Assiduous 64. Assimilate

12. Abase

지위를 떨어뜨리다, 비하하다. to humiliate or degrade (someone else or one-self)

A (ad, to), base (lower)

abase oneself 자신을 비하하다.

The president is not willing to **abase** himself before the nation, and admit that he made a mistake. 대통령은 국민 앞에 자신을 낮추려 하지 않았으며 자기가 저지른 실수를 인정하려 하지 않았다.

13. Abate

1. 감하다 a (ad, intensive), bate (beat) 때려서 약화시키다
<u>abate</u> part of a price 값을 얼마간 깎다.
2. 약하게 하다 to become or make less strong or severe
<u>abate</u> the pain 고통을 완화하다
The storm showed no signs of <u>abating</u>.
폭풍은 누그러질 기미가 전혀 보이지 않았다.

14. Abbreviate

단축하다 to shorten
ab (ad, to), brev (short, brief, brevity 간결)

In writing, the title 'doctor' is **abbreviated** to 'Dr'.
작문에서 doctor 타이틀은 Dr. 로 단축된다.

15. Abet

선동하다, 교사하다. especially law to help or encourage someone to do something wrong, especially to commit an offence.
A (ad, to), bet (bait) <u>미끼로 유인하다</u>.

abet a person in crime 범죄를 교사하다.

208

aid and **abet** …을 방조하다.

He was arraigned on charges of aiding and **abetting** terrorists.

그는 테러리스트들을 도와주고 선동한 혐의로 기소됐다.

16. **Abridge**

…을 단축하다, 생략하다 to make (a book, etc) shorter

A (ad, to), bri (bre, short)

He's currently **abridging** his book so that it can be made into a film.

그는 현재 자신의 책이 영화로 제작될 수 있도록 줄거리를 요약하는 중이다.

17. **Accede**

동의하다 to take office, especially (as accede to the throne) to become king or queen. to agree

Ac (ad, to), ced (go, concede 인정하다, 양보하다) -쪽으로 가다.

accede to the chancellorship 재무장관에 취임하다

They will not lightly **accede to** his request.

그들이 그의 요청에 쉽게 동의하지는 않을 것이다.

18. **Accomplice**

공모자 someone who helps another commit a crime

ac (ad, to), com (together), pli (fold) 나쁜 일에 연관됨

The police arrested him and his two **accomplices.**

경찰은 그와 두 명의 공범을 체포했다.

19. **Accost**

가까이 가다, 매춘부가 손님을 끌다. to offer to have sexual intercourse with someone in return for money.

She was **accosted** in the street by a complete stranger.

그녀는 길거리에서 전혀 낯선 사람의 접근을 받았다.

20. **Acquiesce**

묵인하다, 마지못해 따르다 (usually acquiesce in or to something) to accept it or agree to it without objection

Ac (ad, to), quies (quiet) <u>조용히 인정하다.</u>

His parents will never **acquiesce** in such an unsuitable marriage.

그의 부모들은 그런 부적합한 결혼을 결코 받아들이지 않을 것이다.

21. **Addict**

중독자 someone who is physically or psychologically dependent on the habitual intake of a drug such as alcohol, nicotine, heroin, etc. 중독되다.

Ad (to), dict (say) <u>-에 대해 말하다.</u>

addict oneself to …에 빠지다.

be **addicted** to …에 빠지다, 탐닉하다.

I'm a shopping **addict.** 나는 쇼핑 중독자이다.

Don't **addict** yourself to gambling. 도박에 몰두하지 마라.

22. **Adjacent**

근접한, 이웃의 (often adjacent to something) lying beside or next to it

Ad (to), jac (ject, throw, abject 비참한, deject 낙담시키다) <u>가까이에 던져진</u>

My house is **adjacent** to the school. 우리 집은 학교에 인접해 있다.

the Medical School and the **adjacent** Medical Centre.

의과대학과 부설 의료기관.

23. Adjourn

휴회하다. to put off (a meeting, etc) to another time.

Ad (to), journ (day, journal 일기, journey 여행) 날짜를 뒤로 늦추다.

The National Assembly voted to **adjourn** the meeting until the following day. 국회는 다음날까지 정회하기로 표결하였다.

24. Adjunct

1. 부속물. something attached or added to something else but not an essential part of it.

Ad (to), junc (join) 결합되어 있는 것

The scheme was designed as an **adjunct** to existing health care facilities. 그 설계는 기존 건강관리 시설의 부속물로 고안되었다.

2. 부가 사. In 'He came willingly,' 'willingly' is an **adjunct.**

'He came willingly'에서 'willingly'는 부가사이다.

25. Admonish

권고하다 to warn. to scold or tell someone off firmly but mildly. to advise or urge.

Ad (to), mon (advice, premonition 예고, summon 소환하다) 충고하다. 동의어 exhort, reprove, rebuke 주의,

He was frequently **admonished** by his teachers for being late.

그는 지각한다고 선생님한테서 자주 꾸중을 들었다.

26. Adore

숭배하다, to love someone deeply.

Ad (to), or (speak, oral 입의) 우러러 말하다.

I **adore** swimming. 나는 수영을 매우 좋아한다.

John **adores** Sally, but he can't reach first base with her. She won't even speak to him. 존은 샐리에게 완전히 반했지만, 그녀에게 한 걸음도 다가갈 수 없다. 그녀는 그에게 말을 걸려고 하지도 않는다.

27. **Adulterate**

…의 품질을 떨어뜨리다 to debase something or render it impure, by mixing it with something inferior or harmful

ad (to), ulter (alter, other, alternative 양자택일의) 다른 물질을 집어넣다. adulterated milk 물을 탄 우유

28. **Adumbrate**

어렴풋이 …의 윤곽을 드러내다, to suggest or indicate (something likely to happen in the future); to foreshadow.

ad (to), umbra (shadow, umbrella)

The play opens with a fierce storm which **adumbrates** the violence to follow. 그 연극은 다음에 이어질 폭력을 예시하는 맹렬한 폭풍으로 시작한다.

29. **Advent**

도래 coming or arrival; first appearance.

ad (to), vent (come, covenant 계약, revenue 소득)

the **advent** of modern technology 현대 기술의 출현

30. **Adverse**

적대하는 unfavourable to one's interests.

ad (to), vers (vert, turn)

adverse weather conditions 불리한 기후 조건

adverse circumstances 역경

31. Advert

언급하다 to refer to it or mention it in speaking or writing

Ad (to), vert (turn) <u>주의, 관심을 돌리다.</u>

advert to a person's opinion. 남의 의견에 주목하다.

32. Advocate

지지하다 someone who supports or recommends an idea, proposal, etc.

Ad (to), voc (speak) <u>-을 위해 말하다.</u>

Gandhi was an **advocate** of nonviolence. 간디는 비폭력의 주창자였다.

He was a skillful and experienced **advocate.** 그는 능숙하고 노련한 변호사였다

I **advocate** a policy of gradual reform. 나는 점진적인 개혁 정책을 주장한다.

33. Affable

붙임성 있는 pleasant and friendly in manner; easy to talk to

Af (ad, to), fa (speak, fable 우화, ineffable 말로 형언할 수 없는, fabulous 멋진)
<u>말 붙이기 쉬운</u>

He found her parents very **affable.**

그는 그녀의 부모님들이 매우 친근감이 있다는 것을 알았다.

34. Affiance

약혼시키다. (usually be affianced to someone) become engaged to be married to them

Af (ad, to), fia (fid, trust) <u>신뢰를 주다.</u>

affiance oneself to somebody. -와 약혼하다.

35. Affiliate

…을 합병하다, to connect or associate a person or organization with a group or a larger organization

af (ad, to), fil (son, filial 자식의, filicide 자식살해) <u>아들로 삼다.</u>

A number of local groups want to **affiliate** with the union. 많은 지역 단체가 그 조합에 가입하고 싶어 한다.

affiliate members 소속 회원

36. Affinity

친근감, 인천관계 a strong natural liking for or feeling of attraction or closeness towards someone or something.

Af (ad, to), fin (end, infinite 무한한, confine 한정하다, final, finish, define 정의하다.) <u>서로 경계가 비슷한 것, 유사한 것</u>

There's an **affinity** between two persons.

두 사람 간에는 인척 관계가 있다.

There is an **affinity** between the two languages.

그 두 언어 사이에는 유연관계가 있다.

People really feel an **affinity** for dolphins and want to help them.

사람들은 돌고래에 정말로 친근감을 느끼며 그들을 도와주고 싶어 한다.

37. Affluent

부유한 having more than enough money; rich

Af (ad, to), flu (flow) <u>흘러넘치는,</u>

유사 어는 wealthy, abundant, copious, opulent

반대말은 impecunious

His parents were very **affluent.** 그의 부모님은 매우 부유하셨다.

38. Affront

모욕하다, an insult, especially one delivered in public

af (ad, to), front (앞, confront 맞서다) 면전에서 면박을 주다.

His speech was an **affront** to all decent members of the community.

그의 연설은 그 지역의 모든 점잖은 구성원들에게 무례한 언동이었다.

39. Aggravate

악화시키다 to make (a bad situation, an illness, etc) worse.

Ag (ad, to), grav (heavy, gravity 중력) 무거운 것을 올려놓다.

Some of his remarks really **aggravate** me.

그의 몇몇 발언들은 나를 정말 화나게 만들었다.

He **aggravated** his condition by leaving hospital too soon.

그는 너무 일찍 퇴원함으로써 자신의 상태를 악화시켰다.

215

40. Aggregate

총계…(total).

ag (ad, to), greg (flock, congregate 모이다. Segregate 분리하다.) 떼 지어 모이다.

the complete **aggregate** of unemployment figures

실업자 수의 완전한 총계

aggregate data 전체 자료

41. Alleviate

완화시키다 to make (pain, a problem, suffering, etc) less severe

Al (ad, to), levi (light, elevate 올리다, levy 세금부과하다 levity 가벼움, lever 지렛대) 가볍게 하다.

The drugs did nothing to **alleviate** her pain.

그 약들은 그녀의 통증을 진정시키는 데 아무 효과가 없었다.

42. **Allocate**

…을 할당하다 to give, set apart or assign something to someone or for some particular purpose

Al (ad, to), locate (place) 각자의 몫을 놓다.

He **allocated** each of us our tasks.

그가 우리들 각자에게 할 일을 할당해 주었다.

43. **Allude**

언급하다, 암시하다. to mention it indirectly

Al (ad, to), lude (play, collude 공모하다, delude 속이다) 장난치듯 이야기 하다.

allude to the problem 그 문제를 언급하다

You **alluded** in your speech to certain developments, what exactly did you mean? 당신은 연설에서 특정한 전개 상황을 넌지시 비추셨는데, 그게 정확히 뭘 말씀하신 겁니까?

44. **Allure**

꾀어내다 to attract, charm or fascinate

al (ad, to), lure (미끼, 유혹)

the false **allure** of big-city life 대도시 생활의 헛된 매력

45. **Alluvial**

충적의 formed by soil left by flowing water, deposited

Al (ad, to), luv (lav, wash, ablution 목욕재개, lavatory 화장실) 물에 씻겨 조금씩 쌓인

Some **alluvial** deposits are a rich source of diamonds.

어떤 충적기 퇴적물들은 다이아몬드의 풍부한 원천이다.

46. Annex

첨가하다. add to a larger thing.

An (ad, to), nex (net, bind, nexus 유대, 관계, disconnect 연락을 끊다) 하나로 묶다.

annex a neighbouring state 이웃 주를 합병하다

Crete was formally **annexed** to Greece in 1913.

크레타 섬은 1913년에 그리스에 공식적으로 병합되었다.

47. Annihilate

몰살시키다. destroy completely

an (ad, to), nihil (noting, nihilism 허무주의, annul 무효로 하다.) 아무것도 없도록 만들어 버리다.

The enemy was completely **annihilated.** 적은 완전히 진멸되었다.

48. Aplomb

평정. calm self-assurance and poise

A (ad, to), plomb (lead, plumb 연추, 조사하다 plumber 배관공) 납처럼 무겁고 차가운

He performed the duties of a president with great **aplomb.**

그는 대통령으로서의 의무를 아주 침착하게 수행했다.

49. Appall

소름끼치게 하다 fill with horror, terrify

ap (ad, to), pal (pale, pallid 창백한)

We heard about the **appalling** news about the earthquake.

우리는 지진에 대한 소름끼치는 소식을 들었다

50. **Apparition**

유령 a sudden unexpected appearance, especially of a ghost.

Ap(ad, to), appear

동의어 ghost, phantom, spectrum, specter

You look as though you've seen an apparition.

넌 마치 유령이라도 본 것 같구나.

51. **Append**

…을 덧붙이다 to add or attach something to a document, especially as a supplement, footnote, etc

ap (ad, to), pend (hang, impending 임박한)

<u>append</u> an extra clause to the contract 계약서에 추가 조항을 부가하다

52. **Apposite**

적절한 suitable; well chosen; appropriate

Ap (ad, to), ops (place) 가까이에 위치해 있는

This answer is apposite to the question.

이 답은 그 질문에 딱 들어맞는다.

53. **Appraise**

평가하다 to put a price on (a house, property, etc), especially officially

Ap (ad, to), prais (price, precious 귀중한) 가격을 매기다.

I had an expert appraise the house beforehand.

미리 전문가에게 그 집을 평가하게 했다.

54. **Apprehend**

1. 체포하다. take into police control, arrest

   Ap (ad, to), prehen (seize) 붙잡다.

apprehend a thief 도둑을 체포하다.

2. 이해하다 readily **apprehend** the meaning of …의 뜻을 쉽게 이해하다

3. 염려하다 It is **apprehended** that the bridge will be washed away in the flood. 홍수로 다 리가 떠내려갈 우려가 있다.

55. Apprentice

도제 someone, usually a young person, who works for an agreed period of time, often for very low pay, in order to learn a craft or trade;

Ap (ad, to), pren (seize, impregnable 난공불락의) 배우려고 꽉 붙잡는 사람

Most of the work was done by **apprentices**.

대부분의 작업은 수습공들이 한다.

56. Approbation

허가 approval; consent

ap (ad, to), prob (prove)

receive official **approbation** 공적인 인가를 받다

57. Arbitrary

1. 제멋대로인 capricious; whimsical.

ar (ad, to), bit (it, go) 자기가 가고 싶은 곳에만 가는

an **arbitrary** interpretation 제멋대로인 해석.

2. 전제적인 said of a government or of someone in a position of power: dictatorial, authoritarian or high-handed.

an **arbitrary** government 전제 정치.

3. 임의의 discretionary; based on subjective factors or random choice and not on objective principles.

an **arbitrary** decision 자의적 결정.

58. **Arrogant**

건방진 aggressively and offensively self-assertive; having or showing too high an opinion of one's own abilities or importance; impudently over-presumptive

Ar (ad, to), rog (ask) 강제로 요구하는

We found him **arrogant** and overbearing.

우리는 그가 거만하고 으스댄다는 것을 알았다.

59. **Ascribe**

…의 탓으로 하다. to attribute; assign

a (ad, to), scribe (write)

He **ascribed** his failure to bad luck.

그는 자기의 실패를 불운 탓으로 돌렸다.

This play is usually **ascribed** to Shakespeare.

이 연극은 통상 셰익스피어 작품이라고 일컬어지고 있다.

60. **Asperse**

…을 중상하다 spread damaging or false reports about, slander

a (ad, to), sper (sprinkle, disperse 흩뜨리다. sparse 드문드문한) 물을 뿌리듯 퍼붓다.

asperse a person with bitter reproaches. 신랄한 악담을 퍼붓다.

61. **Aspire**

열망하다 to have a strong desire to achieve or reach (an objective or ambition)

A (ad, to) spire (breathe, inspire 격려하다 expire 만기되다) -향해 숨 쉬다.

Few people who **aspire** to fame ever achieve it.

명성을 열망하는 사람들 중 그것을 성취하는 사람은 극소수이다.

62. Assent

동의하다, consent or approval, especially official

as (ad, to), sent (feel, consent 승낙하다 dissent 반대하다) -에 감정을 느끼다.

give one's **assent** to a proposal 제안에 동의하다

63. Assiduous

근면한 hard-working

As (ad, to), sid (sed, sit, dissident 적수, insidious 음흉한, 잠행성의) -에 꾸준히 앉아 있는

The book was the result of ten years **assiduous** research.

그 책은 10년간의 주도면밀한 연구의 결과이다.

64. Assimilate

동화하다, 소화하다, 이해하다 to become familiar with and understand (facts, information, etc) completely

as (ad, to), simil (simul, imitate) 같아지게 하다.

Children need to be given time to **assimilate** what they have been taught. 아이들은 배운 것을 소화시킬 시간이 필요하다.

This is not an easy concept for non-believers to **assimilate**.

이것은 믿지 않는 사람이 이해하기 쉬운 개념이 아니다.

3. 접두어 AN[184]

접두어 an-은 <u>부정(not) 의 의미</u>를 지닌다. 자음 앞에서는 A로 변화에 주의!

65. **Agnostic**

불가지론자 someone who believes that one can know only about material things and so believes that nothing can be known about the existence of God

A (an, not), gno (know, diagnosis 진단, prognosis 예측) <u>신의 존재를 모르는 사람</u>

Although he was born a Catholic, he was an **agnostic** for most of his adult life. 그는 가톨릭교도로 태어났지만, 성인이 된 후에는 대부분 불가지론자로 지냈다.

66. **Amnesty**

사면 a general pardon, especially for people convicted or accused of political crimes

a(an), mnes(remember, amnesia 건망증) <u>과거의 죄를 기억안함</u>

Most political prisoners were freed under the terms of the **amnesty**. 대부분의 정치범들이 사면 협정에 의해 자유의 몸이 되었다.

67. **Amorphous**

무정형의 without definite shape or structure.

a (an), morph (shape, metamorphosis 변형, morphology 형태론)

an **amorphous** organization 무정형의 조직

---

184) 65. Agnostic 66. Amnesty 67. Amorphous 68. Anarchy 69. Anecdote 70. Anomalous 71. Anonymous 72. Apathy 73. Atheist 74. Atrophy

68. Anarchy

무정부상태 confusion and lack of order because of the failure or breakdown of law and government;

An (without), arch (ruler, monarch 군주, patriarch 족장)

The country has been in a state of _anarchy_ since the inconclusive election. 그 나라는 결론이 나오지 않는 선거를 치른 이후 무정부 상태에 빠져 있다.

69. Anecdote

일화 a short entertaining account of an incident

an (not), ec (ex, out), do (give) <u>밖으로 들어나지 아니한 이야기</u>

He's always telling us _anecdotes_ about his childhood in India.

그는 항상 우리들에게 인도에서 보낸 어린 시절의 일화늘을 들려준다.

70. Anomalous

이례적인 different from the usual; irregular; peculiar

an, normal

He is in an _anomalous_ position as the only part-time worker in the firm. 그는 회사 내의 유일한 비정규직으로서 이례적인 위치에 있다.

71. Anonymous

익명의 having no name, incognito

An, onym (name, synonym 동의어, antonym 반의어)

An _anonymous_ benefactor donated 2 million dollars.

한 익명의 은인이 2백만 달러를 기증했다.

72. **Apathy**

무관심 lack of interest or enthusiasm.

A (an), path (feeling, sympathy 공감, 동정, antipathy 반감, 혐오)

The citizens' **apathy** to local affairs resulted in poor government.

지역 일에 대한 시민들의 무관심으로 형편없는 정부가 생겨났다.

73. **Atheist**

무신론자 unbeliever

A (an), the (god, theology 신학, pantheism 범신론)

She has been a confirmed **atheist** for many years.

그녀는 오랜 세월 확고한 무신론자였다.

74. **Atrophy**

감퇴 to make or become weak and thin through lack of use or nourishment.
A (an), troph (nourishment, dystrophy 영양실조, eutrophy 부 영양 상태) Can
the U.S. allow its basic industries to atrophy and still remain a major industrial and military power? 미국이 기간산업을 위축시키고도 산업 및 군사 대국의
구실을 할 수 있겠는가?

4. 접두어 BE[185]

접두어 be-는 <u>동사형성(,do, make)의 의미</u>

75. **Befall**

일어나다 happen to, occur

be (do), fall (떨어지다 fallacy 오류, infallible 확실한)

We prayed that no harm should <u>befall</u> them. 우리는 그들에게 나쁜 일이 일어나지 않게 해 달라고 기도했다.

76. **Beget**

1. 아버지가 자식을 보다(*어머니에 대해서는 bear를 쓴다).

   He **begot** one son and two daughters. 그는 아들 하나와 두 딸을 두었다.

2. …을 생기게 하다 Hate <u>begets</u> hate. 증오는 증오를 낳는다.

   War **begets** misery and ruin. 전쟁은 불행과 황폐를 초래한다.

77. **Beguile**

1. 속이다 Be (do), guile (기만, guileless 순진한)

   beguile a person by flattery 감언이설로 남을 속이다

   He **beguiled** them into accepting it.

   그는 그들을 속여 그것을 받아들이게 했다.

   beguile a person of his money 남의 돈을 사취하다

2. 즐겁게 보내다 She **beguiled** her child with tales.

   그녀는 이야기를 해주어 아이를 즐겁게 했다

---

185) 75. Befall 76. Beget 77. Beguile 78. Behold 79. Belated 80. Belie 81. Belittle 82. Bereave 83. Beseech 84. Beset 85. Betroth 86. Bewitch

78. **Behold**

보다 look at

Be, hold (keep) 관심을 가지고 계속 지켜보다

The new bridge is an incredible sight to **behold.**

새 다리는 대단한 볼거리이다.

79. **Belated**

늦은 delayed

The **belated** letter arrived at last. 늦어진 편지가 마침내 도착했다.

80. **Belie**

어긋나다. give a false idea of

Practical experience **belies** this theory.

실제적인 경험과 이 이론은 일치하지 않는다.

81. **Belittle**

과소평가하다. to treat something or someone as unimportant, or of little or no significance; to speak or write disparagingly about it or them

Don't belittle yourself. 너 자신을 과소평가 하지 마라.

82. **Bereave**

1. 빼앗다, 잃게 하다 bereavement 사별, bereaved 가족을 잃은 bereft 희망, 재산 을 잃은

be utterly **bereft** 어찌할 바를 모르다

2. 죽음이 근친·형제를 앗아가다.

She was **bereaved** of her parents by a traffic accident.

=The traffic accident bereaved her of her parents.

그녀는 교통사고로 부모를 잃었다.

83. Beseech

간청하다 to ask someone earnestly; to beg

Be, seech(seek 추구하다)

I **beseech** you to forgive him. 그를 용서해 주시기를 간청합니다.

84. Beset

1. 포위하다 the forest that **besets** the village 마을을 둘러싸고 있는 숲.

2. …을 괴롭히다. The task was **beset** with[or by] difficulties.

   그 일에는 여러 가지 어려움이 따랐다.

85. Betroth

약혼시키다. engage 발음: 비츄로우드

be, troth(truth)

They were **betrothed** to each other at an early age.

그들은 어렸을 때에 서로 혼약이 되었다.

86. Bewitch

마법을 걸다, 매혹시키다. to charm, fascinate or enchant

The wicked fairy **bewitched** the prince and turned him into a frog.

그 사악한 요정은 왕자에게 마법을 걸어 개구리가 되게 했다.

5. 접두어 CIRCUM[186]

접두어 circum-은 <u>주위, 둘레(around)의 의미</u>

87. Circumlocution

완곡어법 an unnecessarily long or indirect way of saying something

Circum, locu (loqu, speak, obloquy 치욕, 불명예, colloquy 대담)

Politicians are experts in **circumlocution.**

정치가들은 에둘러 말하기의 전문가들이다.

88. Circumscribe

제한하다. confine

circum, scrib (write, conscript 징집하다, prescribe 규정, 처방하다.)

laws passed to **circumscribe** the power of the government

정부의 권력을 제한하기 위해 통과된 법률

89. Circumspect

신중한 cautious

Circum, spec (look, conspicuous 눈에 띄는 , perspicuous 명료한)

Forty years of twists and turns in politics have taught them to remain **circumspect.** 그들은 40년의 정치적 우여곡절 끝에 신중을 배웠다.

90. Circumvent

d a way of getting round or evading (a rule, law, etc).

---

186) 87. Circumlocution 88. Circumscribe 89. Circumspect 90. Circumvent

circum, ven (come, intervene 중재하다, convention 집회, 관례) avoid,

Ships were registered abroad to <u>circumvent</u> employment and safety regulations. 고용수칙 및 안전수칙을 회피하기 위해 배들은 외국에서 등록했다.

6. 접두어 COM[187]

접두어 com-은 <u>함께(together)</u> 의미이다.

91. **Coalition**

연합 a combination or temporary alliance, especially between political parties

co (com), ali (ales, grow, coalesce 연합하다, adolescence 청년기)

form a **coalition** 연합을 형성하다

92. **Cognate**

동족의, 동계 언어 descended from or related to a common ancestor.

co (com), gn (gen, born, progenitor 선조, progeny 자손)

French and Italian are **cognate** languages.

프랑스어와 이탈리아어는 동계 언어이다.

93. **Cognition**

인식 the mental processes, such as perception, reasoning, problem-solving, etc, which enable humans to experience and process knowledge and infor-

---

187) 91. Coalition 92. Cognate 93. Cognition 94. Collateral 95. Collude 96. Commensurate 97. Commiserate 98. Compassion 99. Compatible 100. Compensate 101. Complement 102. Compunction 103. Concede 104. Concoct 105. Condescend 106. Condole 107. Condone 108. Confine 109. Confront 110. Congenial 111. Congenital 112. Congregate 113. Conjecture 114. Conjure 115. Conscript 116. Consecrate 117. Console 118. Conspire 119. Construe 120. Consummate 121. Contagious 122. Contort 123. Contrite 124. Convene 125. Convivial 126. Convoke 127. Convoy

mation

Co (com), gn (gno, know, diagnosis 진단, incognito 익명의)

One of the things we try to do in therapy is to help clients to minimize their negative **cognitions.** 우리가 치료에서 시도하려는 것 중 하나는 고객들이 자신의 부정적 인식을 최소화하도록 도와주는 것이다.

94. Collateral

부수적인, 담보물 additional; secondary in importance; subsidiary.

Col (com), later (side, bilateral 양측의, multilateral 다각적인)

collateral benefits 부수적인 혜택

a **collateral** branch of the family 가족의 방계

So when **collateral** requirements were loosened up, women automatically began applying for these programs. 그런데 담보 조건이 완화되자, 여성들은 자연 이들 프로그램에 신청서를 내기 시작했습니다.

95. Collude

공모하다 to plot secretly with someone, especially with a view to committing fraud

Col (com), lude (play)

His sisters **colluded** in keeping it secret.

그의 자매들은 그 일을 비밀로 하기로 결탁했다.

96. Commensurate

같은 크기의 in equal proportion to something; appropriate to it.

Com, mens (measure, dimension 치수, 크기 immense 막대한)

The salary will be **commensurate** with age, experience and position.

월급은 나이, 경험, 지위에 상응할 것이다.

97. Commiserate

동정하다 sympathize

Com, miser (pity, miserable 비참한, miser 구두쇠)

I was just **commiserating** with Don over the loss of his pet rabbit.

나는 돈이 애완 토끼를 잃은 것을 동정할 따름이었다.

98. Compassion

동정 a feeling of sorrow and pity for someone in trouble

Com, pass (feeling, impassive 냉정한)

The government hasn't shown much **compassion** for the sufferers.

정부는 피해자들에게 별로 동정을 보이지 않았다.

99. Compatible

양립할 수 있는 able to associate or coexist agreeably. com (together), pat (feel, passionate 열정적인, dispassionate 냉정한)

We decided to separate when we realized we were not really **compatible.** 우리는 우리가 실지로 어울리지 않는다는 것을 깨닫고 헤어지기로 결정했다.

This printer is **compatible** with most microcomputers.

이 프린터는 대부분의 소형 컴퓨터에 사용 가능하다.

100. Compensate

보상하다. to make amends to someone for loss, injury or wrong, especially by a suitable payment.

Com, pens (pay, expenditure 지출, pension 연금)

She was **compensated** by the insurance company for her injuries.

그녀는 부상에 대해 보험회사로부터 보상을 받았다.

101. Complement

보완 물, 보완하다. something that completes or perfects; something that pro-vides a needed balance or contrast

Com, ple (fill) 보충, 전 인원

Rice makes an excellent **complement** to a curry dish.

밥은 카레 요리와 훌륭하게 어울린다.

We've taken on our full **complement** of new trainees for this year.

우리는 올해 견습생들을 정원수대로 모두 고용했다.

102. Compunction

양심의 가책 a feeling of guilt, remorse or regret

Com, punc (pung, prick, punctual 시간을 엄수하는)

I have no **compunction** for what I have done.

내가 한 일을 조금도 후회하지 않는다.

103. Concede

인정하다. admit as true

Com, cede (go, cede 양도하다, accede 동의, 취임하다) 함께 가려면 상대방을 인정하여야 한다.

She grudgingly had to **concede** defeat.

그녀는 억지로 패배를 인정해야 했다.

104. Concoct

만들다. make by mixing

Con, coc (cook)

He **concocted** a surprisingly tasty supper of pasta and vegetables.

그는 파스타와 야채로 놀랍도록 맛있는 저녁 식사를 조합해 내었다.

105. Condescend

자신을 낮추어 - 하다. to act in a gracious manner towards those one regards as inferior.

Con, descend 내려오다 에서 자신을 낮추어 -하다, 친절을 베풀다

I do wish he wouldn't **condescend** to the junior staff in his department. 나는 정말 그가 자기 부서의 나이 어린 직원들한테 생색 좀 안 냈으면 좋겠어.

She actually **condescended** to say hello to me in the street today.

그녀는 사실 오늘 길에서 내게 겸손하게 인사를 했다.

106. Condole

애도하다. to express sympathy

Con, dole (grieve, doleful 슬픔에 잠긴, indolent 나태한)

<u>condole</u> with someone on the death of a parent

···에게 부모의 죽음에 대한 조의를 표하다.

107. Condone

용서하다 to pardon or overlook

Con, done (give, pardon 용서하다)

If the government is seen to **condone** violence, the bloodshed will never stop. 만약 정부가 폭력을 용인하는 것으로 비친다면 유혈 참사는 결코 멈추지 않을 것이다.

108. Confine

제한하다 to restrict or limit.

Con, fin (limit, define 정의를 내리다)

I wish the speaker would <u>confine</u> himself to the subject.

연설자가 연설을 주제에만 국한해 주었으면 좋겠다.

Isn't it cruel to <u>confine</u> a bird in a cage?

새를 새장에 가둬 놓는 것은 잔인하지 않은가요?

109. Confront

대항하다. to face someone, especially defiantly or accusingly.

con, front정면 affront 모욕하다

She knew she'd have to **confront** her parents when she got home.

그녀는 집에 도착하면 부모와 맞서야 하리라는 것을 알고 있었다.

110. Congenial

같은 성질의 compatible; having similar interests

con, gen (spirit)

a **congenial** companion 마음 맞는 친구

111. Congenital

선천적인 inborn

con, gen (birth) genesis 발생

congenital defects 선천성 결함

a **congenital** liar 타고난 거짓말쟁이

112. Congregate

모이다. to gather together into a crowd

con, greg (flock, egregious , gregarious 사교적인)

A crowd quickly **congregated** round the speaker.

연설자 주위로 관중이 재빨리 모여들었다

113. Conjecture

추측(하다) guess

con, ject (throw, abject 비참한, adjacent 인접한)

a mere **conjecture** 단순한 추측

114. Conjure

마술로-하다. to perform magic tricks, especially ones which deceive the eye
or seem to defy nature.

con, jur (swear) 맹세와 함께 불러내다

learn how to **conjure** 마술 쓰는 법을 배우다

a **conjuring** trick 마술 묘기

115. Conscript

징집하다. draft

con, script (write, ascribe 탓으로 하다, inscribe 글자를 새기다)

conscript soldiers 징집 병

116. Consecrate

신성하게하다. hallow

Con, secra (sacred, desecrate 신성을 모독하다, execrate 저주하다)

The new church was **consecrated** by the Bishop of Chester.

그 새 교회는 체스터 주교에 의해 축성되었다.

117. Console

달래다 soothe

Con, sole (comfort, solace 위로하다)

Nothing could **console** her grief.

아무것도 그녀의 슬픔을 달랠 수는 없었다.

118. Conspire

공모하다. plot

Con, spire (breathe, aspire 야망을 품다, expire 죽다)

They were charged with **conspiring** to pervert the course of justice.

그들은 정의의 진행을 왜곡시키려는 음모를 꾸민 혐의를 받았다.

119. Construe

해석하다. interpret

Con, strue (struct, build)

Her remarks were wrongly **construed**. 그녀의 발언은 잘못 해석되었다.

120. Consummate

완성하다. accomplish

Con, summa (highest, summit 정상)

With her he would lead a life of **consummate** happiness.

그녀와 함께라면 그는 완전히 행복한 삶을 살 것이다.

121. Contagious

전염성의 infectious

Con, tag (touch, contiguous 인접한, contingent 우연의)

Laughter is **contagious**. 웃음은 옮기 쉽다.

122. Contort

비틀다. distort

Con, tort (twist, torment 고통을 주다, torture 고문하다)

His face **contorted**, then relaxed. 그의 얼굴은 일그러졌다가 퍼졌다.

123. Contrite

깊이 뉘우치는 penitent

con, tr (ter, rub, attrition 마찰, 마모) 양손을 마구 비벼대는 에서 깊이 뉘우치는, 회한의

Gloria looked **contrite**, even distressed.

Gloria는 회개하는 듯, 심지어 비통해 하는 듯 보였다.

tears of **contrition** 회오의 눈물

124. Convene

모이다. assemble

Con, vene (come, advent 도래)

The committee will **convene** at 9.30 tomorrow morning.

위원회는 내일 아침 9시 30분에 소집합니다.

125. Convivial

유쾌한 delightful

con, viv (live, vital 생기 넘치는, 절대 필요한, vivid 생생한)

convivial companions 유쾌한 동료들

126. Convoke

소집하다. assemble

con, voke (voc, call, invoke 호소하다, evoke 감정을 불러일으키다) **convoke**

Parliament 국회를 소집하다

127. Convoy

호송하다. escort

Con, voy (via, way, convey 운반하다) 함께 길을 가다에서 호송(호위)하다. Escort, accompany, go with

The **convoy** was attacked by submarines.

호위대는 잠수함들의 공격을 받았다.

7. 접두어 CONTRA[188]

접두어 contra-, counter- 는 반대(against) 의미를 지닌다.

128. **Contraband**

밀수품 the smuggling of goods prohibited from being imported or exported.
contra (against), ban (prohibition, banish 추방하다, bandit 강도, 불량배) **con traband** goods 금제품.

129. **Contraception**

피임 the deliberate prevention of pregnancy by artificial or natural means
Contra, cep (take) 피임 birth control

Impartial advice on **contraception** is available if you feel you need it.

당신이 필요하다고 느낀다면 피임에 편견 없는 조언을 구할 수 있습니다.

130. **Contradict**

반박하다. 모순되다. deny, be contrary to
Contra, dic (speak, verdict 평결, valediction 고별사)

Recent evidence has tended to **contradict** established theories on this

---

188) 128. Contraband 129. Contraception 130. Contradict 131. Contravene 132. Counterfeit 133. Countermand

subject. 최근의 증거는 이 주제에 관해 이미 확립된 이론과 모순되는 경향이 있다.

131. Contravene

반대하다. 위반하다 oppose, violate

contra, ven (come, convene 소집하다) 반대하다, 위반하다

a blatant **contravention** of the treaty 노골적인 조약 위반

132. Counterfeit

위조의 fake

Counter, feit (fac, make, forfeit 벌금, 몰수당하다, surfeit 과식하다)

This note is a poor **counterfeit.** 이 지폐는 조잡하게 만든 가짜다.

133. Countermand

취소하다. revoke

Counter, mand (order, mandate 명령, 통치의 위임, mandatory 강제적인) As a junior officer you have no right to undermine my authority by **counter manding** my orders. 하급 장교인 당신은 내 명령을 취소함으로써 내 권위를 훼손할 권리가 없다.

8. 접두어 DE[189]

접두어 de-는 <u>아래(down) 분리, 이탈(off) 강조(intensive) 의 의미</u>

134. **Debase**

저하시키다. degrade

De (down), base (lower, bastard 서자) degrade, depreciate

You **debase** yourself by telling such lies.

너는 그런 거짓말을 해서 너의 격을 떨어뜨리고 있어.

135. **Debilitate**

쇠약하게하다. weaken

de (down), bil (strong) 쇠약하게 하다 weaken

Parkinson's disease is a **debilitating** and incurable disease of the nervous system. 파킨슨씨병은 사람을 쇠약하게 하는, 신경계통의 불치병이다.

136. **Deceased**

죽은 dead

de (off), cease 생명이 끝난

the near relations of the **deceased** 고인의 가까운 친척

137. **Decipher**

해독하다. decode

De, cipher 숫자의 영, 가치 없는 것, 암호

---

189) |134. Debase 135. Debilitate 136. Deceased 137. Decipher 138. Deduce 139. Defer 140. Defunct 141. Degenerate 142. Dejected 143. Delegate 144. Delinquent 145. Delude 146. Demolish 147. Demur 148. Demure 149. Denounce 150. Depict 151. Deplete 152. Deport 153. Depose 154. Despise 155. Destitute 156. Deviate 157. Devour

They were part of a team whose job was to **decipher**.

그들은 암호해독이 주 업무인 팀에 속해 있었다.

138. **Deduce**

추론하다. to think out or judge on the basis of what one knows or assumes to be fact

De (down), duc (lead, conducive 도움이 되는) 아래로 파고들어 결론을 끌어내다

From this we **deduce** a method for the construction.

이것을 바탕으로 하여 그 건조법이 도출된다.

139. **Defer**

여기하다. 복종하다. to put off something or leave it until a later time(usually defer to someone, etc) to yield to their wishes, opinions or orders

de (down), fer (carry, confer 협의하다, 수여하다)

I couldn't help but **defer** departure. 나는 출발을 연기하지 않을 수 없었다.

On technical matters, I **defer to** the experts.

기술적 문제는 전문가에게 맡깁니다.

140. **Defunct**

죽은 deceased

De, funct (perform)

He belonged to a now **defunct** political party.

그는 지금은 존재하지 않는 정당에 소속되어 있었다.

141. **Degenerate**

퇴화하다. physically, morally or intellectually worse than before.

De, gen (birth, progeny 자손, eugenics 우생학)

His health is **degenerating** rapidly. 그의 건강이 급격히 나빠지고 있다.

The march **degenerated** into a riot. 그 행진은 폭동으로 변질되었다.

142. **Dejected**

낙심한 depressed

De, jec (throw, abject 비참한)

She looked very **dejected** when she was told that she hadn't got the job. 그녀는 취직이 안 되었다는 말을 듣자 몹시 낙담한 것 같았다.

143. **Delegate**

위임하다. to give (part of one's work, power, etc) to someone else.

De, leg (send, relegate 좌천시키다)

The job had to be **delegated** to an assistant.

그 일은 조수에게 위임될 것이다.

144. **Delinquent**

비행의, 체납된 remiss, overdue

de, linq (leave, relinquish 포기하다)

a juvenile **delinquent** 비행 청소년

a tax **delinquent** 세금 체납자

145. **Delude**

속이다. deceive

De, lud (play, allude 암시하다, collude 공모하다)

You're **deluding** yourself if you think things will get better.

사정이 나아질 것이라고 생각한다면 당신은 스스로를 기만하는 것이다.

146. Demolish

부수다. destroy

De, mol (grind, molest 괴롭히다, emolument 관직의 봉급)

They're **demolishing** the old buildings.

그들은 그 낡은 건물들을 부수고 있다.

147. Demur

반대하다. object

They accepted my proposal without **demur**.

그들은 내 제안을 이의 없이 받아들였다.

148. Demure

얌전한 quiet, modest and well-behaved

a very **demure** young lady 매우 얌전한 젊은 아가씨

243

149. Denounce

비난하다. to inform against or accuse someone publicly

She **denounced** the government's handling of the crisis.

그녀는 정부의 위기관리 처리를 비난했다.

150. Depict

묘사하다. to describe something, especially in detail.

Her novel **depicts** the life of country people.

그녀의 소설은 시골 사람들의 삶을 묘사한다.

151. Deplete

고갈시키다. exhaust

De, ple (fill, replete 가득 찬, plenary 절대적인, 전원 출석의)

The election has severely **depleted** the party's funds.

선거로 그 당의 자금이 극심하게 소모되었다.

152. Deport

추방하다. banish

He was convicted of drug offences and was **deported**.

그는 마약 범죄로 기소되어 국외로 추방되었다

153. Depose

1. 면직하다, 퇴위시키다.

The king was **deposed** by the revolution.

왕은 혁명으로 왕좌에서 쫓겨났다.

2. 증언하다. He **deposed** that he had seen the accused before.

그는 피고를 이전에 본 일이 있다고 증언했다.

154. Despise

경멸하다. to look down on someone or something with scorn and contempt

de, spi (look)

You should not **despise** a man just because he is poorly dressed.

사람을 옷차림이 남루하다는 이유만으로 경멸해서는 안 된다.

155. Destitute

빈곤한 lacking money, food, shelter, etc; extremely poor.

De, stit (stand)

He's **destitute** of common sense. 그는 상식이 결핍되어 있다.

The floods have left thousands of people in the area **destitute**.

홍수로 그 지역 주민 수 천 명은 가난하게 되었다.

156. **Deviate**

벗어나다. to turn aside or move away from what is considered a correct or normal course, standard of behaviour, way of thinking, etc

de, via (way, via 경유하여, obviate 미연에 방지하다)

Her behavior **deviates** from the rules.

그녀의 행동은 규칙에서 벗어나고 있다.

157. **Devour**

게걸스럽게 먹다.

De, vor (eat, voracious 게걸스러운, omnivorous 잡식성의)

He **devours** all the books he can lay his hands on.

그는 닥치는 대로 무슨 책이든 탐독한다.

10. 접두어 EX[190]

접두어 ex- 는 <u>밖(out) 의 의미</u>

158. **Eccentric**

이상한 strange

Ec (ex, out), cent (center, concentrate 집중하다)

She had an **eccentric** habit of collecting stray cats.

그녀는 집 없는 고양이들을 모으는 유별난 취미를 갖고 있었다.

---

190) 158. Eccentric 159. Efface 160. Effigy 161. Elucidate 162. Elude 163. Emancipate 164. Enumerate 165. Eradicate 166. Erudite 167. Evacuate 168. Evade 169. Evoke 170. Excavate 171. Excerpt 172. Exempt 173. Exhort 174. Exile 175. Exorbitant 176. Expedient 177. Expedite 178. Expend 179. Expire 180. Explicit 181. Extrude

159. Efface

지우다 erase

The whole country had tried to **efface** the memory of the old dictatorship. 나라 전체가 옛 독재의 기억을 지우려고 노력했다.

160. Effigy

형상 a crude doll or model representing a person, on which hatred of, or contempt for, the person can be expressed, eg by burning it.
Ef (ex), fig (form, figure, figurative 상징적인)

They hanged the dictator in **effigy**.

그들은 그 독재자의 형상을 만들어 교수형에 처했다.

161. Elucidate

명료하게 하다. clarify
E, lucid (light, luxury 사치품, 쾌락)

You have not understood; allow me to **elucidate**.

당신이 이해를 못하셨군요. 설명을 해 드릴게요.

162. Elude

교묘히 피하다. to escape or avoid something by quickness or cleverness.
E, lud (play, delude 속이다, ludicrous 우스운)

"Sorry, your name **eludes** me."

"죄송합니다만, 당신의 이름이 생각나질 않는군요."

163. Emancipate

해방시키다. release

e, man (hand, manipulate 조작하다)

be **emancipated** from colonialist rule 식민지 통치에서 해방되다

164. Enumerate

열거하다. to list one by one.

She **enumerated** her objections to the proposals.

그녀는 그 제안들에 대한 자신의 반대 이유를 열거했다.

165. Eradicate

근절하다. to get rid of something completely

E, radic (root, radical 급진적인)

He has promised to **eradicate** the last vestiges of military rule.

그는 군사 통치의 잔재를 완전히 제거하겠다고 약속했다.

166. Erudite

박식한 learned

E, rude 무례한

He's the author of an **erudite** book on Scottish history.

그는 스코틀랜드 역사에 대한 학문적인 책의 저자이다.

167. Evacuate

대피시키다. withdraw

e, vacu (empty, vacuum, vacant)

help **evacuate** flood victims 수재민들을 대피시키는 것을 돕다

168. Evade

피하다. avoid

e, vad (go, invade 침입하다, pervade 널리 퍼지다)

You cannot **evade** your responsibility. 너는 네 책임을 피할 수 없다.

169. Evoke

불러일으키다. to bring (a memory or emotion, etc) into the mind.

E, vok (call, provoke 자극하다, revoke 취소하다)

That smell always **evokes** memories of my old school.

저 냄새는 언제나 내가 옛날에 다닌 학교의 추억을 불러일으킨다.

170. Excavate

발굴하다. dig

E, cav (cave, cavity 충치)

They spent seven years **excavating** in the Middle East.

그들은 중동에서 발굴을 하며 7년을 보냈다.

171. Excerpt

인용 extract

ex (out), crept (pluck)

An **excerpt** from her new thriller will appear in this weekend's maga-

zine. 그녀의 신작 스릴러의 발췌문이 이번 주말 잡지에 실릴 것이다.

172. Exempt

면제 된, 면제하다. release

a tax-**exempt** savings scheme 비과세 저축 안

exempt from military service 군복무가 면제된

173. Exhort

권고하다. advise

ex, hort (urge, hortative 권고의)

The teacher kept _exhorting_ us to work harder.

선생님은 우리들에게 더 열심히 공부하라고 계속 타일렀다.

174. Exile

추방 banishment

Ex (out), il (sed, sit, assiduous 근면한)

He came back after an _exile_ of ten years.

그는 10 년간의 망명 생활 끝에 돌아왔다.

175. Exorbitant

터무니없는 excessive

Ex, orbit 궤도

The price of food here is _exorbitant_. 여기 식품 값은 터무니없다.

176. Expedient

1. 시기적절한. Ex, speed

You'll find it _expedient_ to see him.

그를 만나보는 것이 상책이라는 것을 알게 될 것이다.

2. 편의적인, **a temporary _expedient_** 임시방편

resort to an _expedient_ 편법을 강구하다.

177. Expedite

촉진하다. quicken

ex, speed 재촉하다 expedition 은 신속, 긴 여행

The government plans to **expedite** the emergency relief plan.

정부는 긴급 구호계획을 조기에 실시할 계획이다.

178. **Expend**

쓰다. spend

He had already **expended** large sums in pursuing his claim through the courts. 그는 법정에서 자사의 주장을 관철시키는데 많은 돈을 들였다.

179. **Expire**

만료되다. terminate

Ex, pire (spire, breathe, conspire 공모하다 inspire 고무하다)

When does the patent **expire**? 그 특허는 언제 기한이 만료되는가?

180. **Explicit**

명백한 stated or shown fully and clearly.

Ex, plic (fold, complicate 복잡하게 하다, implicit 은연중에)

He was quite **explicit** on that point.

그는 그 점에 대해서 조금도 숨김이 없었다.

181. **Extrude**

내밀다. push

Ex, trud (thrust, intrude 간섭하다, obtrude 강요, 강제하다)

extrude glue from a tube 튜브에서 풀을 짜내다.

11. 접두어 IN191)

접두어 in- 은 <u>부정(not)의 의미</u>를 지닌다.

182. Enmity

증오 hostility

en (in, not), m (am, love, amiable 호감을 주는,) 사랑하지 아니함

He has **enmity** against me. 그는 나에게 앙심을 품고 있다.

183. Ignoble

비열한, 비천한 without honor, humble

Ig (in), noble 귀족

To betray a friend is **ignoble**. 친구를 배신하는 것은 비열하다.

(251)

184. Ignominious

수치스러운 shameful

ig, nomin (name, anonym 익명, nominal 명목상의)

an **ignominious** defeat 불명예스러운 패배

185. Illegible

읽기 어려운 hart to read

Your handwriting is so **illegible** that I can't read it.

너의 필체가 너무 알아보기 어려워서 나는 읽을 수가 없다.

---

191) 182. Enmity 183. Ignoble 184. Ignominious 185. Illegible 186. Illiterate 187. Immaculate 188. Immortal 189. Impartial 190. Impecunious 191. Impunity 192. Incongruous 193. Indolent 194. Infirm 195. Inhospitable 196. Insolvent 197. Intrepid 198. Irrevocable

186. **Illiterate**

문맹의 ignorant

il, literate 읽고 쓸 수 있는, obliterate 지우다, 말살하다, literal 문자 그대로

an **illiterate** child 글을 모르는 아이

187. **Immaculate**

완전한 without a spot

Macula 흠, 오점 maculate 얼룩지게 하다

He gave an **immaculate** performance as the aging hero.

그는 늙어가는 주인공으로서 완벽한 연기를 보여 주었다.

188. **Immortal**

불멸의 everlasting

Im, mortal (death, mortgage 저당 mortify 수치스럽게 하다)

The Greek gods were **immortal** and so could not die.

그리스의 신들은 불멸의 존재이므로 죽을 수가 없었다.

189. **Impartial**

공평한 fair

It's an admirably objective and **impartial** report.

그것은 존경스러울 만큼 객관적이고 공정한 보도이다.

190. **Impecunious**

가난한 needy

im, pecuni (money, peculate 횡령하다 pecuniary 금전의)

impecunious circumstances 무일푼인 상황

191. Impunity

무사 free from any punishment

You cannot break the law with **impunity.** 무사히 법을 어길 수는 없다.

192. Incongruous

어울리지 않는 inconsistent

In, con, gru (grow)

Such traditional methods seem **incongruous** in this modern technical age. 그러한 전통적인 방법은 이러한 현대의 과학적인 시대에는 어울리지 않는 것처럼 보인다.

193. Indolent

게으른 idle

He was a fat and **indolent** person. 그는 뚱뚱하고 나태한 사람이었다.

194. Infirm

허약한 feeble

His grandfather was old and **infirm.** 그의 할아버지는 늙고 허약했다.

195. Inhospitable

불친절한 unkind

It was **inhospitable** of you not to offer her a drink.

네가 그녀에게 음료수를 대접하지 않은 것은 불친절한 행동이었다.

196. Insolvent

파산한 bankrupt

They lost orders and were **insolvent** within weeks.

그들은 환어음을 잃어 버려 몇 주 안 되어 파산했다.

197. **Intrepid**

용감한 dauntless

an **intrepid** explorer 용맹스러운 탐험가

198. **Irrevocable**

취소할 수 없는 irreversible

an **irrevocable** decision 취소할 수 없는 결정

11. 접두어 IN (안)[192]

접두어 in-은 <u>안(in)의 의미</u>

199. **Illuminate**

조명하다, 설명하다 lighten, explain

il (in, 안), lumen (light) 안에 불을 밝히다

illuminate a difficult passage in a book 책 속의 어려운 구절을 설명하다.

illuminated signs 조명 표지

---

192) 199. Illuminate 200. Imbibe 201. Impart 202. Impassioned 203. Impending 204. Imperative 205. Impetuous 206. Impose 207. Impoverish 208. Inborn 209. Indigenous 210. Infuriate 211. Ingrained 212. Inmate 213. Innate 214. Inscribe 215. Insidious 216. Instigate 217. Insurrection 218. Intimidate 219. Intrude 220. Inundate

200. Imbibe

마시다 drink in

Plants **imbibes** moisture from the soil.

식물은 토양으로부터 수분을 흡수한다.

201. Impart

주다, 전하다. bestow, make known

im, part 나누다

You have to **impart** your information to them.

당신은 당신의 정보를 그들에게 전해야만 한다.

202. Impassioned

감동적인 full of strong feeling

an **impassioned** speech 정열적인 연설

203. Impending

절박한 imminent

Im, pend 안에 불안하게 매달려 있는

Let's discuss the **impending** matter first.

우선 시급한 문제부터 협의합시다.

204. Imperative

긴급한 urgent

im, pera (command)

It is absolutely **imperative** that we make a quick decision.

우리가 빨리 결정을 내리는 것이 절대적으로 필요하다

205. Impetuous

성급한 impulsive

Im, pet (rush, petulant 화 잘 내는, 까다로운)

Don't be so **impetuous**! 그렇게 성급하게 굴지 마라!

206. Impose

부과하다 put a burden

im, pose 안에 놓다 에서 부과하다, 강요하다

A dictator can **impose** his will on the people.

독재자는 자기의 의지를 국민에게 강요할 권력을 지니고 있다.

207. Impoverish

가난하게하다. make very poor

im, pover (poor, poverty 가난)

impoverished farmers 곤궁해진 농부들

208. Inborn

타고난 innate

That statesman has an **inborn** ability to lead the masses.

저 정치가는 대중을 이끄는 타고난 재능을 가지고 있다.

209. Indigenous

토착의 native

Indi (in 안), gen (birth)

The kangaroo is **indigenous** to Australia.

캥거루는 오스트레일리아가 원산지이다.

210. Infuriate

격분하다. enrage

In, fury 격노

It was **infuriating** to have to wait another hour.

한 시간을 더 기다려야 한다는 것은 화나는 일이다.

211. Ingrained

깊이 베어든 rooted

In, grain (gran, seed, grain 곡물, granary 곡물 창고) 땅 속에 씨가 깊이 박힌

Distrust was **ingrained** in her from childhood.

불신은 어린 시절부터 그녀에게 뿌리깊이 박혀 있었다.

212. Inmate

수감자 prisoner

In, mate 동료

He said that **inmates** were forced to live in dirty condition.

그는 수용자들이 더러운 환경에서 살기를 강요받고 있다고 말했다.

213. Innate

타고난 inborn

In, nat (born)

Looking back over the many years, Cyril's most impressive quality, for me, was his **innate** goodness. 지난 여러 해를 뒤돌아보니, 나한테 시릴의 가장 인상적인 성격은 그의 타고난 선량함이었다.

214. Inscribe

쓰다 engrave

inscribe one's name in a book 책에 이름을 새기다.

215. **Insidious**

음흉한, 잠행성의 sly, working secretly

in, sid (sit, preside)

an **insidious** disease 잠행 성 질병

Jealousy is **insidious.** 질투는 모르는 사이에 진행된다.

216. **Instigate**

선동하다. urge

in, stig (prick) 하도록 찔러대다

instigate a strike 파업을 부추기다

217. **Insurrection**

폭동 revolt

In, sur (surg, rise)

Insurrection was seen as the only way of changing the government.

반란은 정부를 바꾸는 유일한 방법으로 보였다.

218. **Intimidate**

위협하다. frighten

in, timid 겁 많은 frighten, terrify

I find Mr. Kitson very **intimidating.** I'm always terrified when he

comes over to my desk. 난 킷슨 씨가 참 무서워요. 내 책상 가까이 오기만

해도 겁이 난다니까요.

219. **Intrude**

밀어 넣다. force

In, trud (thrust, extrude 밀어내다, protrude 불쑥 나오다)

Don't **intrude** yourself on her privacy. 그녀의 사생활에 끼어들지 마시오.

220. Inundate

범람시키다. overflow

In, und (flow, redundant 여분의)

If the dam breaks, it will <u>inundate</u> large parts of the town.

만약 댐이 무너지면 그 마을의 대부분 지역이 물에 잠길 것이다.

12. 접두어 OB[193]

접두어 ob-는 <u>반내, 저항(against)의 의미</u>

221. Obdurate

고집 센 inflexible

Ob, dur (harden, endurance 인내력, duration 지속)

The President remains **obdurate** on the question of cutting taxes.

대통령은 세금 삭감 문제에 대해 완고한 입장을 고수하고 있다.

222. Obese

비만인 very fat

Ob, es (de, eat, edible 먹기에 좋은)

Obese people are more at risk from diabetes and heart disease.

비만한 사람들은 당뇨병과 심장병에 걸릴 위험이 더 많다.

---

193) 221. Obdurate 222. Obese 223. Obliterate 224. Oblivion 225. Obloquy 226. Obscene 227. Obsequious 228. Obsess 229. Obstruct 230. Obtrude 231. Obviate 232. Opponent

223. Obliterate

삭제하다 delete

Ob, liter (letter, illiterate 문맹의)

She tried to **obliterate** the memory of her childhood.

그녀는 어린 시절의 기억을 지워 버리려고 애썼다.

224. Oblivion

망각 forgetfulness, Ob, liv

His work fell into **oblivion** after his death.

그의 작품은 그가 죽은 이후 망각되었다.

225. Obloquy

불명예 dishonor

ob, loquy (loqui, speak, colloquialism 구어체, loquacious 수다스런)

In the face of public **obloquy**, he was forced to resign.

대중적인 비방에 직면하여 그는 사직해야만 했다.

226. Obscene

음란한 salacious

Stanley was arrested for making **obscene** phone calls.

스탠리는 음란 전화를 한 죄목으로 체포되었다.

227. Obsequious

아부하는 flattering

Ob, sequ (follow, consecutive 연속적인)

She is almost embarrassingly **obsequious** to anyone in authority.

그녀는 권력자라면 아무한테나 거의 당황스러울 정도로 굽실거린다.

228. Obsess

망상이 들다. haunt

On, sess (sit, assiduous 근면한, dissident 적)

The idea of finding her real mother seemed to <u>obsess</u> her.

진짜 어머니를 찾겠다는 생각이 그녀를 사로잡고 있는 듯이 보였다.

229. Obstruct

막다. hinder

Ob, struct (build, construct 건설하다)

He was charged with <u>obstructing</u> the highway.

그는 고속도로 차단혐의를 받았다.

230. Obtrude

강요하다. intrude

Ob, trud (thrust, abstruse 난해한 intrusion 강요, 침입) -을 향해 밀고 나가다

Don't <u>obtrude</u> your opinions on others.

남에게 자신의 의견을 강요하지 마라.

231. Obviate

미연에 방지하다. eliminate

ob, via (way, deviate 빗나가다,) 길 위에 방해되는 것을 없애다

A peaceful solution would <u>obviate</u> the need to send a UN military

force. 평화롭게 해결된다면 유엔 군사력을 파견하지 않아도 될 것이다.

232. Opponent

상대자 antagonist

Op (ob, against), pon (place,) antagonist, adversary, con, foe

반대말은 proponent

He was my **opponent** in the debate.

그는 나의 논쟁 상대였다.

13. 접두어 PER[194]

접두어 per-는 <u>관통, 통과(through) 의미</u>

233. **Peremptory**

절대적인, 단호한 imperative

per, empt (take, preempt 선점하다, redemption 되찾음, 구조)

She finally lost patience with his incessant **peremptory** demands.

그의 끊임없는 강제적인 요구에 마침내 그녀는 인내심을 상실했다.

234. **Perennial**

계속되는 perpetual

Per, enn (ann, year)

Jim Boren is representative of another kind of **perennial** presidential candidate. 짐 보렌은 만년 대통령 후보 중 또 다른 종류의 대표적 인물이라고 할 수 있다.

235. **Perfidy**

배반, 불성실 betrayal

per, fid (faith, defiant 도전적인) betrayal

---

194) 233. Peremptory 234. Perennial 235. Perfidy 236. Persecute 237. Perspicacious 238. Pervade 239. Pervert

Such **perfidy** cannot be forgiven. 그런 배신은 결코 용서될 수 없다.

236. Persecute

박해하다. torment

Per, secu (sequ, follow, prosecute 기소하다) 끝까지 따라가서 못하게 굴다.

He accused the media of **persecuting** him and his family.

그는 언론이 자신과 자신의 가족을 괴롭힌다고 비난했다.

237. Perspicacious

통찰력이 있는 astute

per, spic (spec, look, circumspect 신중한)

a **perspicacious** remark 통찰력 있는 발언

238. Pervade

퍼지다. permeate

Per, vad (go, evade 피하다 invade 침입하다)

An intense poetic quality **pervades** her novels.

강렬한 시적 특질이 그녀의 소설 곳곳에 퍼져 있다.

239. Pervert

타락시키다. 왜곡하다. debase, distort

Per, vert (turn, subvert 전복시키다, divert 전환하다) 나쁜 쪽으로 바꾸다 에서
타락하다, 왜곡하다 debase, distort

pervert the truth 진실을 왜곡하다

Do pornographic books **pervert** those who read them?

도색 서적은 그것을 읽는 사람들을 도착자로 만드는가?

15. 접두어 PRE[195]

접두어 pre-는 <u>앞(before)의 의미</u>

240. **Precept**

교훈 maxim

Pre, cep (take, conception 개념, 임신)

Practice is better than <u>precept</u>. 실행은 교훈보다 낫다.

241. **Preclude**

막다. prevent

Pre (before), clud (shut, include 포함하다)

Financial constraints <u>preclude</u> excavation of more than part of the site. 재정적 압박 때문에 그 지역 일부분 이상을 발굴하는 것이 불가능하다.

242. **Precursor**

선구자 forerunner

pre, cur (run, concur 일치하다)

small disturbances that were precursors of the revolution to come 다가올 혁명의 선봉이 된 소규모 소동들

243. **Predilection**

편애 preference

---

195) 240. Precept 241. Preclude 242. Precursor 243. Predilection 244. Pregnant 245. Preposterous 246. Prerogative 247. Prescribe

pre, di (dis, apart), lect (choose, elect 선출하다, select 선택하다) 좋아하는 것
을 미리 선택함

have a **predilection** for Japanese food 일본 음식을 특별히 좋아하다

244. Pregnant

임신한 having an unborn young in the body

Pre, gn (gen, birth)

She is **pregnant** with her first child. 그녀는 첫 아이를 임신했다.

245. Preposterous

앞뒤가 바뀐, 터무니없는 absurd

pre, post (after) 앞뒤가 뒤바뀐, 터무니없는

He described it as **preposterous.** 그는 그것을 상식 밖이라고 말했다.

246. Prerogative

특권 privilege

Per, rog (ask, abrogate 취소하다)

It is the prime minister's **prerogative** to decide when to call an election. 언제 선거를 요청할 것인지를 결정하는 것은 수상의 특권이다.

247. Prescribe

규정하다. 처방하다 order

pre, scribe (write, describe 묘사하다, inscribe 새기다)

Ask her to **prescribe** something for that cough.

그녀에게 그 기침에 복용할 뭔가를 좀 처방해달라고 부탁해라.

Police regulations **prescribe** that an officer's number must be clearly

visible. 경찰 규칙은 경찰관의 번호가 분명히 보이게 되어 있어야 한다고 규정하

고 있다.

You can't **prescribe** fixed standards for art.

예술에 대해서는 일정한 기준을 정할 수가 없다.

15. 접두어 PRO[196]

접두어 pro-는 <u>앞(forth)의 의미</u>

248. **Prodigal**

방탕한 lavish

Pro, ig (drive, agitate 선동하다) 낭비하는,

prodigy 천재, progeny 자손과 비교하여야 한다.

After a thrifty father, a **prodigal** son.

절약하는 아버지 밑에 낭비하는 자식.

249. **Prodigious**

거대한 huge

The government sank **prodigious** amounts of public money into the scheme. 정부는 그 계획에 막대한 공금을 쏟아 부었다.

250. **Profane**

불경스러운 impious

Pro, fan (shine, fan 지지자, fanatic 광신자)

---

196) 248. Prodigal 249. Prodigious 250. Profane 251. Proficient 252. Prognosticate 253. Propensity 254. Proscribe 255. Prosecute 256. Protrude

He uses too much **profane** language.

그는 불경스러운 말을 지나치게 많이 쓴다.

251. **Proficient**

능숙한 skillful

Pro, fic (make)

She is **proficient** at German. 그녀는 독일어에 숙달되어 있다.

252. **Prognosticate**

예언하다. forecast

Pro, gno (know, diagnose 진단하다)

prognosticate a depression 불황을 예측하다.

253. **Propensity**

성향 proclivity

pro, pens (hang, impending 임박한) 마음이 매달려 있는 상태, 보통 나쁜 뜻으로 성벽

She has a **propensity** to exaggerate.

그녀는 과장하는 경향이 있다.

254. **Proscribe**

금지하다. forbid

proscribed books 금지된 서적

255. **Prosecute**

기소하다. indict

pro, secu (sequ, follow, persecute 박해하다)

The police decided not to **prosecute**. 경찰은 기소하지 않기로 결정했다.

256. **Protrude**

튀어나오다. stick out

Pro, trude (thrust, intrude 방해자, 침입자)

He managed to hang on to a piece of rock **protruding** from the cliff face. 그는 절벽 면에 튀어나온 바위 하나에 간신히 매달렸다.

16. 접두어 RE[197]

접두어 re-는 뒤(back,) 다시(again)의 의미

257. **Reciprocal**

상호의 mutual

reci (re, back), pro (forth) 서로 앞뒤로 오가는

The two superpowers agreed to **reciprocal** reduction of nuclear weapons.

그 두 열강은 핵무기 상호 감축에 동의했다.

258. **Recompense**

보상하다. repay

re, com (together), pense (weigh, expenditure 지출) 보상하다

recompense employees for working overtime

직원들에게 시간외 근무에 대해 보상하다

---

197) 257. Reciprocal 258. Recompense 259. Recondite 260. Recuperate 261. Redolent 262. Reimburse 263. Reiterate 264. Relegate 265. Relent 266. Relinquish 267. Remiss 268. Replete 269. Retail

259. **Recondite**

심오한 profound

Re (back), cond (hide, abscond 도망하다) 뒤로 깊숙이 숨은 에서 난해한

She believes that poetry should be part of the everyday, not a **recondite** preoccupation of academics. 그녀는 시가 학자들의 심오한 학문적 관심사가 아닌, 일상생활의 일부가 되어야 한다고 믿는다.

260. **Recuperate**

회복하다. recover

Re (again), cup (cap, take) 잃었던 것을 다시 잡다. 에서 회복하다 recover, convalesce

She spent a month in the country **recuperating** after the operation.

그녀는 수술을 받은 후 시골에서 한 달간 회복하면서 보냈다.

261. **Redolent**

향기로운 fragrant

re (again), ol (smell, olfactory 냄새의)

The air was **redolent** with the smell of exotic spices.

공기 중에 이국적인 향신료 냄새가 진동했다.

a place **redolent** of history and tradition

역사와 전통을 생각나게 하는 장소

262. **Reimburse**

변상하다. repay

Re, im, burs (purse) 다시 지갑 안에 돈을 넣어주다 에서 변상하다.

We will **reimburse** the customer for any loss or damage.

저희는 고객 여러분께 어떤 손실이나 손상도 배상해 드립니다.

263. **Reiterate**

반복하다. repeat

re, iter (repeat)

Let me **reiterate** that we are fully committed to this policy.

저희는 이 정책에 전적으로 전념하고 있음을 누차 강조하는 바입니다.

264. **Relegate**

좌천시키다. demote

re (back), leg (send) 뒤쪽의 낮은 지위로 보내다

relegate old files to the storeroom 오래된 서류철들을 창고로 이관하다

I have been **relegated** to the role of a mere assistant.

나는 단순히 조수 역할로 전락했다.

265. **Relent**

누그러지다. abate

re (again), lent (slow, lenient 너그러운)

The police will not **relent** in their fight against crime.

경찰은 범죄와의 전쟁을 완화하지 않을 것이다.

266. **Relinquish**

포기하다. give up

re (back), linqu (leave, delinquent 의무태만의, 비행의) 자기 것을 뒤로 하고 떠나다. 에서 포기하다.

relinquish one's position as Governor 총재직을 그만두다

267. **Remiss**

태만한 neglectful

Re (back), miss (send) 일을 뒤로 보내는 에서 태만한

You have been **remiss** in your duties. 당신은 의무를 태만히 해 왔습니다.

268. **Replete**

가득 찬 full

re (again), ple (fill)

a game **replete** with drama and high tension

드라마와 높은 긴장감이 충만한 경기

269. **Retail**

소매 Re (back), tail (cut, entail 수반하다) 커다란 것의 뒤를 잘라 판매함

Do you sell by wholesale or <u>retail?</u>

당신은 도매로 팝니까? 소매로 팝니까?

17. 접두어 SUB[198]

접두어 sub-는 <u>아래(under)의 의미</u>

270. **Subjugate**

정복하다. conquer

sub, jug (yoke)

a **subjugated** race 정복당한 인종

271. **Subordinate**

하위의 subject

---

198) 270. Subjugate 271. Subordinate 272. Subscribe 273. Subside 274. Subsidiary 275. Subsist 276. Subtract 277. Succumb 278. Supplicate 279. Surrogate

sub, ordin (order)

be in a **subordinate** position to the head of the department

부서장의 하위직에 있다

272. **Subscribe**

1. 기부하다, **subscribe** $ 100 for the new gymnasium

신설체육관에 100달러를 기부하다.

2. 동의하다. **subscribe** a contract 계약서에 동의하다.

3. 서명하다. President **subscribed** his name to the document.

대통령은 그 문서에 서명했다.

273. **Subside**

가라앉다. abate

sub, sid (sit)

The police are hoping that the violence will soon **subside**.

경찰은 폭력이 곧 진정되기를 바라고 있다.

274. **Subsidiary**

보조의

a **subsidiary** business 부업.

subsidiary payments 보조금

275. **Subsist**

살아가다 live

Sub, sist (stand) 살아가다

He **subsisted** mainly on vegetables and fruit.

그는 주로 채소와 과일로 연명했다.

Part 5
어근분석

01 The _____ between good and evil

a. anatomy   b. epitome   c. dichotomy   d. appendectomy

02 Nothing could _____ his thoughts from his mother's sudden death.

a. convert   b. converse   c. conversant   d. divert

03 The court has no _____ over foreign diplomats.

a. malediction   b. valediction   c. valedictory   d. jurisdiction

04 He managed to hang on to a piece of rock _____ing from the cliff face.

a. extrude   b. intrude   c. obtrude   d. protrude

05 This regulation is not _____ to this case.

a. explicit   b. replica   c. supplicate   d. applicable

06 He had the _____ to demand more money.

a. affront   b. confront   c. effrontery   d. frontier

07 Some reptiles _____ through their skin.

a. conspire   b. suspire   c. expire   d. respire

08 The police are hoping that the violence will soon _____.

a. subside   b. reside   c. resident   d. residue

09 "After a thrifty father, a _____ son."

a. ambiguous   b. agitate   c. cogent   d. prodigal

10 She went to the mountains to _____ after leaving hospital.

a. ambivalence   b. available   c. convalesce   d. equivalent

11 This is strictly _____.

a. confident   b. confidential   c. fidelity   d. infidelity

12 "Sorry, your name _____ me."

a. collude   b. allude   c. elude   d. delude

13 He lived alone on his old-age _____.

a. recompense   b. expenditure   c. pension   d. expense

14 Higher salaries are _____ing many teachers into industry.

a. aqueduct   b. educe   c. subdue   d. seduce

15 Do you _____ to any magazines?

a. proscribe   b. subscribe   c. describe   d. transcribe

16 The police _____ his car as evidence.

    a. expound   b. impound   c. compound   d. propound

17 I _____ that he had failed in his business.

    a. demise   b. surmise   c. emissary   d. remit

18 Kate _____ on th bench.

    a. repose   b. impose   c. impound   d. composure

Part 5 어근분석

1. **abstemious**[199]

폭음, 폭식하지 아니하는, 절제 있는 not eating and drinking too much, moderate; **tem (tom)은 cut** 라는 것을 atom에서 알 수 있다.
abstemious in the use of tobacco 담배를 절제하는

anatomy (해부학), **the anatomy of the frog** 개구리의 해부학적 구조

epitomize (발췌하다) epitome 요약 summary, outline 전형 representative,
the epitome of a perfect soldier, 완벽한 군인의 전형

dichotomy (양분법) the act of dividing into two parts
the dichotomy between good and evil 선과 악의 이분법

appendectomy (애펀댁터미) (맹장수술)
An appendectomy is a medical operation to remove appendix.
맹장절제술은 충양 돌기를 제거하는 의료적 수술 행위다.

2. **avert**[200]

가. 돌리다 turn away, **vert(vers)는 turn**이다.
He averted his eyes from the horrible sight.
그는 그 잔혹한 관경에서 그의 시야를 돌려버렸다.
나. 피하다, 막다 prevent, avoid,
Many highway accidents can be averted
많은 고속도로 사고들은 막을 수 있다.

averse (싫어하는/반대의) **Fear made her averse to fighting.** 겁이 나서 그녀는 싸움을 꺼리게 되었다.

---

199) 1. abstemious anatomy epitomize dichotomy appendectomy

200) 2. avert averse adverse adversity convert converse conversant divert diverse

adverse (불리한) <u>adverse</u> winds 역풍

adversity (역경) She was always cheerful in <u>adversity</u>. 그녀는 역경 속에서도 항상 유쾌했다.

convert (개종하다) <u>convert</u> a barn into a garage 헛간을 차고로 개조하다.

converse (대화하다/거꾸로) <u>converse</u> fluently in a foreign language 외국어로 유창하게 대화하다. I wanted to appear friendly and approachable, but I think I gave the <u>converse</u> impression. 나는 친근하고 접근하기 쉬운 사람으로 보이고 싶은데 내 생각엔 정반대의 인상을 풍기는 것 같다.

conversant (정통한) familiar with, having a knowledge of
<u>conversant</u> with a subject 한 과목을 잘 알고 있는

divert (전환하다) Nothing could <u>divert</u> his thoughts from his mother's sudden death. 그의 생각을 어머니의 갑작스러운 사망에서 딴 데로 돌릴 수 있는 것이 아무 것도 없었다.

diverse (다양한) <u>Diverse</u> opinions were expressed at the meeting. 모임에서는 다양한 의견들이 나왔다.

3. abominable[201]

몹시 싫은, 무서운 hateful, horrible. <u>om(hom)은 man</u>이다.
The weather was <u>abominable</u>. 날씨가 지독했다.

homage (존경) We pay <u>homage</u> to the genius of Shakespeare. 우리는 셰익스피어의 천재성에 경의를 표한다.

---

201) 3. abominable homage humane humiliate homicide humble

humane (자비의) It's not <u>humane</u> to treat people like that. 사람들을 그렇게 대하는 것은 비인간적이다.

humiliate (굴욕감을 주다) We didn't just win, we <u>humiliated</u> them! 우리는 그냥 이긴 게 아니라 그들의 코를 납작하게 해주었어!

homicide (살인) He was convicted of <u>homicide</u>. 그는 살인 혐의로 기소되었다.

humble (겸손한) He is <u>humble</u> in his manner. 그의 태도는 겸손하다.

4. **ab<u>dic</u>ate**[202]

포기하다, 물러나다 abandon, resign, **<u>dic(dict)</u>은 say** 이다.
<u>abdic</u>ate from the throne 왕관을 양위하다.

addict (중독) Don't <u>addict</u> yourself to gambling. 도박에 몰두하지 마라.

predict (예언하다) It's too early to <u>predict</u> the outcome of the meeting. 그 회동의 결과를 예측하기에는 너무 이르다.

indict (기소하다) They <u>indicted</u> people they knew to be innocent. 그들은 그들이 무죄라고 알았던 사람들을 기소했다.

contradict (반박하다) The facts <u>contradict</u> the theory. 그 사실은 이론과 상반된다.

verdict (평결) The jury returned a unanimous <u>verdict</u> of guilty after a short deliberation. 배심원들은 짧은 토론 끝에 만장일치의 유죄 평결로 답신했다.

interdict (금지하다) an official order forbidding someone to do something.

202) 4. abdicate addict predict indict contradict verdict interdict benediction malediction valediction valedictory jurisdiction

benediction (축복) a prayer giving blessing, especially at the end of a religious service.

malediction (저주) a curse or defamation.
valediction (고별사) the act of saying farewell; a farewell.

valedictory 졸업식의 고별사 an address of farewell at the ceremony of graduation from school.

jurisdiction (재판권) **The court has no jurisdiction over foreign diplomats.** 그 법원은 외국 외교관에 대하여 사법권이 없다.

5. abrogate[203]

폐지하다 abolish, repeal, **rog는 ask** 이다.
abrogate a treaty 조약을 폐지하다.

arrogate (사칭하다) take something to oneself without right, 탓으로 돌리다 attribute without good reason,
arrogate bad motives to other people.
나쁜 동기를 다른 사람의 탓으로 돌리다.

arrogant (건방진) **It was arrogant of them to expect us to do all the work.** 우리가 그 모든 일을 다 할 것으로 기대하다니 그들은 오만했다.

prerogative (특권) **It is a woman's prerogative to bear children.**
아이를 낳는 것은 여성의 특권이다.

derogate (데러게잇) (손상시키다) take away fame, detract,

---

203) 5. abrogate arrogate arrogant prerogative derogate interrogate

<u>derogate</u> from one's authority. 권위를 손상시키다.

interrogate (조사하다) examine by questioning.

6. **avocation**[204]

부업, 취미 an occupation besides one's regular work, hobby

<u>voc(vok)는 voice, call</u> 이다.

convoke (소집하다) <u>convoke</u> Parliament 국회를 소집하다

provoke (성나게 하다) make angry, stir up, irritate,
She was <u>provoked</u> at his remark. 그녀는 그의 말에 화가 났다.

evoke (불러일으키다) **That smell always <u>evokes</u> memories of my old school.** 저 냄새는 언제나 내가 옛날에 다닌 학교의 추억을 불러일으킨다.

advocate (지지하다, 옹호자), **Gandhi was an <u>advocate</u> of nonviolence.** 간디는 비폭력의 주창자였다.

invoke (빌다) **<u>Invoking</u> morality on this occasion would not be appropriate.** 이 상황에서 도덕성에 호소하는 것은 적절치 않을 것이다.

revoke (취소하다) **He had his sentence <u>revoked</u>.** 그는 그의 판결을 파기했다.

7. **abound**[205]

풍부하다 be rich in, <u>und는 wave</u> 이다.
Fish <u>abound</u> in this river.

---

204) 6. avocation convoke provoke evoke advocate invoke revoke
205) 7. abound inundate redundant undulate

inundate 이넌데잇 (범람시키다) **The river burst its banks and inundated near by villages.** 강물이 강둑을 허물어서 근처의 마을을 침수시켰다.

redundant (여분의) **In the sentence 'She is a single unmarried woman,' the word 'unmarried' is redundant.** '그녀는 독신의 결혼하지 않은 여성이다'라는 문장에서'결혼하지 않은'은 불필요한 말이다.

undulate (물결치다) **undulating hills** 기복이 심한 산

8. **abstruse**[206)]

난해한, difficult to understand, **trus(trud)는 thrust** 이다.
abstruse questions 어려운 질문들

extrude 익스츄르드 (밀어내다) **extrude glue from a tube** 튜브에서 풀을 짜내다.

intrude (침입, 강요하다) **Don't intrude yourself on her privacy.** 그녀의 사생활에 끼어들지 마시오.

obtrude (강요하다) **push one's opinions forward against other's will, force oneself upon others, Don't obtrude your opinions upon others.** 너의 의견을 다른 사람들에게 강요하지 마라.

protrude (불쑥 내밀다) **He managed to hang on to a piece of rock protruding from the cliff face.** 그는 절벽 면에 튀어나온 바위 하나에 간신히 매달렸다.

9. **abase**[207)]

지위나 품격 따위를 떨어뜨리다, make lower in rank, position. humble,

---

206) 8. abstruse extrude intrude obtrude protrude
207) 9. abase debase baseless

base 는 기초이다.
He was abased for his crimes. 그는 그의 범죄로 품위가 떨어졌다.

debase (타락시키다) You debase yourself by telling such lies. 너는 그런 거짓말을 해서 너의 격을 떨어뜨리고 있어.

baseless (근거 없는) All the Chadian allegations are baseless, spokesman Ibrahim added. 이브라힘 대변인은 차드 정부의 주장은 모두 근거 없는 것이라고 일축했습니다.

10. access[208]

ces(ced)는 go이다.

accede (동의, 접근하다) They acceded to our demands. 그들은 우리의 요구에 따랐다.

concede (마지못해 동의하다) He finally conceded the election to his opponent. 그는 결국 상대 후보의 당선을 인정했다.

proceed (나아가다) The storm forbids us to proceed. 폭풍우 때문에 우리는 전진하지 못한다.

precede (앞서다) the events that preceded this 이것에 선행된 사건들

precedent (선례) There is no precedent for it. 그것에 대한 전례가 없다.

recede (퇴각하다) As the tide receded from the shore we were able to look for shells. 해변에서 물이 빠져나가자 우리는 조개껍질을 찾을 수 있었다.

---

208) 10. access accede concede proceed precede precedent recede recess proced

recess (휴식) The National Assembly is in <u>recess</u>. 국회는 휴회 중이다.

procedure <u>프로씨저</u>, (순서, 절차) It's a <u>complicated</u> procedure. 이는 복잡한 절차입니다.

11. acclaim²⁰⁹⁾

갈채를 보내다 welcome with praise and applause along with loud shouts.
<u>claim</u> 은 <u>cry out</u> 이다.
<u>acclaim</u> the victor. 그 승리에 갈채를 보내다.

declaim (항의, 비난하다) A preacher was <u>declaiming</u> against the ills of modern society. 한 설교자가 현대사회의 해악들에 대해 비난을 퍼붓고 있었다.

disclaim (포기하다) We <u>disclaim</u> all responsibility for this disaster. 우리는 이 재난에 대한 모든 책임을 부인한다.

proclaim (선언하다) The president <u>proclaimed</u> to the nation that new currency would be issued. 대통령은 국민에게 새로운 통화가 발행될 것임을 공표했다.

exclaim (외치다) He <u>exclaimed</u> that he was innocent. 그는 자신이 결백하다고 외쳤다.

reclaim (개간, 교정하다) I went to the station to <u>reclaim</u> my suitcase from the left luggage office. 나는 잔류 수하물 사무소에서 여행 가방을 되찾기 위해 역으로 갔다.

clamorous (소란스러운) The newspaper devoted 7 pages to a <u>clamorous</u> call for independence. 그 신문은 독립에 대한 소리 높은 요구에 7 페이지나 할애했다.

---

209) 11. acclaim declaim disclaim proclaim exclaim reclaim clamorous

12. **accomplice**[210]

공범자 a person who helps another in a wrong act,

<u>pli(ply)는 fold</u> 이다.

an <u>accomplice</u> in murder 살인사건의 공범자

complicity (공모) He was suspected of <u>complicity</u> in her murder. 그는 그녀의 살인에 공모 혐의를 받았다.

complicate (복잡하게 하다) Her refusal to help <u>complicates</u> matters. 그녀가 돕기를 거절해서 일이 더 복잡하게 되었다.

apply (적용, 신청하다) Those interested should <u>apply</u> immediately. 희망자는 즉시 신청하시오.

explicit 익스플리씻 (명백한) He was quite <u>explicit</u> on that point. 그는 그 점에 대해서 조금도 숨김이 없었다.

replica (복사) She was a cheerful <u>replica</u> of her mother. 그녀는 신기할 정도로 엄마를 빼쏘았다.

supplicate (간청하다) to humbly and earnestly request it.

applicable (적용할 수 있는) This regulation is not <u>applicable</u> to this case. 이 규정은 이 경우에는 적용되지 않는다.

13. **accord**[211]

가. 주다, give, <u>cord 는 heart</u> 이다.

They <u>accorded</u> a hearty welcome to me.

---

210) 12. accomplice complicity complicate apply explicit replica supplicate applica

211) 13. accord concord discord cordial

그들은 나에게 가슴에서 우러나오는 환영을 해 주었다.

나. 일치하다 agree,

His account of the day accords with yours.

그 날에 대한 그의 설명은 너의 설명과 일치하지 않는다.

concord (조화) 칸코드 **There was complete concord among the delegates.** 대표들 간에 완전한 의견의 일치를 보았다.

discord (불화) **The letter caused discord between uncle and nephew.** 그 편지는 숙부와 조카 사이의 불화를 초래했다.

cordial (진심에서의) **Ties between the two nations have always been described as friendly and cordial.** 양국 관계는 항상 가깝고 우호적인 것으로 알려져 왔다.

14. **accommodate**[212]

가. 조화시키다 make fit, adapt, **mod는 fit** 이다.

accommodate oneself to circumstances

나. 숙박시키다 have rooms for,

The hospital can accommodate 300 patients.

modish (유행의), stylish; fashionable

demode (구식의), outmoded

moderate (절제하는), **They were moderate in their demands.** 그들의 요구에는 무리가 없었다.

commodious (널찍한) **a commodious house** 널찍한 집

---

212) 14. accommodate modish demode moderate commodious

15. **accrue**[213]

더 해지다, come as a natural result, **cru(cre)는 grow** 이다.
이자가 생기다 interest accruing from principal
increment (이윤), **You will receive annual salary increments every Septem
ber.** 당신은 매년 9월에 연중 봉급 인상을 받게 될 것입니다.

crescent (초승달) (크레쓴) **The moon was a brightly shining crescent.** 초승달
이 밝게 빛나고 있었다.

16. **acquisitive**[214]

탐내는 eager to get and keep as one's own, **quisit 는 ask** 이다.
an acquisitive collector 욕심 많은 수집가

inquisitive (호기심이 많은), sour to learn, curious,
Children are inquisitive.

disquisition (논문), a long and detailed discussion of a subject in speech or
writing

requisite (필수의), 레쿠어짓, **have the requisite experience for the job**
그 일자리에 필요한 경험을 가지다

prerequisite (선행조건) **A degree is a prerequisite for employment at this
level.** 이런 수준의 취업에는 학위가 필수조건이다.

---

213) 15. accrue increment crescent
214) 16. acquisitive inquisitive disquisition requisite prerequisite

17. acquit[215]

무죄 방면하다 set - free from a charge of crime or from duty, <u>qui</u>는 quiet 이다.

They <u>acquitted</u> him of the charge.

acquiesce (순종하다), 엑쿠이에스, His parents will never <u>acquiesce</u> in such an unsuitable marriage. 그의 부모들은 그런 부적합한 결혼을 결코 받아들이지 않을 것이다.

disquiet (불안하게 하다), The rising crime figures are certainly <u>disquieting</u>. 범죄 증가 수치는 분명히 걱정스럽다.

quietude (고요, 정적), quietness; tranquillity

quiescent (고요한), 큐이에쓴트, / It is unlikely that the terrorists will remain <u>qui</u> <u>escent</u> for long. 테러범들이 한동안 활동을 안 할 것 같지는 않다.

18. aff<u>a</u>ble[216]

상냥한 friendly and polite, <u>fa</u>는 say 이다.

He has a very <u>affable</u> manner.

fable (우화), Even adults have a taste for <u>fable</u>, fantasy and magic. 성인들도 우화와 판타지, 마술에 취미를 가진다.

ineffable (형언할 수 없는), unable to be described or expressed in words, especially because of size, magnificence, etc

---

215) 17. acquit acquiesce disquiet quietude quiescent

216) 18. affable fable ineffable fabulous defame defamation

fabulous (엄청난, 전설적인), <u>fabulous</u> wealth 엄청난 재산

<u>fabulous</u> heroes 전설적인 영웅

defame (비방하다), The article is an attempt to <u>defame</u> an honest man. 그 기사는 정직한 사람을 중상하려는 시도이다.

defamation (명예훼손) He is suing for <u>defamation</u> of character. 그는 명예 훼손으로 소송을 제기한다.

19. **adjacent**[217)]

인접한 next to, <u>jac(ject)는 throw</u> 이다.

The garage is <u>adjacent</u> to our house.

abject (비참한), They live in <u>abject</u> poverty. 그들은 극빈 속에 산다.

inject (주사하다), He tried to <u>inject</u> some life into the club. 그는 그 클럽에 다소 활기를 불어넣으려 했다.

conjecture (추측하다), Her <u>conjecture</u> that the election would be a landslide proved to be true. 선거에서 압승을 거둘 것이라는 그녀의 추측이 옳았음이 증명되었다.

eject (추방하다), <u>eject</u> an invading army 침입해오는 군대를 몰아내다

reject (거절하다) He had the presumption to <u>reject</u> the proposal. 그는 건방지게도 그 제의를 거절했다.

---

217) 19. adjacent abject inject conjecture eject reject

20. advent[218]

도래 arrival / vent는 come 이다.

adventitious (우연의), 애드벤티셔스, happening by chance; accidental.

intervene (중재하다), I tried to intervene between the two friends. 나는 두 친구 사이를 중재하려고 애썼다.

revenue (세입), 레버뉴, Taxes provide most of the government's revenue. 세금이 정부 세입의 대부분을 차지한다.

supervene (잇달아 일어나다), She was working well until illness supervened. 그녀는 병이 찾아들 때까지는 일을 잘 하고 있었다.

convene (소집하다), The committee will convene at 9.30 tomorrow morning. 위원회는 내일 아침 9시 30분에 소집합니다.

contravene (위반하다), The penalties for contravening that law are very serious. 그 법을 위반하면 처벌이 매우 중하다.

venue (개최지) Her lawyer requested a change of venue. 그녀의 변호사는 재판장소의 변경을 요구했다.

21. affinity[219]

가. 유사 likeness, fin은 end 이다.
나. 좋아함, liking
There's an affinity between two persons.
두 사람 간에는 인척 관계가 있다.

---

218) 20. advent adventitious intervene revenue supervene convene contravene venu

219) 21. affinity finite definite confine define definitive

finite (제한된), Human understanding is <u>finite</u>. 인간의 이해력은 한정되어 있다.

definite (명확한), She was <u>definite</u> about it. 그녀는 그것에 대해서 확신하고 있었다.

confine (제한하다, 감금하다), Please <u>confine</u> your remarks to the fact. 그 사실에만 국한해서 발언해 주시오.

define (정의를 내리다), It is very difficult to <u>define</u> the concept of beauty. 미의 개념을 정의하기란 너무 어렵다.

definitive (최종적인) There are no <u>definitive</u> answers to this problem. 이 문제에는 명확한 답이 없다.

22. **<u>affront</u>**[220]

모욕하다 insult someone openly and on purpose, <u>front</u> 은 <u>face,</u>
He <u>affronted</u> her before her husband.

confront (직면하다), <u>confront</u> a prisoner with a witness 형사 피고인을 목격자와 대면시키다.

effrontery (뻔뻔스러움), He had the <u>effrontery</u> to demand more money. 그는 뻔뻔스럽게도 돈을 더 요구했다.

frontier (국경지대), <u>frontier</u> disputes 국경 분쟁

---

220) 22. affront confront effrontery frontier

23. **aggravate**[221]

가. 악화시키다 make worse, **grav는 heavy** 이다.

나. 성나게 하다 make angry

He **aggravated** his condition by leaving hospital too soon.

그는 너무 일찍 퇴원함으로써 자신의 상태를 악화시켰다.

grave (무덤, 무거운), **This could have grave consequences.** 이 일이 중대한 결과를 초래할 수도 있다.

grievous (슬픈), **She was crying over the grievous news.** 그녀는 그 슬픈 소식을 애통해 하고 있었다.

gravity (중력), **Things fall to the ground because of gravity.** 물체는 중력 때문에 땅으로 떨어진다.

(293)

24. **allege**[222]

증거 없이 주장하다 assertion without proof, **leg는 send** 이다.

The two men **allege** that the police forced them to make false confessions.

그 두 남자는 경찰이 강제로 거짓 자백을 하게 만들었다고 주장했다.

delegate (대표자, 위임하다), He **delegated** his responsibilities to a deputy. 그는 자신의 책무를 대리인에게 위임했다.

relegate (좌천시키다), send someone to a lower position, **relegate an agitator beyond the city limits.** 소요 선동자를 도시 범위 밖으로 내 보내다.

legacy (유산), **An elderly cousin had left her a small legacy.** 중년을 지난 사촌

한 사람이 그녀에게 작은 유산을 물려주었다.

25. allegiance[223]

충성 loyalty, <u>leg</u>는 law 이다.
She proudly recited the Oath of <u>Allegiance.</u>
그녀는 자랑스럽게 충성 맹세를 암송했다.

legal (합법의), Fishing is not <u>legal</u> in this area. 이 지역은 낚시 금지 구역이다.

privilege (특권, 특권을 주다), <u>privilege</u> him to receive secret information.
그에게 비밀정보를 입수할 수 있는 특권을 주다.

legislate (법률제정하다), He promised to <u>legislate</u> against abortion.
그는 임신 중절을 금하는 법을 제정하겠다고 약속했다.

legitimate (합법적인) Both regimes claimed to be Korea's <u>legitimate</u> government. 양 정권은 각기 자신들이 한국의 합법적인 정부라고 주장했다.

26. alleviate[224]

완화하다 lighten, <u>lev</u> 는 light, lift 이다.
The drugs did nothing to <u>alleviate</u> her pain.
그 약들은 그녀의 통증을 진정시키는 데 아무 효과가 없었다.

levy (부과하다), They are going to <u>levy</u> some new taxes.
그들은 몇 가지 새로운 세금을 징수하려고 한다.

elevate (들어 올리다), She hoped to <u>elevate</u> the minds of her young students

---

by reading them religious stories. 그녀는 어린 학생들에게 종교적인 이야기를 읽어 줌으로써 그들의 마음을 고양할 수 있기를 바랐다.

27. allay[225)]

진정시키다. lessen, mitigate, <u>ly(li, lig)</u>는 <u>bind</u> 이다.
The government is desperately trying to <u>allay</u> public concern about the spread of the disease. 정부는 필사적으로 그 질병의 확산에 대한 일반 시민들의 우려를 진정시키려 하고 있다.

liable 가. -할 경향이 있는 apt or likely to do, He is <u>liable</u> to catch cold.
나. 책임이 있는 be responsible legally, **He is <u>liable</u> to pay his wife's debts.**

liability (책임), **We assumed full <u>liability</u> for our children's debts.**
우리는 우리 아이들이 빌린 돈에 대해 전적으로 책임을 졌다.

rely (의지하다), **You can <u>rely upon</u> him.** 그는 믿을 수 있다.

reliance (신뢰), **Don't place too much <u>reliance</u> on others.**
남을 지나치게 신뢰하지 마라.

oblige 가. (강요하다), force or compel , **I am <u>obliged</u> to leave early to catch my train.**
나. 친절을 베풀다 <u>oblige</u> me by shutting the door.

obligation (의무) **A delinquent person is one who fails to do what law or <u>ob ligation</u> requires.** 직무 태만한 사람이란 법이나 의무가 요구하는 바를 이행하지 못하는 사람이다.

---

28. **append**[226]

첨가하다 attach, add, pend(pens)는 hang 이다.

append an extra clause to the contract 계약서에 추가 조항을 부가하다

appendix (부록), The book has a long appendix. 그 책에는 부록이 길게 붙어 있다.

appendage (부가 물), The elephant's trunk is a highly versatile appendage. 코끼리의 코는 대단히 쓸모가 많은 부속기관이다.

compendium (요약), outline, a compendium of modern medicine 개론

pending (미결의), Her application is pending. 그녀의 신청서는 보류중이다.

impending (절박한), Let's discuss the impending matter first. 우선 시급한 문제부터 협의합시다.

suspend (정지하다) One measure will suspend payments on foreign loans for six months. 조치들 중 하나는 앞으로 6개월간 외국의 외채 상환을 중단하는 것입니다.

29. **apprise**[227]

알리다 inform, prise는 take 이다.

I was apprised of the committee's decision. 난 위원회의 결정을 통고 받았다.

comprise (포함하다), The committee comprises six members.

---

226) 28. append appendix appendage compendium pending impending suspend

227) 29. apprise comprise reprisal imprison enterprising

그 위원회는 여섯 명의 위원으로 이루어져 있다.

reprisal (보복), They shot 10 hostages in reprisal.
그들은 보복조치로 인질 10명을 사살했다.

imprison (투옥하다), The men were imprisoned and tortured.
그 남자들은 투옥되고 고문을 받았다.

enterprising (진취적인) He is an enterprising businessman. 그는 진취적인 실업가다.

30. aspirant[228]

야심가 an ambitious person, spire는 breathe 이다.
aspirants to the presidency 대통령 지망자

aspiring (포부 있는), He is an aspiring and hard-working young manager. 그는 포부가 있고 부지런한 젊은 부장이다.

conspire (공모하다), They were charged with conspiring to pervert the course of justice. 그들은 정의의 진행을 왜곡시키려는 음모를 꾸민 혐의를 받았다.

suspire (한 숨 쉬다)
expire (기간이 다하다), When does the patent expire? 그 특허는 언제 기한이 만료되는가?

respire (숨 쉬다) Some reptiles respire through their skin. 일부 파충류는 피부로 호흡한다.

---

228) 30. aspirant aspiring conspire suspire expire respire

31. **assent**[229]

동의하다 agree to, **sent(sens)**는 **feel** 이다.
give one's **assent** to a proposal 제안에 동의하다

dissent (의견차이), In those days, religious **dissent** was not tolerated.
그 시절에는 종교적 반대는 용납되지 않았다.

presentiment (예감), She had a **presentiment** that an accident would happen. 그녀는 사고가 일어날 것이라고 예감했다.

resent (분개하다), I **resent** his being too arrogant. 나는 그가 너무 오만한 것에 분개한다.

sensible (분별 있는), The **sensible** solution to this problem is to talk about the disagreements and try to compromise. 이 문제에 대한 현명한 해결 방안은 의견의 불일치에 대해 토의하고 타협하려고 노력하는 것이다.

sensual (관능적인), of the pleasure of the bodily senses, not mental or spiritual, **sensual** pleasures, 관능적(육체적) 쾌락

32. **assess**[230]

평가하다 determine the value of, **sess(sed)**는 **sit**이다.
I'd **assess** your chances as extremely low.
나는 당신의 가능성을 매우 낮게 평가합니다.
obsess (홀리다), fill the mind with a fear, **She is always obsessed by the idea of her own inferiority.**

---

229) 31. assent dissent presentiment resent sensible sensual
230) 32. assess obsess obsession session sedentary supersede sediment

obsession (강박관념), Her fear is bordering on obsession.
그녀의 공포는 강박관념에 근사해지고 있다.

session (학기), The Senate is in session. 상원은 개회중이다.

sedentary (앉아있는), My doctor says I should start playing sport because my lifestyle is too sedentary. 내 주치의는 내 생활 방식이 너무 앉아만 있는 것이라서 운동을 시작해야 한다고 말한다.
supersede (대신하다), to take the place of

sediment (침전) There was a brown sediment in the bottom of the bottle.
그 병의 바닥에는 갈색 침전물이 있었다.

33. assiduous[231]

근면한 diligent, sid는 sit 이다.
The book was the result of ten years assiduous research.
그 책은 10년간의 주도면밀한 연구의 결과이다.

insidious (음흉한, 잠행성의), You'd be better be careful of his insidious character. 당신은 그의 음흉한 성격을 조심하는 것이 좋을 것이다.

preside (의장이 되다, 사회보다), Who will preside over the meeting?
누가 회의의 사회를 맡게 되는가?

subside (누그러지다), The police are hoping that the violence will soon subside. 경찰은 폭력이 곧 진정되기를 바라고 있다.

reside (살다), They reside in London. 그들은 런던에 살고 있다.

---

231) 33. assiduous insidious preside subside reside resident residue

resident (거주자), I don't have a social security number. I'm not a U.S. resident. 사회보장 번호가 없는데요. 미국 시민이 아니거든요.

residue (나머지) The <u>residue</u> of the estate goes to his daughter.
이 토지의 잔여분은 그의 딸에게 넘어간다.

34. **attain**[232]

달성하다 reach, <u>tain(ten)</u>은 <u>hold</u> 이다.
It is now impossible to <u>attain</u> your ambition.

abstain (삼가다), You should <u>abstain</u> from smoking in the office. 사무실에서는 금연이다.

sustain (유지하다), We do not have sufficient resources to <u>sustain</u> our campaign for long. 우리에게는 우리의 캠페인을 오랫동안 지속할 만한 충분한 재력이 없다.

contain (포함하다), What does that box <u>contain</u>? 그 상자에는 무엇이 들어 있니?

pertain (속하다), Your remark does not <u>pertain</u> to the question.
너의 발언은 그 문제와는 관계가 없다.

pertinent (적절한), Is it <u>pertinent</u> to cite those facts?
그 사실들을 인용하는 것이 적절합니까?

detain (억류하다), He was <u>detained</u> for questioning.
그는 심문을 받기 위해 억류되었다.

---

232) 34. attain abstain sustain contain pertain pertinent detain retain retentive

retain (보유하다), Sign and date the form at the bottom and <u>retain</u> the pink copy for your records. 용지 하단에 서명을 하고 날짜를 기입한 후 분홍색 용지는 보관해 두세요.

retentive (보유하는) She has a <u>retentive</u> memory. 그녀는 뛰어난 기억력의 소유자이다.

35. **attenuate**[233]

약화시키다 lessen, <u>tenu는 thin</u> 이다.

<u>attenuated</u> limbs 쇠약한 팔다리

tenuous (엷은), I found an excuse to phone her, but it was rather <u>tenuous</u>. 그녀에게 전화할 구실을 찾긴 했지만 좀 빈약했다.

extenuate (정상참작하다) Nothing can <u>extenuate</u> his guilt. 그의 죄과에는 정상을 참작할 여지가 없다.

36. **attribute**[234]

탓으로 하다 , 속성 , <u>tribute 는 give</u> 이다.

I <u>attribute</u> my success to hard work.

나는 나의 성공이 열심히 노력한 덕분이라고 생각한다.

contribute (공헌하다), Science has <u>contributed</u> much to modern technology. 과학은 현대 과학기술에 많은 기여를 했다.

retribution (보복), Some people saw her death as divine <u>retribution</u> for her crimes. 어떤 이들은 그녀의 죽음을 두고 그녀가 저지른 범죄에 대해 하늘이 내린 벌이라고 생각했다.

---

233) 35. attenuate tenuous extenuate

234) 36. attribute contribute retribution distribute tribute

distribute (분배하다), The instructor <u>distributed</u> the test papers to the students. 교사가 학생들에게 시험지를 나누어주었다.

tribute (공물) A large portion of the <u>tribute</u> was paid in money.
공물의 상당 부분은 돈으로 지불됐다.

37. agnostic[235]

불가지론자, <u>gno는 know</u> 이다.
Although he was born a Catholic, he was an <u>agnostic</u> for most of his adult life. 그는 가톨릭교도로 태어났지만, 성인이 된 후에는 대부분 불가지론자로 지냈다.

ignoble (비천한), To betray a friend is <u>ignoble</u>. 친구를 배신하는 것은 비열하다.

ignominious (수치스러운), an <u>ignominious</u> defeat 불명예스러운 패배

prognostic (예견하는), belonging or relating to a prognosis

prognosticate (예언하다), to foretell.

cognition (인식) One of the things we try to do in therapy is to help clients to minimize their negative <u>cognitions</u>. 우리가 치료에서 시도하려는 것 중 하나는 고객들이 자신의 부정적 인식을 최소화하도록 도와주는 것이다.

38. ambiguous[236]

애매한 obscure, <u>ig(g, ag)는 drive</u>이다.
Her speech was deliberately <u>ambiguous</u> to avoid offending either side.
그녀의 연설은 어느 쪽도 자극하지 않으려고, 의도적으로 애매했다.

---

235) 37. agnostic ignoble ignominious prognostic prognosticate cognition
236) 38. ambiguous agitate cogent prodigal exigency navigate intransigent

agitate (동요시키다), <u>agitate</u> for tax reform 세제 개혁을 요구하다

cogent (설득력 있는), He produced <u>cogent</u> reasons for the change of policy.
그는 정책 변화에 대해 설득력 있는 이유를 내놓았다.

prodigal (방탕한), "After a thrifty father, a <u>prodigal</u> son." 절약하는 아버지 밑
에 낭비하는 자식.

exigency (급박), Economic <u>exigency</u> obliged the government to act. 경제적
위기 때문에 정부가 나설 수밖에 없었다.

navigate (항해하다), They will <u>navigate</u> throughout the Pacific. 그들은 태평
상 횡단 항해를 할 것이다.

intransigent (비타협적인 사람) Owing to their <u>intransigent</u> attitude we were
unable to reach an agreement. 그들의 비합리적인 태도 때문에 우리는 협정에
도달할 수 없었다.

39. amb<u>i</u>valence[237]

이중의식, 우유부단, <u>val</u>은 <u>value</u>이다.
There is much <u>ambivalence</u> about our involvement in the war.
우리가 전쟁에 연루되는 것에 대해 많은 상반되는 감정이 공존하고 있다.

available (유용한), You will be informed when the book becomes
available. 그 책을 구입할 수 있을 때, 알려 드리겠습니다.

convalesce (건강회복하다), She went to the mountains to <u>convalesce</u> after
leaving hospital. 그녀는 퇴원해서 산으로 요양을 하러 갔다.

---

237) 39. ambivalence available convalesce equivalent prevail evaluate invalidate

equivalent (동등한), These two diamonds are <u>equivalent</u> in value. 이 두 개의 다이아몬드는 동등한 값어치를 지니고 있다.

prevail (우세하다), Such ideas <u>prevail</u> these days. 그런 생각들이 우세하다.

evaluate (평가하다), He was evaluated as unfit for military service. 그는 병역 부적격 판정을 받았다.

invalidate (무효로 하다) The Nepal's Cabinet said it will <u>invalidate</u> legislation, appointments, decrees and other actions taken since the monarch took absolute power in February 2005. 네팔 내각은 지난 2005년 2월 국왕이 절대 권력을 장악한 이후 취해진 입법과 정치적 임명, 명령 및 행동들을 취소할 것이라고 말했습니다.

40. beneficence[238]

(선행) <u>fic (fict)</u>는 do, make 이다.

fictitious (허위의), The actor has dismissed the recent rumors about his private life as <u>fictitious</u> and malicious. 그 배우는 자신의 사생활에 관한 최근의 소문을 거짓되고 악의적인 것이라고 일축했다.

efficacious (유효한), 에퍼케이서스, She decided it would be more efficacious to remain silent. 그녀는 잠자코 있는 것이 더 효력이 있겠다고 맘먹었다.

munificent (아낌없이 주는), A former student has donated a <u>munificent</u> sum of money to the college. 예전에 그 대학의 학생이었던 사람이 학교에 돈을 아낌 없이 기부했다.

beneficial (유익한), Using computers has a beneficial effect on children's

---

238) 40. beneficence fictitious efficacious munificent beneficial beneficiary deficient officiate officious

learning. 컴퓨터 이용이 어린이들의 학습에 유익한 영향을 미친다.

beneficiary (수익자), (베너피쉬에리) Her husband was the chief beneficiary of her will. 그녀의 남편이 그녀가 남긴 유언의 최고 수혜자였다.

deficient (모자라는), She is <u>deficient</u> in common sense. 그녀는 상식이 부족하다.

officiate (사회보다), The bishop will <u>officiate</u> at the wedding. 주교가 그 결혼식을 집전할 것이다.

officious (참견하는) I'm tired of being pushed around by <u>officious</u> civil servants. 나는 간섭하기 좋아하는 공무원들에게 둘러싸여 압박 받는 것에 질렸다.

41. benign[239]

친절한 kind, 양성의 반대말은 malignant, **gn(gen)은 <u>birth</u>** 이다.
On a warm sunny day the river seems placid and <u>benign</u>.
따뜻하고 햇볕 나는 날에는 그 강은 평온하고 온화해 보인다.

generate (발생시키다), Solar cells <u>generate</u> electricity directly when struck by sunlight. 태양 전지들은 햇빛을 받으면 곧 전기를 발생시킨다.

degenerate (타락하다), His health is <u>degenerating</u> rapidly. 그의 건강이 급격히 나빠지고 있다.

regenerate (갱생시키다), Some animals can <u>regenerate</u> lost parts of the body. 어떤 동물은 손상된 몸의 일부를 재생시킬 수도 있다.

ingenuous (솔직한), 인제뉴어스, Children are more <u>ingenuous</u> than adults.

---

239) 41. benign generate degenerate regenerate ingenuous congenial congenital cognate

아이들은 어른들보다 솔직하다.

congenial (같은 성질의), He was <u>congenial</u> to company. 그는 일행과 마음이 맞았다.

congenital (선천적인), **A <u>congenital</u> liar is someone who is always lying.** 타고난 거짓말쟁이란 언제나 거짓말을 일삼는 사람을 말한다.

cognate (같은 기원의), cognate language

42. bona fide[240]

성실한 sincere, <u>fide</u>는 <u>trust</u>이다.
His <u>bona fides</u> remain unproven. 그의 진실은 증명되지 않았다.

confide (신뢰하다), **You can <u>confide</u> in his good faith.** 그의 성실성은 믿을 만하다.

confidence (신용), **He lacks <u>confidence</u>.** 그는 자신감이 부족하다.

confident (확신하는), **We were <u>confident</u> of success.** 우리는 성공을 확신하고 있었다.

confidential (기밀의), 칸피덴셜, / **This is strictly <u>confidential</u>.** 이것은 극비 사항이다.

fidelity (충실), **Marital <u>fidelity</u> is not valued as highly as it once was.** 부부간의 정절이 옛날만큼 귀하게 여겨지지 않는다.

---

240) 42. bona fide confide confidence confident confidential fidelity infidelity diffident perfidious

infidelity (배신), She tolerated her husband's frequent infidelities.
그녀는 그녀 남편이 종종 바람피우는 것을 참았다.

diffident (자신 없는), an able but diffident young student 능력은 있지만 내성적인 학생

perfidious (배반하는) She described the new criminal bill as a perfidious at tack on democracy. 그녀는 새 형법을 가리켜 민주주의를 배반하는 공격이라고 묘사했다.

43. **bisect**[241]

이등분하다, sect는 cut이다.
The new road will bisect the town.
새 도로는 그 도시를 두 부분으로 나눌 것이다.

insect (곤충), The insect simulates the appearance of a leaf. 그 곤충은 잎으로 가장한다.

vivisect (생체해부하다),

dissect (해부하다), The film has been minutely dissected by the critics.
그 영화는 비평가들에 의해 세세히 분석되었다.

intersect (가로지르다) This street intersects with the main road. 이 거리는 중심 도로와 교차 한다.

---

241) 43. bisect insect vivisect dissect intersect

44. collude[242]

공모하다, <u>lud(lus)</u>는 <u>play, laugh</u>이다.
His sisters <u>colluded</u> in keeping it secret.
그의 자매들은 그 일을 비밀로 하기로 결탁했다.

allude (언급하다), You <u>alluded</u> in your speech to certain developments, what exactly did you mean? 당신은 연설에서 특정한 전개 상황을 넌지시 비추셨는데, 그게 정확히 뭘 말씀하신 겁니까?

elude (회피하다), "Sorry, your name <u>eludes</u> me."
"죄송합니다만, 당신의 이름이 생각나질 않는군요."

delude (속이다.), You're <u>deluding</u> yourself if you think things will get better.
사정이 나아질 것이라고 생각한다면 당신은 스스로를 기만하는 것이다.

illusion (착각) He cherished the <u>illusion</u> that she loved him, but he was wrong. 그는 그녀가 자신을 사랑한다는 환상을 품고 있었지만, 사실은 그렇지 않았다.

45. commend[243]

칭찬하다, <u>mend(mand)</u>는 <u>order</u>이다.
The book has much to <u>commend</u> it. 그 책은 칭찬할 것이 많다

command (명령하다, 언어구사하다), The officer <u>commanded</u> his men to stop shooting. 장교가 병사들에게 사격중지를 명령했다.

commandeer (징발하다), <u>commandeering</u> private cars to transport troops

---

242) collude allude elude delude illusion
243) 45. commend command commandeer commanding demand remand mandate

군대를 수송하기 위해 개인 승용차를 징발하는

commanding (지휘하는, 위풍당당한), **a commanding voice** 위풍당당한 목소리

demand (요구하다), **The people demanded a republican system of govern ment.** 국민들은 공화 정치를 요구했다.

remand (하급법원에 환송하다, 다시 구류하다), **remanded in custody** 재 구류된 (=sent back to prison).

mandate (위임통치하다) a mandated territory.

46. **commotion**[244]

소요, mot는 move이다.
The children are making a lot of commotion.
아이들이 야단법석을 떨고 있다.

demote (강등시키다), **He was demoted to the rank of corporal.**
그는 하사 계급으로 강등되었다.

locomotion (운동), **A fish uses its fins for locomotion.** 물고기는 지느러미를 이용해 이동한다.

promote (승진시키다), **They have reformed their business regulations to promote foreign investment.** 그들은 해외 투자를 장려하기 위해 사업 규정을 개정했다.

emotion (감정), **Her writing appeals more to the intellect than the emotion.**
그녀의 글은 감정보다는 지성에 더 호소한다.

---

remote (먼) Robots are operated by <u>remote</u> control. 로봇은 원격 조정으로 작동된다.

47. **compassion**[245)]

연민, 동정, <u>pass(path)</u>는 <u>feel, suffer</u> 이다.

The government hasn't shown much <u>compassion</u> for the sufferers.

정부는 피해자들에게 별로 동정을 보이지 않았다.

passionate (열정적인), The Spanish are very <u>passionate</u>. 스페인 사람들은 매우 열정적이다.

dispassionate (냉정한), calm; unemotional

compatible (양립할 수 있는) We decided to separate when we realized we were not really <u>compatible</u>. 우리는 우리가 실지로 어울리지 않는다는 것을 깨닫고 헤어지기로 결정했다.

310

48. **compensate**[246)]

갚다, <u>pens(pend)</u>는 <u>pay</u>이다.

Nothing can <u>compensate</u> for the death of a loved one.

사랑하는 사람의 죽음을 보상할 수 있는 것은 아무것도 없다.

expend (소비하다), He had already <u>expended</u> large sums in pursuing his claim through the courts. 그는 법정에서 자사의 주장을 관철시키는데 많은 돈을 들였다.

recompense (갚다), 레컴팬스, pay back, reward, <u>recompense</u> employees for working overtime 직원들에게 시간외 근무에 대해 보상하다

---

245) 47. compassion passionate dispassionate compatible

246) 48. compensate expend recompense expenditure pension expense

expenditure (지출), <u>Expenditure</u> outgoes income. 지출이 수입보다 훨씬 많다.

pension (연금), He lived alone on his old-age <u>pension</u>. 그는 노령 연금을 받고 혼자 살았다.

expense (지출, 비용) A car is a great <u>expense</u>. 자동차는 돈이 많이 든다.

49. compliant[247]

순종하는, <u>pli(ple)</u>는 <u>fill</u>이다.
a more <u>compliant</u> attitude 더 순종적인 태도

compliment (칭찬), Thank you for your <u>compliment</u>. 칭찬해 주서서 감사합니다.
complimentary (무료의), Wine is <u>complimentary</u>. 포도주는 무료입니다.

complement (보충 물, 보충하다) Rice makes an excellent <u>complement</u> to a curry dish. 밥은 카레 요리와 훌륭하게 어울린다.
supplement (보충), something added to complete a thing.
Reader comments will be published in a later <u>supplement</u>. 독자 평은 차후 증보판에 실릴 것이다.

implement (도구, 이행하다) It is increasingly difficult to implement the agreement. 그 협약을 이행하기가 점점 더 어려워지고 있다.

50. concede[248]

양보하다, <u>cede(cess)</u>는 <u>go</u>이다.
I was forced to <u>concede</u> that she might be right.
나는 그녀가 옳을 지도 모른다고 인정해야만 했다.

---

247) 49. compliant compliment complimentary complement supplement implement

248) 50. concede intercede incessant unprecedented excess

intercede (중재하다), He had tried to <u>intercede</u> with the authorities for me. 그는 나를 위해 당국과 중재하려고 애썼다.

incessant (끊임없는), We had <u>incessant</u> rain last month. 지난달에는 끊임없이 비가 왔었다.

unprecedented (전례 없는, 언프레써댄티드), This century has witnessed environmental destruction on an <u>unprecedented</u> scale. 이 세기에 들어 우리는 환경파괴가 전례 없는 규모로 진행되는 것을 목격했다.

excess (과잉) He's drinking to <u>excess</u>. 그는 과도하게 술을 마신다.

51. **concur**[249]

동의하다, <u>cur</u>는 <u>run</u>이다.
I don't <u>concur</u> with you on this point.
이 점에서는 너와 의견이 같지 않다.

incur (자초하다), <u>incur</u> debts 빚을 지다
recur (재발하다) The symptoms tend to <u>recur</u>. 그 징후들은 재발하는 경향이 있다.

52. **condole**[250]

위로하다, <u>dole</u>은 <u>grieve</u> 이다.
<u>condole</u> with someone on the death of a parent
…에게 부모의 죽음에 대한 조의를 표하다.

doleful (슬픔에 잠긴), The dog looked at me with a <u>doleful</u> expression.

249) 51. concur incur recur
250) 52. condole doleful indolent dolorous

그 개는 슬픔에 잠긴 표정으로 나를 바라보았다.

indolent (나태한), **He was a fat and indolent person.** 그는 뚱뚱하고 나태한 사람이었다.

dolorous (슬픈) **Her music always has a faintly dolorous feel.** 그녀의 음악은 언제나 어렴풋이 슬픈 느낌이 든다.

53. conducive[251]

도움이 되는, duc(duct)는 lead 이다.
Temperance is conducive to long life. 절제는 장수를 가져온다.

aqueduct (수로, 엑쿠어덕), a channel or canal that carries water, especially one that is in the form of a tall bridge across a valley, river, etc

(313)

educe (끌어내다), to bring out or develop

subdue (정복하다), **The fire burned for 8 hours before the fire crews began to subdue it.** 그 화재는 소방 요원들이 진압하기 전까지 8시간 동안 타올랐다.

seduce (꼬드기다) **The promise of huge profits seduced him into parting with his money.** 엄청난 수익을 약속한다는 유혹에 넘어가서 그가 자기 돈을 내어놓았다.

54. confer[252]

가. 수여하다, fer 는 carry 이다.
The Queen conferred knighthoods on several distinguished men.

---

251) 53. conducive aqueduct educe subdue seduce
252) 54. confer defer differ differential deferment deference differentiate indiffe

여왕은 몇 몇 뛰어난 사람들에게 기사 작위를 수여했다.

나. 협의하다. **I should like sometime to <u>confer with</u> my lawyer.**
내 변호사와 협의하고 싶습니다.

defer (연기하다), **I couldn't help but <u>defer</u> departure.** 나는 출발을 연기하지 않을 수 없었다.

differ (구별되다), **We <u>differ</u> over many things.** 우리는 많은 것들에 대해 의견이 다르다.

differential (차별하는), <u>differential</u> **treatment of prisoners** 죄수의 차별 대우

deferment (연기), **Every male citizen is required to initiate military service within two years of graduation from high school, unless arrangements are made for a <u>deferment</u>.** 남자들은 징집 연기를 한 경우를 제외하고는 누구나 고등학교 졸업 이후 2년 내로 군 복무를 시작해야 한다.

deference (복종, 존경), **show <u>deference</u> to a judge** 판사에게 경의를 표하다

differentiate (구별하다, 디퍼렌쉬엣), **Language <u>differentiates</u> man from animals.** 언어의 유무가 사람과 동물을 구별 짓는다.

indifference (무관심) **He is angry at the <u>indifference</u> of the authorities to his plight.** 그는 그의 어려움에 무관심한 당국에 화가 났다.

55. **consecrate**[253]

신성하게 하다, <u>secr(sacr)</u>은 <u>holy</u> 이다.
The new church was <u>consecrated</u> by the Bishop of Chester.

---

253) 55. consecrate desecrate sacred execrate

그 새 교회는 체스터 주교에 의해 축성되었다.

desecrate (신성모독하다), **It's a crime to <u>desecrate</u> the country's flag.**
국기를 욕되게 하는 것은 범죄이다.

sacred (신성한), **Temples and churches are <u>sacred</u> buildings.**
사찰과 교회는 신성한 건물이다.

execrate (저주하다), to feel or express hatred or loathing of something.

execrable (저주할 만한) **I've never heard such an <u>execrable</u> performance of the concerto** (컨체토우, 협주곡). 나는 그렇게 지겨운 협주곡 연주를 들어본 적이 없다.

56. **consequence**[254]

결과, <u>seque</u>는 <u>follow</u>이다.
The accident was the inevitable <u>consequence</u> of carelessness.
그 사고는 부주의에서 발생한 필연적 결과였다.

consequential (결과로서 일어나는, 칸씨   셜), **She was injured and suffered a <u>consequential</u> loss of earnings.** 그녀는 부상을 입었고 그에 따른 수입 손실을 겪었다.

inconsequent (일관성이 없는), not following logically or reasonably; illogical.

subsequent (차후의, 후속적인), <u>Subsequent</u> events vindicated his innocence.
그 뒤의 사건이 그의 무죄를 입증했다.
obsequious (아첨하는, 업씨퀴이어스) **She is almost embarrassingly obsequi**

---

254) 56. consequence consequential inconsequent subsequent obsequious

<u>ous</u> to anyone in authority. 그녀는 권력자라면 아무한테나 거의 당황스러울 정도로 굽실거린다.

57. **conspicuous**[255]

현저한, <u>spic</u>는 <u>look</u>이다.

There was no <u>conspicuous</u> road sign in that highway.
그 도로에는 눈에 들어오는 도로 표지가 없었다.

auspicious (길조의), Our first meeting was no <u>auspicious</u>, we had a huge argument. 우리의 첫 모임은 순조롭지 못했다.

inauspicious (흉조의), an <u>inauspicious</u> occasion 불길한 경우

suspicious (수상쩍은), <u>suspicious</u> behaviour 수상쩍은 행동

despicable (비열한), It was <u>despicable</u> of him to desert his family.
그는 비열하게도 가족을 버렸다.

perspicuous (명백한), clearly expressed and easily understood

perspicacious (총명한) He was <u>perspicacious</u> enough to realize that things were soon going to change. 그는 대단히 선견지명이 있어서 사태가 곧 변화리라는 것을 인식했다.

58. **constrain**[256]

억제하다, <u>strain</u>은 <u>tie</u> 이다.

Men and women are becoming less <u>constrained</u> by stereotyped roles.

---

255) 57. conspicuous auspicious inauspicious suspicious despicable perspicuous perspicacious

256) 58. constrain distrain restrain strain

남녀는 정형화 된 스타일에 덜 얽매이게 되었다.

distrain (압류하다), law to seize (eg property) as, or in order to force, payment of a debt

restrain (억제하다), **He was so angry he could hardly restrain himself.**
그는 너무 화가 나서 거의 자제할 수가 없었다.

strain (긴장시키다) **According to its critics, the bill will generate mountains of red tape and lawsuits, strain diplomatic ties with close allies, and diminish the chances of a peaceful political transition.** 비판자들의 말에 따르면 그 법안은 무수히 많은 형식적 행정절차와 소송을 야기하고, 가까운 동맹국들과의 외교 관계상 긴장을 초래하며, 평화적 정치 변화의 가능성을 감소시킬 것이다.

59. **contend**[257]

317

다투다, **tend는 stretch**이다.
There are three world-class tennis players contending for this title.
이 타이틀을 얻기 위해 경쟁하는 세계적인 테니스 선수들이 세 명이나 있다.

distend (팽창시키다), **starving children with huge distended bellies**
엄청나게 배가 부풀어 오른 굶주린 아이들

intensive (집중적인), **She needed intensive care for three weeks.**
그녀는 3주간의 집중 치료가 필요했다.

pretend (가장하다), **The man pretended to be dead.** 그 사람은 죽은 시늉을 했다.
extend (연장하다), **extend a deadline** 기한을 연장하다

---

257) 59. contend distend intensive pretend extend extensive pretentious

extensive (넓은), The school has <u>extensive</u> grounds. 그 학교에는 아주 넓은 운동장이 있다.

pretentious (허세부리는) The novel deals with grand themes, but is never heavy or <u>pretentious</u>. 그 소설은 웅장한 주제들을 다루지만 그렇다고 다루는 방법이 결코 엄숙하거나 과장되지 않았다.

60. <u>contiguous</u>[258]

이웃의, <u>tig (tag, tact)</u>은 <u>touch</u> 이다.
The city is <u>contiguous</u> to the ocean. 그 도시는 대양에 접해 있다.

contagious (전염성의), Laughter is <u>contagious</u>. 웃음은 옮기 쉽다.

contact (접촉), The two substances are now in <u>contact</u> with each other, and a chemical reaction is occurring. 그 두 물질이 지금 서로 접촉하여 화학 반응이 일어나고 있다.

tact (재주), He had the <u>tact</u> to settle the matter. 그는 재치 있게 그 문제를 해결했다.

intangible (만질 수 없는), <u>intangible</u> assets 무형 재산

tangle (엉킴), Long hair <u>tangles</u> easily. 긴 머리카락은 잘 엉클어진다.

entangle (얽히게 하다), He was <u>entangled</u> in a financial scandal. 그는 독직 사건에 휘말렸다.
disentangle (해결하다) He tried to <u>disentangle</u> himself from the bushes into which he had fallen. 그는 떨어진 덤불 속에서 몸을 빼내려고 애를 썼다.

318

---

258) 60. contiguous contagious contact tact intangible tangle entangle disentangle

61. circumscribe[259]

제한하다, scribe는 write 이다.

laws passed to circumscribe the power of the government
정부의 권력을 제한하기 위해 통과된 법률

ascribe (탓으로 하다), She ascribed her success to hard work. 그녀는 자신의 성공을 열심히 노력한 덕택이라고 생각했다.

inscribe (쓰다), inscribe one's name in a book 책에 자신의 이름을 적어 넣다

prescribe (지시하다), Police regulations prescribe that an officer's number must be clearly visible. 경찰 규칙은 경찰관의 번호가 분명히 보이게 되어 있어야 하다고 규정하고 있다.
proscribe (금지하다), proscribed books 금시된 시적

subscribe (기부하다, 동의하다, 정기구독하다), Do you subscribe to any maga zines? 정기 구독하는 잡지 있어요?

describe (묘사하다), She described the scene to us. 그녀가 그 광경을 우리에게 설명했다.

transcribe (복사하다, 타이프하다) transcribe testimony from a tape 테이프에서 증언을 문자로 표기하다;

62. controversial[260]

논쟁적인, vers(vert)은 turn 이다.

The ruling party proposed the shelving of the controversial property issue.

259) 61. circumscribe ascribe inscribe prescribe proscribe subscribe describe transcribe

260) 62. controversial invert inverse pervert perverse introvert

여당은 논란이 되고 있는 재산 문제를 보류하자고 제안했다.

invert (뒤집다), In questions, the subject and the verb are often <u>inverted</u>. 의문문에서 주어와 동사가 흔히 자리가 바뀐다.

inverse (반대의), Good is the <u>inverse</u> of evil. 선은 악의 반대이다.

pervert (왜곡하다), <u>pervert</u> the truth 진실을 왜곡하다

perverse (외고집의), The <u>perverse</u> child did just what we told him not to do. 고집불통의 그 아이는 우리가 하지 말라고 한 일만 골라 했다.

introvert (내향적인 사람) He used to be very sociable, but he's been an <u>introvert</u> since his wife's death. 그는 매우 사교적이었는데 아내가 죽은 이후 내성적인 사람이 되었다.

63. <u>decad</u>ence[261]

타락, <u>cad (cid)</u>는 <u>fall</u>이다.
the <u>decadence</u> of modern society 현대사회의 퇴폐성

caddish (비열한), ungentlemanly

Occident (서양), (the Occident) the countries in the west, especially those in Europe and America regarded as culturally distinct from eastern countries (the ORIENT).
coincide (동시에 일어나다) Your interests <u>coincide</u> with mine. 너와 나는 이해관계가 일치한다.

---

261) 63. decadence caddish Occident coincide

64. de**lu**ge[262)]

홍수, <u>lu 는 wash</u>이다.

Few people survived the <u>deluge</u>.

그 대홍수에서 살아남은 사람은 거의 없었다.

ablution (목욕), **<u>Ablution</u> is carried out as part of some religious ceremonies.**

세정식이 종교 의식의 일부로서 행해진다.

dilute (묽게 하다) make a liquid weaker or thinner by adding water,

<u>dilute</u> whisky with water.

demolition (분쇄) destruction, **mol은 ground** 이다.

houses scheduled for <u>demolition</u> 철거 예정된 주택들

emolument (봉급), payment, salary

immolate (희생으로 삼다), kill or offer something as a sacrifice,

<u>immolate</u> one's ambition on the altar of duty. 의리를 위해 대망을 버리다.

molar (어금니) any of the large back teeth in humans and other mammals, used for chewing and grinding.

65. de**pose**[263)]

가. 면직하다, <u>pos (pon, pound)은 put</u> 이다.

The king was <u>deposed</u> in a military coup.

그 왕은 군사 쿠데타로 실각 당했다.

---

262) 64. deluge ablution dilute demolition emolument immolate molar

263) 65. depose expose impose compose propose expound impound compound propound exponent imposing component proponent

나. 선서증언하다

expose (노출, 전시하다), She was <u>exposed</u> as an impostor. 그녀는 사기꾼으로 드러났다.

impose (부과하다), <u>impose</u> a fine 벌금을 부과하다.

compose (작곡하다), Beethoven <u>composed</u> nine symphonies throughout his life. 베토벤은 일생 동안 9개의 교향곡을 작곡했다

propose (제안하다), She <u>proposed</u> a new plan to us.
그녀는 우리에게 새로운 계획을 제안했다.

expound (상설하다), She <u>expounded</u> her theory to her colleagues.
그녀는 동료들에게 자신의 이론을 상세히 설명했다.

impound (몰수하다), The police <u>impounded</u> his car as evidence.
경찰이 증거로 그의 차를 압수했다.

compound (합성하다), A medicine is usually a <u>compound</u>. 약은 보통 합성물 이다.
propound (제의하다), <u>propound</u> an idea 생각을 제출하다

exponent (해설자, 옹호자), Huxley was an <u>exponent</u> of Darwin's theory of evolu
tion. 헉슬리는 다윈의 진화론 옹호자였다.

imposing (인상적인), her <u>imposing</u> presence 그녀의 위풍당당한 풍채

component (구성요소), the <u>components</u> of an engine 엔진 부품

proponent (제안자) She was an avid <u>proponent</u> of equal rights for immi grants. 그녀는 이민자의 동등한 권리를 열렬히 지지하는 사람이었다.

66. de<u>stit</u>ute[264]

빈곤한, <u>stit</u>는 <u>stand</u> 이다.
He's <u>destitute</u> of common sense. 그는 상식이 결핍되어 있다.

super<u>stit</u>ion (미신), There's an old <u>superstition</u> that killing a spider brings you bad luck. 거미를 죽이면 불운을 초래한다는 오래된 미신이 있다.

pro<u>stit</u>ute (매춘부), Many of them have been forced to work as <u>prostitutes</u>, others as laborers. 인신매매된 사람들 가운데 많은 사람들은 매춘부로 일하도록 강요당하고, 나머지 다른 사람들은 강제 노동을 강요당합니다.

re<u>stit</u>ution (배상, 반환), <u>restitution</u> claims 배상 요구

sub<u>stit</u>ute (대리인) a <u>substitute</u> parent 대리 부모

67. de<u>tract</u>[265]

가치를 떨어뜨리다, <u>tract</u>는 <u>draw</u> 이다.
No amount of criticism can <u>detract</u> from her achievements.
아무리 많은 비판을 해도 그녀의 업적을 훼손시키지는 못한다.

ab<u>stract</u> (발췌, 추상적인, 추출하다), an <u>abstract</u> painting 추상화

di<u>stract</u> (정신을 산만하게 하다), Please be quiet! You're <u>distracting</u> me.
제발 조용히 해! 너희들 때문에 집중이 안 돼.

---

264) 66. destitute superstition prostitute restitution substitute

265) 67. detract abstract distract extract contract retract tractable attract

extract (발췌하다), herbal <u>extracts</u> 약초 추출물

contract (계약, 수축시키다), I made a verbal <u>contract</u> with him. 나는 그와 구두 계약을 맺었다.

retract (취소하다), <u>retract</u> a promise 약속을 취소하다

tractable (유순한), He's quite a docile, <u>tractable</u> child. 그는 상당히 순하고 다루기 쉬운 아이다.

attract (매혹하다) They aimed to <u>attract</u> industry to the new towns.
그들은 새 도시들에 산업체를 유치할 생각이었다.

68. digress[266)]

주제에서 옆길로 벗어나다 turn away from the main subject in talking or writing, <u>gress</u> 는 <u>go</u> 이다.

Let me <u>digress</u> for a moment and explain what had happened previously.
잠깐 본론을 벗어나서 전에 무슨 일이 일어났었는지 설명하겠다.

aggression (공격), She was always full of <u>aggression</u> as a child. 그녀는 아이였을 때 항상 공격성으로 가득 차 있었다.

egress (출구), outlet

ingress (입구), **a means of <u>ingress</u>** 진입 방법

progress (진보), **the <u>progress</u> of civilization** 문명의 발달

retrogress (퇴보하다), **There is a time in the history of many great civiliza tions when they begin to <u>retrogress</u>.** 많은 위대한 문명의 역사에는 그들이 쇠퇴

---

266) 68. digress aggression egress ingress progress retrogress regress transgress

하기 시작하는 시기가 있다.

regress (역행하다), She regressed to her old habits. 그녀는 옛날 버릇으로 되돌아갔다.

transgress (어기다) violate

69. distortion[267]

왜곡, tort 는 twist 이다.
These accusations are outrageous distortions of the truth.
이러한 비난은 터무니없는 진실의 왜곡이다.

contort (일그러지다), His face contorted, then relaxed. 그의 얼굴은 일그러졌다가 펴졌다.

extort (강탈하다), He had been extorting money from the old lady for years. 그는 수년간 노부인의 돈을 착취해 왔다.
extortionate (비싼), The price of perfume is extortionate. 그 향수 가격은 터무니없다.

torment (심한 고통), It was wicked of you to torment the poor cat. 네가 불쌍한 고양이를 괴롭힌 건 나빴다.

retort (말대꾸), "Nonsense!" she retorted. "말도 안 돼!"라고 그녀는 받아넘겼다.

torture (고문) Torture is used to make people confess. 고문은 사람들로 하여금 자백하게 하기 위해 이용된다.

---

267) 69. distortion contort extort extortionate torment retort torture

70. **emit**[268]

발하다 discharge, mit(mis)는 send 이다.

Fire emits heat and smoke. 불은 열과 연기를 방출한다.

demise (서거), the demise of the country's communist regime 그 나라 공산정권의 종언

surmise (가정하다), guess, suppose,

I surmised that he had failed in his business.

emissary (사자, 에머세리), The government appointed him President's special emissary to China. 정부는 그를 대중국 대통령 특사로 임명했다.

remit (용서하다, 송금하다), Remit the money to me at once. 즉시 송금 바람.

premise (전제. 프레미스), the major premise 대전제

dismiss (해고시키다), dismiss an officer from his position.

remiss (태만한), It was remiss of her to forget to pay the bill.
그녀가 공과금을 안 낸 것은 부주의한 처사였다.

manumit (해방하다) to release (a person) from slavery; to set someone free

71. **extricate**[269]

구출하다, trick은 술책

It took hours to extricate the car from the sand. 차를 모래 밖으로 빼내는데

---

268) 70. emit demise surmise emissary remit premise dismiss remiss manumit
269) 71. extricate intricate intrigue

여러 시간이 걸렸다.

intricate (난해한, 뒤얽힌), The watch mechanism is very <u>intricate</u> and difficult to repair. 시계의 메커니즘은 수리하기에 매우 복잡하고 어렵다.

intrigue (음모를 꾸미다), carry on a secret plot, / He will not <u>intrigue</u> against you.

72. importune[270)]

졸라대다, <u>port는 carry</u> 이다.
<u>importune</u> his mother to increase one's allowance
용돈을 올려 달라고 성가시게 조르다.

opportune (적절한), timely, He appeared at a most <u>opportune</u> moment.

comport (처신하다), behave,
The judge must <u>comport</u> himself blamelessly.
disport (놀다), play, amuse, We <u>disported</u> ourselves on the beach.

purport (취지), meaning, What is the <u>purport</u> of his visit here?

deport (추방하다), banish, <u>deport</u> dangerous aliens.

deportment (행동, 처신), behavior, a model of good <u>deportment</u>.

deportation (추방, 디포테이션) a <u>deportation</u> order 추방령

---

270) 72. importune opportune comport disport purport deport deportment deportation

73. **imposter**[271)]

(사기꾼) <u>pos(pound, post)는 put</u> 이다.

apposite (적절한), apt, suitable, **an <u>apposite</u> remark to the case.**

depose (면직하다, 선서증언하다), **The king was <u>deposed</u> in a military coup.** 그 왕은 군사 쿠데타로 실각 당했다.

repose (휴식), rest, **Kate <u>reposed</u> on th bench.**

impose (부과하다), <u>impose</u> a fine 벌금을 부과하다.
impound (몰수하다), **The police <u>impounded</u> his car as evidence.** 경찰이 증거로 그의 차를 압수했다.

composure (평온, 침착), **He showed remarkable <u>composure</u> in a difficult situation.** 그는 어려운 상황 속에서도 놀라운 침착성을 보여줬다.

propound (제출하다) offer, <u>propound</u> a question 문제를 제기하다.

74. **impunity**[272)]

무사, <u>pun(pen)은 punish</u> 이다.
You cannot break the law with <u>impunity</u>. 무사히 법을 어길 수는 없다.

penal (형벌의, 피늘), <u>penal</u> laws 형법

penance (참회, 페넌스), **They are doing <u>penance</u> for their sins.** 그들은 자기 죄에 대한 참회를 하고 있다.

---

penitentiary (교도소, 페니텐셔리), In big black letters the sign says: "Warning: United States Federal Penitentiary, Alcatraz Island." 표지판에는 검은색의 큼직한 글자로 "경고: 미국 연방 교도소, 알카트라즈 섬"이라고 씌어 있습니다."

repent (후회하다), He soon repented his actions. 그는 곧 자신의 행동을 뉘우쳤다.

repentant (후회하는), She wasn't in the least repentant. 그녀는 조금도 뉘우치지 않았다.

penitent (후회하는), The penitent boy promised not to cheat again. 뉘우치는 그 소년은 다시는 속이지 않겠다고 약속했다.

75. infraction[273]

329

위반, frac(frag, fring)은 break 이다.
Speeding is the infraction of the traffic laws. 과속은 교통법 위반이다.

refractory (고집 센, 난치의), a boy trying to control his refractory pony 다루기 힘든 망아지를 다루기 위해 애를 쓰는 소년

refract (굴절시키다), Light is refracted when passed through a prism. 빛은 프리즘을 통과할 때 굴절한다.

fracture (골절), a fracture of the leg 다리 골절

fractious (까다로운), easily made angry, hard to control,
a fractious child.

---

273) 75. infraction refractory refract fracture fractious fraction fragment infringe

fraction (분수, 작은 부분), The car missed me by a <u>fraction</u> of an inch.
그 차는 나를 정말 아슬아슬하게 비껴갔다.

fragment (조각), The box burst into <u>fragments</u>. 상자가 산산조각이 났다.

infringe (어기다) <u>infringe</u> the regulations 규율을 위반하다

76. ingratitude[274]

배은망덕, <u>grat</u>은 thank, favor 이다.
Tim's parents were rather hurt by his <u>ingratitude</u>.
팀의 부모는 아들의 배은망덕함에 다소 상처를 받았다.

gratify (만족시키다), satisfy, Please <u>gratify</u> my curiosity and tell me what it is. 제발 내 호기심 채울 수 있게 그것이 무언지 말해줘요.

gratuitous (무료의), given or obtained free, gratuitous service, without reason, unnecessary, A lot of viewers complained that there was too much <u>gratuitous</u> sex and violence in the film. 많은 관객들이 그 영화에는 별 이유 없이 섹스와 폭력 장면이 지나치게 많이 나온다고 불평했다.

ingratiate (비위맞추다), bring into favor of, He tried to <u>ingratiate</u> himself with his superiors.

ungrateful (감사할 줄 모르는), How <u>ungrateful</u> of him to say that!
그 따위 소리를 하다니, 배은망덕도 유분수다.

gratitude (감사) She expressed her <u>gratitude</u> to all those who had supported

---

274) 76. ingratitude gratify gratuitous ingratiate ungrateful gratitude

her. 그녀는 자신을 도와줄 모든 사람들에게 감사를 표했다.

77. insurgent[275)

반역자, surge(surrect)은 rise 이다.
an attack by armed insurgents 무장 반군에 의한 공격

resurgent (부활하는), a resurgent economy 소생하는 경제

insurrection (폭동), an armed insurrection 무장 폭동

resurrection (부활) The Resurrection is one of the most crucial doctrines of Christianity. 부활은 기독교 신앙에서 가장 중요한 교리 중 하나이다.

---

275) 77. insurgent resurgent insurrection resurrection

Part 6
영영학습

01 The media often comments on the CEO's business _____.

   a. accretion   b. accolade   c. acumen   d. admonition

02 There was a huge scandal when customers discovered that the health food store had been _____ the wheat grass juice with unknown material.

   a. adulating   b. adulterating   c. ameliorating   d. amalgamating

03 Most people believe that stories of alien abduction are _____.

   a. anomaly   b. antipathy   c. apocryphal   d. apogee

04 Weddings are generally considered _____ occasions.

   a. avaricious   b. auspicious   c. audacious   d. assiduous

05 Tom _____ his rival by accusing him of having been unfaithful.

   a. calumniated   b. cajoled   c. broached   d. blandished

06 A "yes man" is characterized by his _____.

a. chicanery   b. contrite   c. convolution   d. complaisance

07 The _____ of snow this winter increases the likelihood of a drought next summer.

a. debacle   b. derision   c. demur   d. dearth

08 She had been fired because she had threatened to _____ information about the company's mismanagement.

a. divulge   b. disparage   c. edify   d. discreet

09 Even though most of the sect's practices were well-documented by anthropologists, some of its most _____ rites had never been witnessed by outsiders.

a. emollient   b. empirical   c. ephemeral   d. esoteric

10 He _____ed on the subject of his Florida vacation for three hours, accompanied by slides, until we were all crazy with boredom.

a. garner   b. gainsay   c. expurgate   d. expatiate

11 The kite was made out of a _____ substance that seemed hardly substantial enough to let it survive even the lightest of breezes.

a. gregarious   b. indolent   c. inimical   d. gossamer

12 I can't believe she _____d a ticket to the concert; I've been trying to get one for weeks.

a. malinger   b. limn   c. inveigle   d. laud

13 Finding my keys in my pocket _____ed the need for the private investigators I just hired to locate them.

a. mitigate   b. obfuscate   c. begin   d. obviate

14 I couldn't believe my campaign manager's _____ in voting for my opponent.

a. opprobrium   b. oscillation   c. peccadillo   d. perfidy

15 The general's hold on power was _____; at any time another coup could overthrow his young regime.

a. perspicacious   b. petulant   c. polemical   d. precarious

16 Joe was so _____ he refused to do anything he was instructed to do.

a. pugnacious   b. redolent   c. recalcitrant   d. rapacious

17 Carrots are _____ for your eyes, since they contain a lot of vitamin A.

a. salubrious   b. salient   c. sanguine   d. sagacious

18 The brief rain did not provide much _____ to the farmers who were losing their crops to drought.

a. succor   b. shard   c. sundry   d. stymie

19 It was unsafe to drive faster than ten miles an hour on the _____ road down the mountain.

a. tautology   b. tenuous   c. torpid   d. tortuous

20 Because he had been caught stealing from the orphanage's fund, he was immediately dismissed on the grounds of moral _____.

a. veneration   b. veracity   c. turpitude   d. travesty

21 After breaking up with her boyfriend, Jane decided to _____ herself in her work in oder to avoid crying.

    a. immerse   b. resolve   c. reprove   d. reprieve

22 The light was _____ed as it passed through the prism.

    a. remiss   b. relegate   c. refurbish   d. refract

23 She was bored by his music because she felt that it was _____ and that she had heard it before.

    a. deride   b. quell   c. rash   d. derivative

24 The jury's verdict may have been more lenient if the criminal had appeared _____ for his gruesome crimes.

    a. penitent   b. penurious   c. insipid   d. deleterious

25 The doctor trusted that the new medication would _____ her patient's discomfort.

    a. palliate   b. inure   c. inundate   d. carp

26 Years of drinking beer caused his stomach to _____.

a. distend   b. dissuade   c. disseminate   d. discern

27 Not wanting to appear greedy, she _____d her intention to sell her ailing father's stamp collection.

a. mollify   b. dissemble   c. vicissitude   d. vagary

28 The experience of playing with a dolphin is _____.

a. indigent   b. ineffable   c. inimical   d. indolent

29 The judge's decision to set the man free simply because the man was his brother was a _____ abuse of power.

a. fortuitous   b. flagrant   c. flabbergasted   d. fecund

30 Echoing throughout our village, the funeral _____ made the stormy day even more grim.

a. platitude   b. kudos   c. knell   d. facile

31 Even though I had the flu, my family decided to go skiing for the weekend and leave me home alone, feeling _____.

a. feral   b. flaccid   c. flout   d. forlorn

32 Every time Jane was late, her boyfriend went into a long _____ about punctuality.

a. sycophant   b. temerity   c. tirade   d. torrid

33 Wishing his book to be _____ to the common man, Tom avoided using complicated grammar.

a. travesty   b. trepidation   c. pellucid   d. mendacious

34 Jane's scarf _____s her blouse.

a. propagate   b. abrogate   c. complement   d. turpitude

35 Jane's _____ writing style greatly pleased readers who disliked complicated novels.

a. discomfit   b. licentious   c. limpid   d. evanescent

276)1. abate / lessen

aberrant / deviating from the norm

abjure / renounce solemnly

abrogate / abolish

abscond / steal off and hide

accolade / an award

accretion / growth

acerbic / having a sour taste

acumen / accurate insight

admonish / express warning

277)2. adroit / adept, dexterous

adulation / excessive praise

adulterate / reduce purity by combining with inferior ingredients

adumbrate / foreshadow vaguely

aesthetic / dealing with art

amalgamate / combine several elements into a whole

ameliorate / make better

amenable / agreeable

anathema / curse

anodyne / soothing

278)3. anomaly / deviation from the normal order

antipathy / dislike

apocryphal / dubious

apogee / highest point, culmination

276) 1. abate aberrant abjure abrogate abscond accolade accretion acerbic acumen admonish

277) 2. adroit adulation adulterate adumbrate aesthetic amalgamate ameliorate amenable anathema anodyne

278) 3. anomaly antipathy apocryphal apogee apostate apotheosis apposite apprise approbation arcane

apostate / betrayer

apotheosis / deification, the perfect example

apposite / pertinent

apprise / inform

approbation / approbation

arcane / mysterious, abstruse

[279]4. archaic / outdated

arduous / requiring significant effort

asperity / severity

aspersion / an act of maligning

assiduous / diligent

assuage / appease

attenuate / lessen

audacious / recklessly bold

auspicious / favorable

avaricious / greedy

[280]5. baleful / pernicious

bellicose / warlike

blandish / coax with flattery

boisterous / loud

bombastic / pompous

broach / begin to talk about

bucolic / rustic

burgeon / grow rapidly

cajole / inveigle, wheedle, sweet-talk

calumniate / slander

279) 4. archaic arduous asperity aspersion assiduous assuage attenuate audacious auspicious avaricious

280) 5. baleful bellicose blandish boisterous bombastic broach bucolic burgeon cajole calumniate

281)6. chicanery / trickery

coalesce / come together

cogent / convincing

commensurate / proportionate

complaisance / the willingness to comply with the wishes of others

contentious / argumentative

contiguous / adjacent

contrite / regretful

convoluted / complicated

craven / lacking courage

282)7. credulous / tending to believe too readily

culpable / deserving blame

dearth / lack

debacle / complete failure

decorum / politeness

demur / oppose

depredate / plunder

derision / scorn

derivative / unoriginal

desiccate / dry out

283)8. diaphanous / transparent

didactic / instruct

diffident / shy

dilatory / causing delay

---

281) 6. chicanery coalesce cogent commensurate complaisance contentious contiguous contrite convoluted craven

282) 7. credulous culpable dearth debacle decorum demur depredate derision derivative desiccate

283) 8. diaphanous didactic diffident dilatory discretion disparage divulge eclectic edifying effrontery

discretion / ability to make responsible decisions

disparage / belittle

divulge / disclose something secret

eclectic / composed of elements drawn from various sources

edifying / enlightening

effrontery / extreme boldness

[284]9. emollient / soothing

empirical / based on observation or experiment

enervate / weaken

enigmatic / mysterious

ephemeral / brief

epitome / embodiment

erudite / scholarly

esoteric / intended for a small group

evanescent / vanishing

exculpate / exonerate

[285]10. expatiate / discuss at length

expiate / make amends for

expurgate / remove obscenity

facetious / humorous

fetid / having a heavy bad smell

flout / demonstrate contempt for

furtive / surreptitious

gainsay / deny

garner / gather

---

284) 9. emollient empirical enervate enigmatic ephemeral epitome erudite esoteric evanescent exculpate

285) 10. expatiate expiate expurgate facetious fetid flout furtive gainsay garner garrulous

garrulous / talking too much

286)11. gossamer / delicate

gregarious / sociable

halcyon / calm and peaceful

heretical / unorthodox

ignominious / shameful

impecunious / without money

importune / ask incessantly

impunity / immunity from punishment

indolent / lazy

inimical / harmful

287)12. intrepid / courageous

inured / accustomed

inveigle / obtain by deception or flattery

inveterate / ingrained

itinerate / travel from place to place

jejune / vapid

laconic / using few words

laud / praise highly

limn / draw, outline in detail

malinger / feign illness so as to avoid work

---

286) 11. gossamer gregarious halcyon heretical ignominious impecunious importune impunity indolent inimical

287) 12. intrepid inured inveigle inveterate itinerate jejune laconic laud limn malinger

[288]13. mellifluous / sweetly flowing

mitigate / moderate

morose / melancholy

mundane / of the world

nebulous / vague

neologism / a new word

neophyte / beginner

obfuscate / make confusing

obsequious / subservient

obviate / make unnecessary

[289]14. opprobrium / disgrace, scorn

oscillation / the act of swinging back and forth

ossify / change into bone

panegyric / formal expression of praise

peccadillo / a slight offense

penchant / strong inclination

perfidy / intentional breach of faith

peripatetic / itinerant, traveling

pernicious / extremely harmful

[290]15. perspicacious / having keen discernment

petulant / impatient, irritable

placate / appease

plethora / surplus

pluck / courage

---

288) 13. mellifluous mitigate morose mundane nebulous neologism neophyte obfuscate obsequious obviate

289) 14. opprobrium oscillation ossify panegyric peccadillo penchant perfidy peripatetic pernicious

290) 15. perspicacious petulant placate plethora pluck polemical precarious prodigal prodigious prolific

polemical / argumentative

precarious / uncertain

prodigal / lavish

prodigious / huge

prolific / productive

[291)]16. proscribe / prohibit

pugnacious / quarrelsome

pusillanimous / cowardly

quiescence / stillness

quotidian / commonplace

rapacious / greedy

recalcitrant / obstinately defiant of authority

redolent / fragrant, suggestive

relegate / forcibly assign to a lower place

repudiate / disown, refuse

[292)]17. rescind / invalidate

resolute / adamant

reticent / quiet

reverent / respect

sagacious / wise

salacious / causing sexual desire

salient / prominent

salubrious / promoting health or well-being

sanguine / cheerful

sap / enervate

---

291) 16. proscribe pusillanimous quiescence quotidian rapacious recalcitrant redolent relegate repudiate

292) 17. rescind resolute reticent reverent sagacious salacious salient salubrious sanguine sap

Part 6 영영학습

293)18. shard / a piece of broken pottery

solicitous / concerned and attentive

solvent / able to meet financial obligations

soporific / tending to induce sleep

specious / seeming true

squander / waste

stymie / block, thwart

succor / assistance, relief in time of distress

sundry / various

supercilious / arrogant

294)19. superfluous / exceeding what is sufficient

surfeit / feed in excess

sycophant / flatterer

tacit / implied

tautology / a repetition

tawdry / cheap

tenuous / having little substance or strength, flimsy

tirade / a long and extremely critical speech

torpid / lethargic

tortuous / twisting

295)20. tout / publicly praise

tractable / docile

travesty / mockery

turpitude / depravity

---

293) 18. shard solicitous solvent soporific specious squander stymie succor sundry supercilious

294) 19. superfluous surfeit sycophant tacit tautology tawdry tenuous tirade torpid tortuous

295) 20. tout tractable travesty turpitude ubiquitous vacillate venal venerate veracity vilify

ubiquitous / widespread

vacillate / waver

venal / capable of being bribed

venerate / revere

veracity / truthfulness

vilify / defame

[296]21. immutable / not changeable

immerse / absorb, deeply involve, engross

resolve / find a solution

reprove / scold, rebuke, criticize, reprimand, admonish, chide, reproach

reprieve / a temporary delay of punishment 집행유예 pardon, acquittal, ex-
culpation, exoneration

The governor granted hundreds of reprieves to prisoners.

reprehensible / deserving rebuke

repose / rest, lie down

replete / abundant, full

repentant / penitent, sorry, remorseful, rueful, contrite

renunciation / rejection, repudiation, abandonment, denial, refusal

[297]22. renown / honor, acclaim

remiss / negligent, careless, lax

relish / enjoy

relegate / assign to an inferior place, demote, transfer, lower

refurbish / restore, clean up, renovate, renew, revamp, overhaul, repair

The dingy old chair, after being refurbished, commanded (deserved, was
entitled to) a handsome price of $200.

296) 21. immutable immerse resolve reprove reprieve reprehensible repose replete repentant renunciation
297) 22. renown remiss relish relegate refurbish refract redoubtable reclusive reciprocate recapitulate

refract / distort, change

redoubtable / formidable, commanding respect

reclusive / solitary

reciprocate / give in return

recapitulate / sum up, repeat

[298]23. raucous / loud, boisterous

rash / hasty, incautious

quell / control, suppress, put down, quash, conquer

quandary / dilemma, predicament

quagmire / a difficult situation

punitive / involving punishment

pungent / sharp

choreography / the arrangement of dances

derivative / unoriginal

deride / laugh at mockingly, scorn

[299]24. derelict / abandoned

depravity / wickedness, debauchery

deplore / regret, express sorrow

denounce / criticize publicly

demure / quiet, reserved, shy, bashful

delineate / describe, outline

deleterious / harmful

insipid / dull, boring

penurious / miserly, stingy, poor

penitent / remorseful, regretful

---

298) 23. raucous rash quell quandary quagmire punitive pungent choreography derivative deride

299) 24. derelict depravity denounce demure delineate deleterious insipid penurious penitent

[300)]25. partisan / a follower, adherent

parsimony / frugality, stinginess

pariah / an outcast

palliate / reduce the severity of

palatable / agreeable to the taste

inure / become accustomed to a situation

inundate / flood

perfidious / disloyal, unfaithful

carp / complain, find fault

carouse / party, drink and become noisy

[301)]26. disclose / reveal, make public

discern / perceive

diffident / shy

didactic / intended to instruct

diaphanous / light, transparent

dialect / a variation of a language

docile / easily taught or trained

distend / swell, bloat, inflate, expand, enlarge

dissuade / persuade someone not to do something

disseminate / spread widely

[302)]27. dissemble / conceal, fake

vindictive / vengeful

vicissitude / event that occurs by chance, variability

vicarious / experiencing through another

---

300) 25. partisan parsimony pariah palliate palatable inure inundate perfidious carp carouse

301) 26. disclose discern diffident didactic diaphanous dialect docile distend dissuade disseminate

302) 27. dissemble vindictive vicissitude vicarious vivacious venerable vagary mollify polemic poignant

vivacious / lively

venerable / deserving of respect

vagary / an unpredictable action, whim

mollify / soften in temper

polemic / an aggressive argument against a specific opinion

poignant / deeply affecting, moving

[303)]28. pinnacle / the highest point

pillage / seize or plunder

innuendo / an insinuation

iniquity / wickedness

inimical / hostile

ingenious / clever

ineffable / incapable of being expressed

indolent / lazy

indigent / poor

fraught / filled with

[304)]29. foster / stimulate, promote, encourage

fortuitous / happening by chance

forsake / give up, renounce

forestall / prevent, thwart

forage / rummage for food

flagrant / offensive, egregious

flabbergasted / astounded

fickle / shifting in character

fetter / chain, restrain

fecund / fruitful, fertile

---

303) 28. pinnacle pillage innuendo iniquity inimical ingenious ineffable indolent indigent fraught

304) 29. foster fortuitous forsake forestall forage flagrant flabbergasted fickle fetter fecund

305)30. fatuous / silly, foolish

fastidious / meticulous, demanding

fallacious / incorrect, misleading

facile / easy

fabricate / make up, invent

extricate / disentangle, free from difficulty

platitude / cliche, banal statement

placid / calm, peaceful

kudos / praise for an achievement

knell / the solemn sound of a bell, often indicating a death

306)31. interject / insert between

inoculate / vaccinate, immunize, inject, give a shot

inchoate 인코이트 / unformed or formless, in a beginning stage, emergent, embryonic / The country's government is still inchoate and, because it has no great tradition, quite unstable.

harrowing / greatly distressing, vexing

harangue / give a lengthy speech

forlorn / lonely, abandoned, hopeless, miserable

foil / thwart, frustrate, defeat

flout / disobey, defy

flaccid / lacking vitality, not firm or strong

feral 피럴 / wild, savage

307)32. execrable / detestable, very bad

emollient / soothing

353

---

305) 30. fatuous fastidious fallacious facile fabricate extricate platitude placid kudos knell

306) 31. interject inoculate inchoate harrowing harangue forlorn foil flout flaccid feral

307) 32. execrable emollient emaciated sycophant tantamount temerity tirade torrid tortuous tractable

emaciated / very thin

sycophant / one who flatters for self-gain

tantamount / equivalent in value

temerity / audacity, recklessness

tirade / a long speech marked by harsh or biting language

torrid / giving off intense heat, passionate

tortuous / winding

tractable / easily controlled

[308]33. transgress / violate

transmute / change

travesty / imitation

trepidation / fear

pallid / lacking color

pathology / study of disease

pellucid / easily intelligible, clear

ruminate / contemplate, reflect

mendacious / having a lying, false character

quotidian / daily

[309]34. propagate / multiply, spread out

profane / lewd, indecent

abstruse / hard to comprehend

abrogate / abolish

compunction / distress caused by feeling guilty

complement / complete, make perfect

collusion / secret agreement, conspiracy

---

308) 33. transgress transmute travesty trepidation pallid pathology pellucid ruminate mendacious quotidian

309) 34. propagate profane abstruse abrogate compunction complement collusion cognizant cogent turpitude

cognizant / aware

cogent / convincing

turpitude / moral corruption

³¹⁰⁾35. artifact / a remaining piece from an extinct culture

conundrum / puzzle, problem

expiate / make amends for, atone

exhort / urge

excursion / trip

evanescent / fleeting

limpid / clear, transparent

licentious / displaying a lack of moral

embezzle / steal money

discomfit / baffle, thwart

---

310) 35. artifact conundrum expiate exhort excursion evanescent limpid licentious embezzle discomfit